THE FIGHTER

Tim Parks studied at Cambridge and Harvard. He lives near Verona with his wife and three children. His novel *Europa* was shortlisted for the Booker Prize. *Destiny* and *Judge Savage* were longlisted in 2000 and 2003.

D1246592

ALSO BY TIM PARKS

Fiction

Tongues of Flame
Loving Roger
Home Thoughts
Family Planning
Goodness
Cara Massimina
Mimi's Ghost
Shear
Europa
Destiny
Judge Savage
Rapids
Cleaver
Talking About It
Dreams of Rivers and Seas

Non-fiction

Italian Neighbours
An Italian Education
Adultery & Other Diversions
Translating Style
Hell and Back
A Season with Verona
Medici Money

TIM PARKS

The Fighter

Essays

VINTAGE BOOKS
London

Published by Vintage 2008

2 4 6 8 10 9 7 5 3 1

Copyright © Tim Parks 2007

Tim Parks has asserted his right under the Copyright, Designs
and Patents Act 1988 to be identified as the author of this work

This page should be read in conjunction with the places and dates of
first publication of these pieces given on pp. 277–8

This book is sold subject to the condition that it shall not,
by way of trade or otherwise, be lent, resold, hired out,
or otherwise circulated without the publisher's prior
consent in any form of binding or cover other than that
in which it is published and without a similar condition,
including this condition, being imposed on the
subsequent purchaser

First published in Great Britain in 2007 by Harvill Secker

Vintage
Random House, 20 Vauxhall Bridge Road,
London SW1V 2SA

www.vintage-books.co.uk

Addresses for companies within The Random House Group Limited can be
found at: www.randomhouse.co.uk/offices.htm

The Random House Group Limited Reg. No. 954009

A CIP catalogue record for this book
is available from the British Library

ISBN 9780099513322

The Random House Group Limited supports The Forest Stewardship
Council (FSC), the leading international forest certification organisation.
All our titles that are printed on Greenpeace approved FSC certified paper
carry the FSC logo. Our paper procurement policy can be found at
www.rbooks.co.uk/environment

Typeset in Galliard by Palimpsest Book Production Limited,
Grangemouth, Stirlingshire

Printed and bound in Great Britain by
CPI Bookmarque, Croydon CR0 4TD

To Bob Silvers and all his team at the *NYR*

Contents

The Fighter

[D. H. Lawrence]

'Now a book lives', wrote D. H. Lawrence, 'as long as it is unfathomed. Once it is fathomed . . . once it is *known* and its meaning is fixed or established, it is dead.'

If this is the case, Lawrence need not have feared for his own works. Seventy-seven years after his death they are all in print and the critics continue to debate, often to fight, over what they might mean. The proliferation of biographies is likewise remarkable, this despite the fact that Lawrence had as little desire to have his life 'fathomed' as his books: 'I hate "understanding" people,' he wrote in 1921, 'and I hate more still to be understood. Damn understanding more than anything.'

But if we are not to understand Lawrence, what is our relationship with him to be? Perhaps we can find a clue in the man's belligerence. Whether dealing with his dog, his doctors, his wife or his closest friends, Lawrence's relationships were characterised by an alternation between intense intimacy and ferocious conflict. In general, the more important a relationship was to him, the more likely it was to be punctuated by violent, even traumatic battles. The present essay will be nothing more than an attempt to understand if not Lawrence, then at least his literary longevity as a function of his passion for conflict. 'I've just done the last proofs of Lady C [*Lady Chatterley's Lover*]' he wrote in 1928. 'I *hope* it'll make 'em howl – and let 'em do their paltry damnedest, after.'

As might be expected, the fighting started at home. 'When I was a small boy, I remember my father shouting at my mother: "I'll make you tremble at the sound of my footstep!"' Fourth of five children born to a Nottinghamshire coal-miner in 1885, the young David

1

Herbert was terrified, but also 'felt it was splendid and right'. His mother was not impressed. 'Which boots will you wear?' she asked her husband wryly. The man was deflated. The boy learns that threats without action are empty. Sick in bed in his early thirties, Lawrence wrote to a friend of his relationship with his wife: 'I suppose I'll get strong enough again one day to slap Frieda in the eye, in the proper marital fashion. At present I am reduced to vituperation.'

Any battle can be seen from at least two sides. In the fictionalised version of his parents' relationship in *Sons and Lovers* (1913), Lawrence wrote of a sensitive, middle-class mother obliged to wrest her children's upbringing from a brutish working-class father. The young writer himself had not been wanted by his parents, was merely the result of Father's drunken, animal lust. Later in life, he could invert the situation: in some of Lawrence's writings, the mother is a manipulative snob who imposes her self-righteous, middle-class values on a simple man with honest male instincts, so monopolising the children's affection that their father becomes an exile in his own home.

For biographers recounting such bitter clashes, it's hard not to take sides. In *D. H. Lawrence: A Biography*, Jeffrey Meyers is pleased to quote research that brings new ammunition to the father's defence: Lawrence's mother was *not* it seems, as we all grew up believing, from a higher class than her husband. The myth of her being a schoolteacher was all airs. Slum-bred, Lydia Beardsall was the merest factory worker when she met the handsome miner, Arthur Lawrence.

Meyers, who loves to close his otherwise excellent chapters, always well documented and convincingly told, with dogmatic little summaries, as if one more period of his subject's life had now been safely stowed away, seems to miss the importance of this discovery. There was no inevitable clash between classes in the Lawrence household. Rather, a spurious class struggle was invented to mask an antagonism of pure wilfulness. 'Their marriage has been one carnal, bloody fight' Lawrence wrote in 1910. Much of his writing would dramatise conflicts between partners – Gudrun's against Gerald's in *Women in Love*, Lou's against Rico's in *St Mawr* – but in such a way as to strip them of social alibis and circumstantial explanations. A typical scene in *Women in Love* describes Gerald, the industrialist, face down on his bed refusing to speak and Gudrun the bohemian artist determined not to let him escape confrontation in this way: 'Her mind wondered over his rigid, unloving body. She was bewildered, and insistent, only her will was set for him to speak to her.' With this prevalence of the individual will over social setting, the characters in Lawrence's novels can seem shrill and insubstantial, or, alternatively, they gather the archetypal force of figures in myth. Either way, they are never Dickensian.

Two questions force themselves on biographers: how was it that the son of a coal-miner became one of England's foremost intellectual and cosmopolitan writers? And what prompted a man brought up in the rigid moral framework of English Methodism, who 'had the Bible poured every day into my helpless consciousness', to become a prophet of sexual revolution?

Lawrence's elder brother, William Earnest, the second son and his mother's favourite, died when Lawrence was sixteen. David Herbert, or Bert as he was called, replaced him, her favourite at last, but only after a rival had been seen off. The boy's chronic lung problems and general physical frailty made it easier for his mother to draw him away from his father's world of sweat and coal dust. When Bert proved too weak even for the position of clerk in a surgical appliances manufacturer, he could be sent to train as a teacher.

Thus Lawrence's education was part of Mother's struggle against Father. Far from being a neutral quality, heightened consciousness was understood to be in direct opposition to masculine instinct. His sickliness assisted his mother's project, and so was soon associated with intellectuality. The boy's choice of friends fitted too. Mother accepted his relationship with Jessie Chambers and her family on a farm outside their mining village because the boy and girl seemed to spend most of their time reading, talking about books and in general procuring themselves an education.

But it wasn't a sex education, and despite all Lawrence's learning and frailty, masculine instinct could not be contained. The problem being that Jessie, like Lawrence's mother, seemed so spiritual. Young Bert was confused. In the event he went off and had sex with another man's wife, which allowed him, at least in the fictional version in *Sons and Lovers*, the added pleasure of a very masculine, potentially erotic fight with the wronged husband, a man who in some ways resembled Lawrence's father. In 1910, long before time and distance might have allowed him to form a less idealised image of her, Lawrence's mother died of cancer. He was heartbroken: 'For me everything collapsed, save the mystery of death and the haunting of death in life.'

Like many people desperately seeking to understand the world but getting nowhere, Lawrence turned out to be an excellent teacher. Between 1908 and 1911 he taught in a working-class school in Croydon, South London. He was full of theories and experimental methods. The pupils were instructed to express themselves freely, but to observe the strictest discipline. Lawrence opposed authority in general, his headmaster observed, except when he himself was imposing it: with the rod. 'School is a conflict,' Lawrence wrote to a friend, 'mean and miserable – and I hate conflicts.' Not many years later he would explain why he had run off with another married woman: 'She [Frieda] is the only possible woman for me, for I must have opposition, something to fight or I shall go under.'

So Lawrence hated fights but needed them to keep him in form for other fights. With sickness for example. In 1911 he fell desperately ill with pneumonia. Just as a previous illness had got him out of clerking, so this one freed him from teaching. Physically, he was fit for nothing, it seemed, but writing. And that would be one long battle from beginning to end.

Alongside the huge body of work (a dozen long novels, many volumes of shorter fiction and poetry, three plays, four travel books, three full-length critical works and scores of essays), Lawrence also found time in his forty-four years to write literally thousands of letters. He could leave no acquaintance, however casual, alone. He was always ready to invite people to join him in some utopian, conflict-free community, or to curse them for refusing to join him, or for having rejected his work, written a bad review, or in some other way not lived up to his standards. Afterwards, he would write again to make up. One had imagined that the wonderful seven-volume Cambridge University Press collection of these letters was complete. Now an eighth volume of addenda has appeared, with hitherto unpublished material from more or less every period of the author's life. Far from trivia, we find gems like this as early as page three: responding, in 1909, to a typescript of Lawrence's first novel, *The White Peacock*, Ford Madox Ford, the first literary man to pay the author any attention, writes: 'As you must probably be aware, the book, with its enormous prolixity of detail, sins against almost every canon of art as I conceive it.' But Madox Ford goes on to say that he believes Lawrence has great talents and a great future.

This ambivalent response to his work would soon become so familiar to Lawrence that he began to adopt it himself. Presenting his second novel, *The Trespasser*, to his publisher, he described it as 'execrable bad art'. Nevertheless he was confident the editor would accept it. 'Lawrence', wrote his close friend (but also bitter enemy) the critic Middleton Murry, 'gave up, deliberately, the pretence of being an artist . . . His aim was to discover authority, not to create art.'

'To discover authority'. What does Murry mean? No novelist has been both so highly praised and so frequently attacked as Lawrence; no literary reputation I can think of is so vast and so compromised. Two new critical introductions to his work, each excellent in its style and scope, *The Cambridge Companion to D. H. Lawrence* and *The Complete Critical Guide to D. H. Lawrence*, both feel the need to include chapters on see-sawing critical reactions to the writer over the years. While he was alive his work was met with incomprehension, contempt, censorship and adoration. His ability to convey a sense of place, to have drama explode from the apparently mundane was undisputed. His candour was admirable if disquieting. But his conclusions, and the violence with which he insisted on them, the lecturing tone he assumes, were, to many, completely unacceptable. Immediately after his death, Middleton Murry wrote a book that dismissed his friend as a psychological cripple destroyed by mother love. Aldous Huxley then attacked Murry's position as 'a slug's eye view'. T. S. Eliot joined the fray announcing that Lawrence might have been a good writer if only he had had a proper education. As it was, he displayed 'an incapacity for what we ordinarily call thinking'.

Eliot's authority threatened to settle the quarrel, until F. R. Leavis declared Lawrence the finest and most 'life-affirming' novelist of the century. Only *Lady Chatterley's Lover* was 'false', Leavis thought, and he declined to give evidence when the book's publisher was tried under the Obscene Publications Act in 1960. Worse than false or obscene, according to Simone de Beauvoir, the novel was irretrievably the work of a male chauvinist. In her book *Sexual Politics* (1969) Kate Millet elaborated de Beauvoir's position and condemned Lawrence as hysterically misogynist. Others ran to his defence. From this point on, the number of studies of Lawrence multiplied. Yet however important and brilliant he is considered, every critic has his or her reservations. The novelist Rebecca West, who compares Lawrence to Dante and St Augustine, nevertheless feels that *Women in Love* was a failure. The biographer Philip Callow greatly admires *Women in Love* but decides that *St Mawr*, which Leavis thought Lawrence's best work, is no more than 'an assault on the reader by plastering contrived symbolism over the tale with impatient crudeness.' Even the English novelist Geoff Dyer, who, in *Out of Sheer Rage* has written one of the most perceptive, idiosyncratic and affectionate accounts of a reader's relationship with Lawrence, remarks that 'some of Lawrence's works would have benefited from thorough, careful revision.'

From Madox Ford's comment on the first typescript right down to the present day, what is remarkable is the critics' assumption that they know what it means to create art and that their irritation on reading much of Lawrence indicates a shortcoming on his part, a refusal to be the artist. Yet rereading his work today one can't help feeling that this embattled critical heritage was *exactly* what Lawrence wanted. Here after all was a man who would start writing spirited responses to the bad reviews he expected even before they appeared. 'All truth', he wrote, '– and real living is the only truth – has in it the elements of battle and repudiation.' A book, for Lawrence, marked the beginning of a fight. Art, in the sense of the tidy, the manageable, the mellifluous, was the bolt-hole of the weak-hearted.

In 1912, recently returned from death's door, Lawrence met Frieda Weekley, née Richthofen, the aristocratic, German-born wife of an English history professor and a mother of three. Six years older than Lawrence, Frieda was bored to death. Less than two months after their meeting, she and the writer ran off together to Germany, then Italy. 'Can't you feel how certainly I love you and how certainly we shall be married . . .' he wrote to her. She couldn't quite, but Lawrence burnt her bridges for her by writing to her husband about the affair. Frieda lost custody of her children. To prove she was a free agent, she betrayed Lawrence immediately and openly. He hung on. So dramatic for both of them was the break with their past, with respectability, with financial common sense, that their relationship and eventual marriage had to be made into a myth to compensate for what both had lost. They were man and woman forged by sex into a couple against the world.

Before meeting Lawrence, Frieda had briefly been the lover of the unorthodox psychoanalyst Otto Gross. She introduced Lawrence to a new range of reading in modern psychology. Over the next five years, under her influence, he wrote his two most substantial novels, *The Rainbow*, an account of changing marital relations over three generations, marking a transition from traditional to modern mores, and *Women in Love*, which picks up the story of two of the young women in *The Rainbow* and brings it into contemporary times. While writing these books Lawrence was formulating the ideas which, with regular variations and volte-faces, would feed his work to the end. They can be crudely summarised thus: the traditional community in which man lived in close relation to the natural world is now for ever gone. The mental life has triumphed over the physical. Freud is the culmination of this disaster, reducing the unconscious as he does to an exclusively mental repository of dirty secrets and simply ignoring the life, conscious and unconscious, of the body.

With nothing natural remaining, society is now divided into the industrialised masses, 'a poor blind, disconnected people with nothing but politics and bank holidays to satisfy the eternal human need of living in ritual adjustment to the cosmos', and an intellectual elite whose exclusive interest is the cultivation of their arid personalities. 'Now men are all separate little entities. While kindness is the glib order of the day . . . underneath this "kindness" we find a coldness of heart . . . Every man is a menace to every other man . . . Individualism has triumphed.'

Lawrence, in short, was anticipating the thinking of those anthropologists (Louis Dumont, for example) who would see the passage from traditional to industrial society as a move to a situation where relationships would inevitably be characterised by conflict. With the old ordering of the world gone, the search was on for some new authority that might transcend mere individual willpower.

Writing in the grim years of World War One, contemplating wholesale slaughter across the Channel, suspected – thanks to his pacifism and his German wife – of being a spy, reduced to poverty, it wasn't difficult for Lawrence to imagine that doomsday was at hand. A futuristic note began to creep into his work. Old codes of behaviour were irrelevant, or at best a weapon to use against those still gullible enough to respect them. Real authority was conspicuous by its absence. The opening of the novella *The Fox* (written, though not published, in 1918) is typical: two young women are sitting in their lonely house on the farm that inexplicably and without any experience they have decided to run. Comes a knock at the door. 'Hello?' Immediately one of the women picks up a gun: menace, conflict.

In the event, it is only a returning soldier who imagined that his grandfather still owned the place. The women are aware that according to the rules of years ago, the man ought to go and find a bed in the village. Instead they offer to put him up. The villagers will gossip, but who cares? After only a few days the soldier abruptly asks one of the women to marry him. The reader, like the woman, is disoriented by the lack of preamble. 'Why shouldn't I?' is the man's constant refrain. There are no rules. He likens his stalking of the woman to his hunt for the fox that has been disturbing the farm animals. Even courtship is conflict.

If English society really was in the state Lawrence described, then of course it had to be saved, or destroyed. Lawrence wasn't sure which. Saved by being destroyed perhaps. In any event something radical was required and where else could it start but with the one-to-one relationship? Here, sex was crucial. Sex was the single thing that might put man and woman, perhaps man and man too, in touch with the deeper forces of nature. It thus became necessary to narrate sexual encounters in candid detail, to follow the interplay between psychology and sensuality, the surrender, or refusal to surrender, of the frantic individual mind.

Very soon Lawrence began to reverse the biblical sense of the verb 'to know' in reference to sex. Rather than 'knowing' another, a positive sexual encounter became an 'unknowing', a shedding of self in oneness. The values he hated, Lawrence was aware, were encoded in the language. He would have to do battle with that too. 'Gudrun lay wide awake, destroyed into perfect consciousness' he says in *Women in Love* when one couple's lovemaking has been nothing more than two wilful individuals rubbing against each other. 'They could forget perfectly' he says of the effect of his preferred kind of sex. Standard syntax and lexical values are attacked, reversed, regenerated. Writing *The Rainbow* Lawrence declared that it was 'a novel in a foreign language I don't know very well.'

But if the goal was 'unknowing', why engage in all this speculation? With Lawrence the intellect is always constructing its own defeat. 'Don't ever mind what I say' he writes in 1913. 'I'm a great bosher and full of fancies that interest me.' The novel, in so far as a story must be grounded in reality, open to incident and multiple interpretation, becomes the vehicle that will disarm his dogmatic theorising, a weapon against himself. 'Never trust the artist, trust the tale' he says.

On the other hand, Lawrence really did want to sort out the question of how a man and woman should behave once they had succeeded in shedding their personalities in sex; the problem being that the society around them was not a traditional one in which such relationships might flourish. What was needed then was a favourable micro-community. Again and again, in novels and life, Lawrence mooted the project of 'a few men with honour and fearlessness' sailing the South Seas or working the land. Or, if that couldn't be arranged – and it never could – he might at least have one male friendship based not on talk and opinions, but on a physical and permanent bond, something that would provide context for the marriage between man and woman. To bemused friends Lawrence proposed a *Blutbrüderschaft*, an eternal friendship that would survive complete frankness, assert stability *despite* conflict. But Lawrence's frankness was notoriously brutal. 'You are a dirty little worm' he wrote to Middleton Murry, perhaps the most serious candidate for blood brother. Not surprisingly, no one came on board.

Meantime, despite their sexual union, man and woman continued to hold different opinions. He would not be bullied, Lawrence yelled at Frieda. She would not be bullied either. They fought bitterly. Lawrence appreciated the comedy in this, the bathos of petty domestic wrangling after the mind-altering sensual experience, the high-flown rhetoric of social regeneration. 'It is the way our sympathy flows and recoils that really determines our lives' he decided. By the time he was writing *Women in Love* this was the rhythm of the novels: the genius lies not in any one scene, and certainly not in the overall form, but in the 'flow and ebb', the constant shifts of tone, biblical apocalypse, sitting-room knockabout.

In 1915 *The Rainbow* was banned for obscenity. 'I curse my country with my soul and body' Lawrence announced. America, he decided, was the place for him. And he began to write *Studies in Classic American Literature*, a book of megalomaniac ambition which offers brilliant insights into, for example, Fennimore Cooper's wish-fulfilment in fantasised friendships between white and native Americans, or, again, Hawthorne's ambivalent presentation of moral purity in *The Scarlet Letter*.

Of course many critics have written perceptively on the literature of another nation without ever visiting it, but what is astonishing about the *Studies* is Lawrence's aggressive confidence, already hinted at in the book's provocative title (many at the time would have seen the collocation of 'classic' with 'American' as oxymoronic), that living as he then was in a remote Cornish village he could grasp not only the essence of this or that author, but the relationship between their writing and the whole dynamic of American history, in short what made these writers 'classically' American.

As always, the book's style is characterised by Lawrence's willingness to offend. Opening with a claim that the original American vision of freedom was nothing more than the escaped slave's eagerness to be rid of a master, he gives us a paragraph that would not seem inappropriate to the present debate about the West's right to impose democracy on every corner of the world:

Men are free when they belong to a living, organic, believing community, active in fulfilling some unfulfilled, perhaps unrealised purpose. Not when they are escaping to some wild west. The most unfree souls go west, and shout of freedom. Men are freest when they are most unconscious of freedom. The shout is a rattling of chains, always was.

In 1917, just when Lawrence had decided he must go to America to assist in turning this negative freedom of escape to the positive freedom of the 'believing community', the British authorities withdrew his passport. He was a possible German sympathiser. In the event it was 1919 before he was able to leave England, never to return except for brief visits.

At this point the writer's story is picked up in the most attractive of recent Lawrence biographies, Philip Callow's *Body of Truth:*

D. H. Lawrence – The Nomadic Years, 1919–1930. Despite the rich detail, a pattern rapidly emerges. Always obliged to count the pennies, suffering from pneumonia, malaria, tuberculosis, Lawrence travels from Italy to Ceylon, to Australia, New Mexico and Mexico in search of communities still in touch with the natural world, still observing older hierarchies and accepting traditional authorities. Wherever they go, he and Frieda seek to establish that small benevolent group of like-minded folk that in some modern way might offer the vital sustenance for their marriage that Lawrence feels is unavailable in mechanised, industrial England.

As it turned out, the only thing that did not disappoint was the landscape, the flora and fauna. For however eager he was to be impressed by pre-modern communities, Lawrence's unsentimental clear-sightedness never failed him. After long observation of the native Indian tribes of New Mexico, he concluded: 'The consciousness of one branch of humanity is the annihilation of the consciousness of another branch . . . And we can understand the consciousness of the Indian only in terms of the death of our consciousness.' The impasse is dramatised in the story 'The Woman Who Rode Away', where a dissatisfied American wife rides off to live with an Indian tribe, only to find herself drugged and sacrificed to native gods in a fertility rite.

In Mexico, meanwhile, so abject, as Lawrence saw it, was the fate of the indigenous people under an alien Christianity, that he wrote a novel describing the rise of a new, local religion that might give hope and positive freedom to the Mexicans. *The Plumed Serpent* mixes Lawrence's flair for observation and description with a tone that is visionary, even apocalyptic. Depending on what one is after in Lawrence, this is the best or the worst of his books. Certainly it is the one where Murry's claim that Lawrence's real aim was 'to discover authority' makes most sense.

But the perplexity generated by the peoples he visited was as nothing to Lawrence's puzzlement with the problems of forming an ideal community of his own. In *Living at the Edge: A Biography of D. H. Lawrence & Frieda von Richthofen*, Michael Squires and his wife Lynn Talbot set out to offer a biography of the marriage. What emerges, though the authors never quite say as much, is Lawrence's one truly massive blind spot in his personal life: while he and Frieda thought of themselves as building a beneficent micro-community, they were in fact seeking in the company of others the friction necessary for keeping their own relationship alive. Ever since Lawrence had taken his wife away from her first husband, their love always fed on the tension provided by a third and interested party. They almost never lived alone.

Middleton Murry and his wife Katherine Mansfield, the poet Witter Bynner, the painters Esther Andrews and Dorothy Brett and the journalist Mabel Dodge Sterne (later Luhan) were among scores of friends invited to live with or near the Lawrences. Obliged to witness the couple's savage, often physically violent marital arguments, they soon found themselves taking sides, becoming confidants, combatants, in some cases even imagining themselves possible future partners of one or the other. But no sooner did a third party presume too much, than he or she was brutally dismissed. Very soon they would be reading unflattering descriptions of themselves in Lawrence's next book. In response, many wrote their own accounts of the experience, all mixing venom, affection and incomprehension. Such was Lawrence's utopia. As a publicity machine for his work, it was extremely effective.

Accused of clumsy repetition in the prose of *Women in Love*, Lawrence came up with the famous response that 'every natural crisis in emotion or passion or understanding comes from this pulsing, frictional to-and-fro which works up to a culmination.' But this appeal to the artist's mimetic function was actually something of an afterthought. Immediately prior to this and rather more belligerently, Lawrence defended his style thus: 'The only answer is that it is natural to the author.'

So what was 'natural' to this author? Fighting. 'Whoever reads me will be in the thick of the scrimmage' Lawrence wrote. Critics take this to mean that he was eager to draw us into the mess of life intensely lived. This is true. But the most urgent scrimmage is between author and reader.

What kind of fight is it and where does it lead? In *Women in Love*, Birkin, the character who most resembles Lawrence, invites his friend Gerald to enter into a *Blutbrüderschaft*. Gerald refuses, but he does agree to wrestle, naked, with Birkin. Needless to say, it is Birkin who chooses the form of combat and teaches Gerald how to fight according to his rules. Gerald is physically stronger, but Birkin is subtle, with an iron will. Nobody wins. At the end both men are so exhausted they fall into a trance, 'quite unconscious', but with Birkin lying on top.

This is the experience Lawrence would like his readers to have at the end of his books. This is the purpose of that rhythmic, seductive, irritatingly repetitive style. It leads us to what can best be described as a catharsis of exhaustion. For the weariness of exhausted combatants is the only oneness, the only brief overcoming of conflict that Lawrence can imagine in the modern world. In her autobiography, Frieda wrote: 'We fought our battles outright to the bitter end. Then there was peace, such peace.'

In 1925 Lawrence suffered his first lung haemorrhage in Oaxaca, Mexico. In a fit of combative energy, between 1926 and 1928 he produced three different versions of *Lady Chatterley's Lover*, proud that his last novel was guaranteed to prove a monumental scandal. Meantime, in a desperate effort to impose authority, he refused to admit that he had tuberculosis, as if belligerent denial could determine the truth. Shortly after his death Frieda and the relatives began to fight over the estate. Then there was a tussle over the future of his ashes. To avoid their being stolen Frieda had them set in cement in a little shrine in Taos. An image of the phoenix was placed on top. Lawrence would rise again from the critical conflagration that was about to begin. Art or no art, nothing, life had taught him, is more seductive than a fight.

Gardens and Graveyards

[Giorgio Bassani]

In the autumn of 1943, 183 members of the Jewish community of Ferrara, a small town in the north-east of Italy, were rounded up, imprisoned and deported to concentration camps in Germany. Only one returned. This atrocity is the grim premise behind almost all of Giorgio Bassani's narrative fiction. He was twenty-seven at the time and had grown up in that community.

Yet the Holocaust as such is never the subject of Bassani's writing, nor is he interested in elaborating a personal denunciation of anti-Semitism or Fascism. There appears to be no political agenda driving his work nor any sensationalism. Rather, his aim is to have life, as he sees it, emerge within the frame of those special circumstances that prevailed in Italy, and in particular in his hometown of Ferrara, in the years of his adolescence and early adulthood.

And life, as Bassani sees it, is complex, rich, comic and very dangerous. Above all, individual psychology and group dynamics can never be neatly superimposed on the great ideological divides of the time. This is the source of the all-pervasive irony in his writing. In 'A Plaque in Via Mazzini', a short story that appeared in 1956, Bassani writes about that one Jewish deportee who did return to Ferrara from Nazi Germany. All his close family killed by Fascism and Nazism, his own health destroyed, Geo Josz nevertheless has only contempt for the anti-Fascist partisans who have taken over his lavish palazzo in the town centre, and very little time either for his optimistic Uncle Daniele with his hopes for world democracy and universal brotherhood. No, the only person whom the anguished Geo is eager to see on arriving home is his Uncle

15

Geremia, a man whose business contacts and enthusiastic participation in the Fascist Party have allowed him to go on playing bridge
with the local shopkeepers' association right through the war. The
fact is presented more as a mystery than a criticism. Geo, eventually,
goes mad with grief.

The Garden of the Finzi-Contini, however, is first and foremost a
love story and an achievement of a quite different order from anything
else Bassani wrote. The action of this largely autobiographical
Bildungsroman is set in the years immediately before the war and
since we are told in the opening pages what the later fate of many
of the characters will be, and in particular of the tragic end that
awaits the story's beautiful and elusive heroine, Micòl Finzi-Contini,
the tension of the novel takes the form of a deepening enigma:
how far, the reader is constantly obliged to wonder, is the strange
and troubled relationship between the narrator and his beloved
Micòl determined by the particular historical situation and how far
by the perversities of the characters themselves? How far, that is –
and this is the puzzle behind all great narrative fiction – is this
unhappiness *necessary*?

The question would be banal if the boy and girl were called Capulet
and Montague, if their families were at war, if there were an unbridge-
able ideological divide between them. But though Ferrara is only
some fifty miles south of Verona, *The Garden of the Finzi-Contini* is
not another *Romeo and Juliet*. Bassani had written about lovers who
must come to terms with both ethnic and class divisions in the story
'A Stroll Before Dinner', in which the celebrated Jewish doctor Elia
Corcos (a historical figure of Ferrara, like so many of the characters
in Bassani's work) marries a nurse from a family of Catholic peasants. But that is a tale of prejudice successfully overcome, albeit at a
price. Instead, in *The Garden of the Finzi-Contini*, both hero and
heroine come from old Jewish families. The Race Laws of 1938 which
forbade Jews and Christians from intermarrying would thus seem
to make the eventual union of two Jews more, rather than less,
'convenient'. And yet . . .

One of the curiosities of Bassani's writing is that while deploring persecution he actually seems to relish the phenomenon of social division, that fizz of incomprehension that occurs when people of different cultures, backgrounds and pretensions are obliged to live side by side. Without division, after all, there would not be the frisson, for the younger generation, of mixing, the sexual lure across the cultural gap. So the first thing we learn about the Jewish community of Ferrara in the 1930s is that, despite its comprising only a few hundred souls, it is far from compact. On the contrary, it thrives on schism. The main synagogue is divided into a first floor following a German style of worship and a second following an Italian style, while a smaller and very secretive Levantine synagogue remains absolutely distinct. Curiously, awareness of these irrational divisions creates a deep complicity among the town's Jews, whichever group they happen to belong to. They are privy to mysteries that the wider Italian community can never even begin to understand.

The psychology Bassani uncovers here is immediately relevant for anyone trying to get a grip on today's multi-ethnic society: 'It was futile', the novel's narrator tells us, 'to attempt to instruct the others [the Gentiles that is], any of them . . . even those playmates infinitely more loved (at least in my case) than Jewish acquaintances, in a matter so private. Poor souls! In this regard you couldn't think of them as anything better than simple plebs, forever condemned to irreparable abysses of ignorance, or rather – as even my father used to say, grinning benignly – "goy niggers".' In this sense it is the Jewish community that excludes the others and not vice versa. Many of the Jewish characters in the novel nourish a superiority complex with regard to goys, a complex actually strengthened when (in 1938) serious persecution begins, if only because that persecution is so evidently brutal and stupid.

The young hero and heroine of *The Garden of the Finzi-Contini*, however, are not only both Jewish but both attend the same synagogue. They are not divided by any sectarian schism. There is no obvious barrier to their relationship. All the same, the positions

17

their families occupy within the Jewish community and with regard to wider Italian society suggest profoundly different attitudes to life, attitudes that will be recognisable in any era or social context.

The narrator of the novel and its main character is never named, but so closely does his biography and family resemble Bassani's that critics have got into the habit of referring to him as B. B's father, an optimist, an erstwhile doctor turned administrator of old family property, has always been eager to become part of modern Italy and wishes the same level of assimilation for his family and for the Jewish community as a whole. He thinks of himself simultaneously as a Jew and an Italian and trusts that he will not be obliged to choose between the two. This outlook seems admirable. B's father is a man who gladly accepts social responsibility. He is president of the committee that maintains the local Jewish cemetery. Yet to participate fully in Italian public life in the 1930s means to become a member of the Fascist Party. In 1933, B's father is delighted that ninety per cent of Ferrara's Jews are card-carrying Fascists. And he is furious that Micòl's father, Ermanno Finzi-Contini, refuses to join the party. When, to spare the rich reclusive man any possible bureaucratic tedium, a membership card is made up for him and taken to his house, the professor – for Ermanno Finzi-Contini is a cultured person, although he holds no university position – tears it up.

The reader will be tempted to side with this refusal to compromise, especially because, on every other occasion, Ermanno is such a gentle, mild-mannered person. Yet his gesture is not the result of a committed anti-Fascist, but part, rather, of a general instinct to isolate himself and his family, not only from wider Italian society, but from the Jewish community as well. So determinedly does he do this, that B's father will paradoxically accuse the Finzi-Contini of anti-Semitism, this despite the fact that when the two families sit one behind the other at the synagogue it is evident that Ermanno Finzi-Contini speaks Hebrew and can repeat all the prayers of the liturgy, while the narrator's more Italianised father can barely mutter a word.

The description of the Finzi-Contini family, at once entirely convincing and magnificently enigmatic, is one of the triumphs of Bassani's literary career. On putting this novel down you feel you could reflect endlessly on the relationship of each family member to the others, on their many contradictions, and above all on what they might or might not represent. To be sure, you will reach no firm conclusions, but all the same the conviction grows that, with the Finzi-Contini, Bassani was seeking to get to grips with a very special product of the modern world, a phenomenon of far wider significance than the structure of society in Ferrara, or even the question of Jewish persecution.

Nevertheless, these people do have to be seen in context. On the annexation of the Papal States into a unified Italy in 1861, the obligation of Ferrara's Jews to live segregated in the town's ghetto was ended. To celebrate his newly won rights, Ermanno's grandfather, Moise Finzi-Contini, a hugely rich man, bought out the property of an impoverished nobleman. The property was large: ten hectares on the edge of town protected by a high wall including a stately home in an advanced state of disrepair. Moise's son Menotti, Ermanno's father, rebuilt and extended the house and took his sophisticated wife to live there. Rather than moving out of the ghetto in order to get into Italian society, the Finzi-Contini have moved out of society altogether and begun to cultivate what B's father sees as absurd pretensions to nobility. (The name Finzi-Contini in Italian might actually suggest 'fake little counts', though it should be said that Finzi is the name of a well known Jewish family.)

The Finzi-Contini vocation for isolation is consolidated in the next generation when Ermanno and his wife, Olga, lose their first-born son, Guido, at six years old, to meningitis. (The doctor who diagnoses the incurable disease is none other than Dr Corcos of 'A Stroll Before Dinner', the man who married down into the most humble strata of Italian society.) Convinced that the death was brought about through contact with others, father and mother decide to have the two children born after Guido, Alberto and

Micòl, educated at home and almost entirely segregated from the world. As a result, B will only ever see Micòl when she and her brother come, as private students, to take their annual state exams at school, or, more regularly, at the synagogue.

Bassani is a master of the dramatic set piece that carries, without ever seeming contrived, a profound significance. Week by week, in the synagogue, the young narrator is fascinated by the Finzi-Contini family sitting on the bench behind him. To control his son, B's father waits for the rabbi to deliver the closing blessing, when each Jewish father drapes his prayer shawl over the heads of his whole family. He then forces his son under the shawl to stop his constant gazing at the family behind. But the shawl is so threadbare that the boy is able to peep through the holes. Charmed by the sound of Ermanno Finzi-Contini chanting the prayers in Hebrew, but with an upper-class Tuscan accent, B exchanges exciting glances with the Finzi-Contini children who seem to be inviting him to come in under their shawl.

So: the father who advocates mixing and assimilation tries in vain to stop his son from mixing with the family who have chosen isolation. Meantime, although the narrator's family is clearly divided within itself, the son rebelling against the father, the Finzi-Contini, on the other hand and for all their social isolation, seem united in casting a spell over the young man, an aesthetic spell, made up of class and caste, beautiful language, beautiful gestures and a beautiful girl. It is a curious and disturbing characteristic of the Finzi-Contini that they never seem to disagree with each other and, with the exception of their attendance at the synagogue, are never to be seen outside the walls of their huge garden. Friends can be invited into that garden, but, for reasons we never quite understand, they can't invite a Finzi-Contini to come out.

B's first invitation into the garden comes on a hot summer day in his early teens. He has just heard that he has failed an exam and is cycling miserably and aimlessly about the town. Astride a high wall, the young Micòl calls to him, suggests he climb over into the garden via a series of footholds. She has placed a ladder on the inside. What do we know about Micòl? That she is blonde and bright-eyed, slim and tall, that her manner is always one of affectionate mockery and that she speaks in a peculiar sing-song, a private language almost, Finzi-Continesque, that she shares with her brother. She is playful, attractive. B is seduced, but scared. Of what? Of the high wall, he says. He would prefer to go into the garden through the main gate. But then the others would know, Micòl objects. At once the boy's fear shifts to the girl's sexuality. Segregated from the world, at one with her close-knit but exclusive family, any openness to others on Micòl's part must be clandestine. What does she want from him? Is it that each member of the family needs occasional victims from outside to make their collective separateness possible? Nervous, the boy fusses over the problem of hiding his bicycle and the moment passes. Inside the garden, Perotti, the gatekeeper, the chauffeur, the butler almost, has spotted the girl on the wall. She must come down.

A word needs to be said here on the wonderfully comic and always sinister figure of Perotti. Employed, together with his wife and children, in the role of family retainer, this ageing factotum of peasant stock has invested even more in the Finzi-Continis' supposed nobility than they have themselves. Officially a servant, he thus begins to function as a prison warder. Manically assiduous, he polishes the family's ancient horse carriage, their old American car, their old American lift. If ever a Finzi-Contini shows any signs of slipping from the role of perfect aristocrat, Perotti will be there to prevent him or her from going too far. A strange hint of the gothic pervades the garden of the Finzi-Contini. It is all the more sinister for being a parodied gothic, a modern gothic, where the cloud hanging over the noble house has a terrible historical reality.

But what is there inside this huge, walled garden and why did Bassani make it the title and focus of his book? Having missed his chance, or escaped the trap perhaps, in his teens, B doesn't get to see beyond the wall until he is in his early twenties. It is the autumn of 1938. The new Race Laws have led to the expulsion of all members of the Jewish community from Ferrara's tennis club. Suddenly, both Alberto and Micòl Finzi-Contini are phoning the narrator to suggest that he could come to play tennis on the court in their garden. Arriving at the great gate to the property, B finds he is not alone. The family have invited half a dozen others. The story proper can begin.

But why this sudden generosity from the Finzi-Contini, demands B's father? He senses danger for his son in this liaison. Why this unexpected openness? Various family members offer inadequate explanations: because we have a tennis court and you have nowhere to play; because the Race Laws have now placed all Jews in the same boat; there can no longer be any distinction between us. But there *is* distinction. It is always the narrator who visits the Finzi-Contini house, never vice versa. The attentive reader smells a rat. What is the reason, then, for this change of attitude?

Bassani's genius is never to be explicit. We cannot separate one strand of life from another. Did the Finzi-Contini really segregate their children because their first son died of meningitis, or was that just a convenient alibi? In 1938 both Alberto and Micòl, now in their early twenties, are at a critical moment in life. Both are officially studying at universities in other towns, while in fact living at home. Like the narrator, both are taking far longer than seems necessary to complete their undergraduate theses and hence their degrees. It is a situation all Italian readers will immediately recognise. The undergraduate thesis, something not required in British or American universities, is a moment of initiation in Italy, a passport to the adult world. All three are shivering on the brink. They are hanging back. What is the point of graduating if society then excludes Jews from the workplace? Your degree is worth nothing.

But there is more to it than that. As with all gothic scenarios, the air is dense with repressed or hidden sexuality. The two young Finzi-Contini, Alberto and Micòl, seem blocked, stalled, marooned, and not only in their studies. Perhaps the political situation is covering some deeper difficulty with facing the world and mixing with life outside their protected garden. By allowing others into their world to play tennis they have found a way to alleviate a tension that would otherwise force them out into adulthood. Sport, after all, offers a pleasant surrogate for life's crueller battles.

In an Indian summer that shines on far into November, the fiercely fought tennis games become a daily ritual. Taking turns to play and rest, B finds himself being shown around the vast grounds by Micòl. He is now hopelessly in love and she has singled him out for friendship. Yet the reader's attention is insistently diverted towards the garden. Immediately we are struck by this reflection: if the Finzi-Contini have refused to mix with the outside world, they nevertheless, in the protected space they live in, have mixed together, generously and heterogeneously, everything that the world has to offer. This is their modernity. Desiring separateness, they seek to possess exoticism, in the security of their own home. Their garden is full of trees from other climes. Micòl can name scores of species. Some have to be protected against the harsh, Po Valley winters by stacking straw against the trunks. The house itself is a bizarre mixture of architectural styles. The food they serve is extravagant in its variety and quantity. It includes kosher food and pork. There is a remarkable library that precludes any need to consult the library in Ferrara. Books on literature and science, Italian history and ancient Judaism, are mixed promiscuously together. The latest American hi-fi equipment abounds. Alberto has personalised his gramophone by separating treble and bass on four different speakers carefully distributed around the antique panelling of his room. Micòl has personalised a recipe she brought back from Austria for something called *Skiwasser*, a hot drink for winter weather. She has added grapes and consumes the concoction ice-cold. She keeps a flask of *Skiwasser* beside her bed, along with a collection of tiny glass ornaments from Venice.

Acquired, segregated and manipulated in this way, the world's abundance is tamed and aestheticised. But that, after all, is what gardens do to nature. The garden is a hybrid space, at once real and unreal, as sport is at once a real engagement, but nothing like the battle to be joined outside the garden only a year hence. In so many ways, the Finzi-Contini foreshadow the modern consumer's obsession with control and security, with possessing the whole world in the safe domestic space, shutting out reality, living in a state of denial. The Race Laws give the family a further excuse for establishing a separate existence. After all, they have the money that makes this possible. Again and again the narrator is surprised to see how the Finzi-Contini, all of them, seem pleased rather than scandalised by the increasingly harsh treatment of the Jews. Isolated together, each has – something unheard of at the time in Italy – a telephone extension in his or her bedroom. 'To protect your freedom,' Micòl tells the narrator, 'there's nothing better than having a good telephone extension.' The subject of the thesis she is taking so long to finish is that most hermetic of poets, Emily Dickinson.

Through the autumn of 1938, the late adolescence of these three Italian Jews is wonderfully and frustratingly protracted in game after game of tennis, walk after walk around the vast grounds. To make matters more complicated and infinitely more ambiguous, a fourth character and tennis player becomes important. Giampiero Malnate already has his degree. He is a few years older than the others. He is a Gentile not a Jew. He comes from the big city of Milan not the provincial backwater of Ferrara. He does not hide a frank and experienced sexuality. He has a job as a chemist with a government project to develop synthetic rubber, this in the hope of making Fascist Italy independent of the wider world. And, ironically, he is a communist. He is optimistic. He believes the world can be improved. He deplores the capitalist basis of the Finzi-Contini wealth. In short, Malnate is everything the other three are not. He has a start in life. He is initiated.

What is this man doing then in the dreamy garden of the Finzi-Contini, a place of eternal suspension, of life delayed? Malnate was originally invited by Alberto, with whom he studied at university. Is it possible that Alberto is homosexual? He shows no interest in women. Bassani will give us no more than the vaguest hints. Or is Giampiero there for Micòl? Are both brother and sister jealous of Giampiero's relationship with the other? At one point Micòl tells the narrator that she would no more have sex with him than with her brother. But perhaps there *is* a sexual attraction between her and her brother. In love with Micòl, the narrator's frustration mounts. So much of what is going on makes no sense. He has fierce political arguments with Giampiero that turn out not to be about politics at all but, obscurely, about the roles the two men have come to occupy within the Finzi-Contini household. While they battle it out, Alberto obsessively adjusts the treble and bass on his hi-fi system, Perotti and his family serve lavish teas. Soon enough the tension reaches the point where some clarifying drama must be at hand. One way or another, these youngsters must become adult.

Three of the finest Italian novels that, in one way or another, deal with the Second War seem obsessed by the choice between action and inaction, which in turn becomes a question of how far and in what way one should or should not become involved in society, since action inevitably means involvement. Despite this similarity of theme, all three are marvellously different. In Dino Buzzati's surreal work *The Tartar Steppe* a young army officer is called to serve in a remote fort at the furthest extreme of his country's borders. High in the mountains, the fort overlooks a vast desert whence the Tartars are expected to attack. Immediately on his arrival, the officer senses that his posting there is a disaster. He has been utterly removed from all social life. He is desperate to leave. But very soon he finds himself strangely enchanted by the fort's military rituals, by a life rendered dramatic by the alpine scenery, and above all by the promise of an eventual Tartar attack. In the end, he rejects an offer to return to his distant hometown, his pretty girlfriend. His whole life passes by. The Tartars fail to show. Military conflict becomes a dream that would give meaning to all he has renounced. He yearns for it but is doomed to frustration. Old and sick, he is leaving the fort for the last time when the Tartar army finally appears en masse. As if conjured up by the officer's disappointment, the catastrophe has finally come. Delivered to the publishers in 1939, *The Tartar Steppe* (or *The Fort* as Buzzati had wanted it to be titled) is an astonishingly timely warning of the dangers of substituting ordinary social involvement with the allure of heroic action and military glory.

Pavese's *The House on the Hill* was written soon after the Second War. Again, the title presents the novel's themes spatially, and again, like Buzzati's fort and Bassani's garden, Pavese's house on the hill is a place of suspension, of action denied. It is 1944 and night after night, a schoolteacher retreats from Turin to a house in the surrounding hills to escape the Allied bombardment. Although he spends his evenings with a group of anti-Fascist activists, admiring their idealism and attracted to their warmth and vitality, he finds himself unable to join them. In Pavese's book, then, unlike Buzzati's, action is abundantly available, the Tartars are everywhere, but the intellectual, pacifist narrator cannot bring himself to participate. Yet he feels guilty for not doing so. He feels unmanned and excluded from life. When his friends are rounded up and imprisoned by the Fascists, the schoolteacher flees. In one memorable scene, he witnesses a partisan ambush of a Fascist military truck. After the fighting is over, he finds it impossible to step over the corpses of the Fascist soldiers on the road. He feels sick, paralysed, and has to turn back.

That a period of social violence and political extremism, such as Italy experienced in the 1920s and 1930s, should oblige the country's writers and artists to reflect on their obligation or otherwise to get involved would seem obvious enough. It was civil war, after all, that inspired Andrew Marvell's great meditation on the merits of the active and contemplative lives in 'An Horatian Ode'. But it is surprising that all three of these Italian novels, each so different in its approach, should constantly entwine the themes of public action and sexual fulfilment, as if rejection of one necessarily implied renunciation of the other. Home on leave from his remote posting, Buzzati's officer is still in time to propose marriage to his

old girlfriend and escape his arid fate in the fort. But it is so difficult to speak to her, he feels so inept. Among the community of
communist activists he visits, Pavese's schoolteacher comes across
an ex-girlfriend. She has a child that may even be his. But the young
mother emphatically excludes him from her life. She will not renew
the relationship and will not let him assume a fatherly role with
the child. In *The Garden of the Finzi-Contini*, communist playboy
Giampiero Malnate brings both a political and sexual urgency into
the otherwise decadent and languid atmosphere of the garden.
Micòl, who has resolved never to marry, mocks him, saying she
doesn't give a damn about his social-democratic future. Speaking
to the narrator about his unhappiness, she freely mixes the vocabulary of love and war, declaring that love is for the bloodthirsty, for
people ready to struggle to get the better of each other day in day
out, a cruel sport, far crueller than tennis. Fully aware that war is
imminent, she concentrates her energies on getting her father to
resurface their deteriorating clay court.

Thus in a highly politicised era, when every publication in Italy
was scrutinised for orthodoxy or heresy on both sides of the ideological divide, all these novelists transmit the truth that individual
political views are the result not of correct or false reasoning, nor
the inevitable expression of a good or evil disposition, but are deeply
connected with the whole personality, the mysteries of identity and
fate.

But beneath every other theme and concern, and whether or
not prompted by the political situation, the question all these three
novels quite explicitly ask is: what does it mean to have lived?
These, after all, were the years of the existentialists. Bassani, or his
narrator, begins his novel with a visit by himself and some friends to
an Etruscan cemetery. We don't feel sad for the dead of antiquity,
someone says, because it is as if they had never lived. A child in
the company, however, reminds everybody that, of course, that is
not true; however long ago, the Etruscans did live, like everybody
else. The tombs bear out that simple reflection with their bas-reliefs

27

showing all the objects they used: hoes, ropes, axes, scissors, spades, knives, bows and arrows. Such are the objects with which one engages in action, whether domestic or military. They are none of them things the Finzi-Contini ever hold in their hands.

From beginning to end, cemeteries are present through the novel, more so perhaps than in any work by Edgar Allan Poe. B's father is responsible for the upkeep of the Jewish cemetery in Ferrara. Ermanno Finzi-Contini has published a collection of all the inscriptions in the famous Jewish cemetery of Venice, where, we discover, he also proposed to his wife. Cemeteries are places of memory and affection, uniting the living and the dead, not places to be shunned or feared. The horror, in this novel, is not death, or even dying young. No, the one truly terrifying thing is to pass from youth to cemetery *without having lived*, without initiation. And that is the fate one risks in the garden of the Finzi-Contini, a gothic world where death and immaturity are magically superimposed and time suspended. Ultimately this will be the fate of Alberto Finzi-Contini, who renounces every form of engagement, political, moral and sexual, and dies of cancer before he can be taken, like his sister and the rest of his family, to the terrible initiation of the Nazi death camps.

We are told nothing of the fate of Bassani's narrator during and after the war; all we know is that he lived to tell the tale. Bassani himself, however, definitely chose the way of engagement and initiation. Having finished his thesis and, like the narrator of the novel, taken his degree in literature in 1939, he joined one of the liberal political groupings that were forming to fight Fascism. It was called *Il partito d'azione*. Arrested in May 1943, Bassani was released in July when Mussolini fled Rome. Days later he married. 'Art,' his narrator remarks in *The Garden of the Finzi-Contini*, 'when it is pure, is always abnormal, antisocial, it can't be used for anything.' In that sense, of course, art and writing have much in common with Micòl's enchanted garden. But, however much the Finzi-Contini might wish to, one does not live in a work of art.

After the Struggle

[Feodor Mikhailovich Dostoevsky]

'You cannot take *a man who was all struggle*', wrote Tolstoy of Dostoevsky, after his great rival's death, 'and set him up on a monument for the instruction of posterity.'*

To which struggle exactly was Count Tolstoy referring? Certainly not the liberal cause that had condemned Dostoevsky to spending four years in a Siberian labour camp and six more as a soldier. In his mid-twenties Feodor Mikhailovich had fallen under the charismatic influence of the revolutionary Nikolay Speshnev and joined his secret society. At once, he was anxious: Speshnev had lent him a large sum of money. How could the young writer ever repay his 'very own Mephistopheles' and escape this compromising and politically dangerous situation? Three days after being arrested and placed in solitary confinement, Dostoevsky tells us, he felt an enormous sense of relief and serenity. Later he would remark: 'penal servitude saved me'.

Such moments of relief, of internal conflict resolved in extreme well-being, feature prominently in Dostoevsky's work. Usually they follow a dramatic surrender of pride by a powerful personality: a murderer confesses, or the great man kneels before the holy hermit, the innocent prostitute, though not before having passed through agonies of uncertainty and rebellion. *Notes from Underground*, however, is unique among Dostoevsky's writings in that it begins with a man whose struggling is long since over and ended in failure: 'I am a sick man . . . I am a wicked man' our anonymous narrator opens his hundred-page monologue. More than any of the writer's other works, this will be Dostoevsky's justification for a life that is indeed all struggle.

Notes is organised in two parts: first, a long statement of the narrator's present situation and vision of the world; second, an account of a dramatic incident in his past. He describes himself as a minor civil servant who has retired on the back of a modest inheritance. In short, a nobody. His sickness and wickedness, we soon learn, are the result of 'intellectual activity', which is always and in every form 'a disease'. It led him to be acutely sensitive to the good and the beautiful while invariably choosing to act in an ugly and repulsive fashion. This painful contradiction caused the narrator years of unhappy struggle as he tried to reconcile egoism with moral sensibility. But at last he is worn out, he has 'lost even the desire to struggle'. More intellectually feverish than ever, he gnashes his teeth in obscurity, consoling himself with the thought that 'it had to be so', that 'this was really my normal state'.

The circumstances in which Dostoevsky wrote this disturbing incipit are worth bearing in mind. Discharged from the army in 1859, aged thirty-eight, he had brought his newly married wife to St Petersburg and begun publishing, together with his brother Mikhail, a political and literary magazine, *Time*. The magazine was successful, the writer's career on the rise, but his marriage was unhappy. Maria Dimitrievna suffered from tuberculosis and frequently accused her husband of being 'a rogue, a rascal and a criminal'. Perhaps to be worthy of her accusations, Dostoevsky began an affair with a twenty-three-year-old and took time off to travel in Europe where he discovered the joys of roulette.

In 1863 the censors closed *Time*, plunging the Dostoevsky brothers into dire financial trouble. But while waiting for permission to publish again, Feodor once more set out to travel in Europe, despite the fact that his wife was now seriously ill. Claiming he needed to consult Western doctors about his epilepsy, he headed for Paris where his young mistress was waiting. His beloved Apollinaria Suslova, however, now decided that there would be no more sex between them. They would travel to Italy as friends, not lovers. Holier than the average adulterer, Dostoevsky went along with this, while making frequent attempts to get the girl back between the sheets. She refused, but generously lent him money to go home when gambling bouts left him penniless.

After three months away, then, Dostoevsky returns to Russia to find his wife at death's door and his brother desperate to gather material for a new magazine that the censors have at last given permission to publish: Feodor Mikhailovich must write something, *at once*. So after months of indulgence and sinful pleasure, Dostoevsky faces a period of labour and renunciation. Perhaps it is not surprising then that in *Notes from Underground* the polarities of good and evil are present throughout but without any possibility of either becoming dominant; instead we have a perverse, self-lacerating enjoyment of their simultaneity and incompatibility. Of his more noble thoughts the narrator tells us:

> These influxes of 'everything beautiful and lofty' used also to come to me during my little debauches; . . . and yet they did not annihilate the little debauch . . . on the contrary, it was as if they enlivened it by contrast and came in exactly the proportion required for a good sauce. The sauce here consisted of contradiction and suffering, of tormenting inner analysis and all these torments and tormenticules lent my little debauch a certain piquancy, even meaning . . .

Yet it would be a mistake to think of *Notes* as primarily a private document. One of the consequences of the strict censorship that made direct statements on many issues impossible was that Russian fiction in this period was always understood as a disguised form of political debate. So no sooner has Dostoevsky established the perverse psychology of his narrator than it is being used in the public arena as an attack on the recent novel *What is to be Done?* by the revolutionary theorist Nikolay Chernyshevsky, an attack that takes up the whole first part of the book.

A word must be said here on Dostoevsky's idiosyncratic style when entering the political fray. Throughout the nineteenth century a fierce debate raged in Russia between westward-looking reformers and tsarist conservatives. At issue were the condition of the serfs, the authority of the tsar. In his editorial for the opening issue of *Time* in 1861 Dostoevsky makes the strange claim that what will distinguish his paper is that he is really convinced of what he says, even if it may sound like 'copybook maxims', while his political opponents are not. In the following editorials he goes on to attack the *ideas* of the westernised liberals, while sympathising with their generous *spirit*, and to support the conservative *ideas* of the tsarist camp while attacking their reactionary harshness. The terms of public debate are thus undermined. No idea can be judged without consideration of the mind and personality that anchors it in reality.

Needless to say, this peculiar approach exercised no political influence, completely confused the censors and was partly responsible for the decision to close down *Time* in 1863. So as Dostoevsky embarks on his first piece for the new magazine, called *Epoque*, he is determined that on this occasion there be no mistake: he absolutely and *implacably* opposes the revolutionary Nikolay Chernyshevsky.

Chernyshevsky was an optimist proposing an ethics of rational egoism. Far from struggling with irreconcilable opposites, the characters in *What is to be Done?* show how a person's real self-interest, when properly understood, is *always* compatible with the general good. Thus the two young heroes of the novel, who are in love with the same woman, are able to sort out their problems without pain or conflict. Thus, if each person acts *selfishly and in his or her own interest*, properly understood, society can be reorganised to the benefit of everyone.

At first glance the target seems too easy to be interesting. 'Oh, what a baby!' our underground narrator exclaims, having summarised Chernyshevsky's position, 'Oh, what a pure innocent child!' And he raises the objection that if one's best interests can be determined by reason and if one then *inevitably* acts in accordance with those interests, all one's actions can be predetermined, a state of affairs man instinctively resists. He himself, the narrator claims, frequently and deliberately acts *against* his best interests, since the highest good is not happiness or material wealth but simply this freedom to do whatever one wishes. As a result of this argument, the first part of the book is often interpreted as a defence of free will over determinism, even if that means accepting unhappy and unattractive phenomena like our sick and spiteful narrator.

But *Notes* is a much more radical and disturbing document than that. For Dostoevsky had the immense good fortune that the enemy of the moment provided him with the stimulus for an exploration of the very possibility of speaking of selfhood and self-interest at all, something that must have been much on the author's mind after his own erratic behaviour of recent months. Here the monologue form is crucial. 'I am a wicked man' the narrator introduces himself. But only moments later he claims: 'as a matter of fact, I was never able to become wicked.' Indeed: 'I never even managed to become anything: neither wicked nor good, neither a scoundrel nor an honest man, neither a hero nor an insect.'

One observes here, as ever, Dostoevsky's habit of seeing only opposite and mutually exclusive alternatives, all equally impossible for our narrator, since, whichever way he leans, his brain is 'swarming' with 'opposite tendencies'. There were thus two related struggles in his past: one between good and evil, or selfishness and renunciation, and, in response to the resulting confusion, the struggle to become someone. It is because our narrator has failed in both struggles that he must remain anonymous. Unable to be bad or good, he is nobody; irretrievably selfish, he has no self worthy of a name. 'An intelligent man of the nineteenth century', he defends himself, 'must be and is morally obliged to be primarily a characterless being.'

Character, the narrator argues, is consolidated in action, good or bad. But the corrosive nature of intellectual thought constantly undermines the basis of action because one senses its futility. Imagining someone who *is* able to act, to take revenge, for example, the narrator remarks:

Well, sirs, it is just such an ingenuous man that I regard as the real, normal man . . . I envy such a man to the point of extreme bile. He is stupid . . . but perhaps a normal man ought to be stupid, how do you know? Perhaps it's even beautiful. And I am the more convinced of this, so to speak, suspicion, seeing that if, for example, one takes the antithesis of the normal man, that is, the man of heightened conscious ness [*sic*], who came, of course, not from the bosom of nature but from a retort (this is almost mysticism, gentlemen, but I suspect that, too) this retort man sometimes folds before his antithesis so far that he honestly regards himself, with all his heightened consciousness as a mouse and not a man. A highly conscious mouse, perhaps, but a mouse all the same, whereas here we have a man, and consequently . . . and so on . . .

Such self-deconstructing reflection not only dismisses centuries of Enlightenment optimism, but opens a wound in the reader's relationship with the narrative voice. Who is it really who is speaking? Since the man who doesn't act has no real relationship with anyone (he admits that the 'gentlemen' he addresses are mere rhetorical constructs), since he constantly contradicts himself, since he is often not sure himself whether he is lying or not, we begin to feel that he is no more than a voice stretched across time. At moments of ellipsis – and there are many – he simply ceases to exist.

The style of *Notes* reinforces our doubts. It is dense with references to scenes and rhetoric from well-known novels of the recent past. This passage is taken from Gogol, that image from Pushkin, or Turgenev. The narrator begins to dream, but then realises he is fantasising something he read somewhere. He frequently refers to his bookish imagination, suggesting that his mind can inhabit well-worn but contradictory positions without any investment in them. Or, worse still, without *knowing* whether he has any investment in them. The statement reminds us of Dostoevsky's perception that his political opponents often put forward positions without really believing in them. At this point, as with the Hollywood habit of quoting interminably from previous films, we have the growing and very modern concern that every statement put before us comes wrapped in a sticky layer of parody. Nothing can be taken seriously except the absence of a convincing seriousness consequent on the disappearance of a reliable identity. The 'struggle' is towards truly holding a position, any position, even if it seems taken from 'copybook maxims'.

When not falling into quotation, Dostoevsky's underground voice invents neologisms and syntactical tics all its own. Language is either private to the point of excluding the listener or so worn out and public as to be meaningless. This puts the translator under considerable pressure. In his introduction to the most recent translation of *Notes* (1993) Richard Pevear attacks the tendency of other translations to normalise the book's style, claiming that he and his translation partner Larissa Volokhonsky have done all they can to reproduce its idiosyncrasies. The problem with such an approach is that the idiosyncrasies of the original arose from the Russian language and in a Russian context. Their meaning, or undermining of meaning, depended on the readers' recognition of a quotation, on the perceived distance between a specific tic and normal usage. Where context is all, translation is arduous. Pevear's aims are admirable and his text always intriguing, but there are times when its oddly shifting registers seem more to do with literal translation than creative prose. If nothing else, however, the problem alerts us to Dostoevsky's anticipation of modernism. When a writer's voice could be confidently public without seeming parodic such difficulties did not arise.

Aside from the roulette table, another form of gambling Dostoevsky indulged in was that of the hazardous publishing contract. Two years after finishing *Notes from Underground* and while working on *Crime and Punishment* he took an advance to write a novel of more than 160 pages. If he failed to deliver by November of the same year he would have to pay a huge fine and if he didn't finish by December, the publisher could have all his work for the next nine years completely free. Why had Dostoevsky agreed to such mad terms? Why did he wait till six weeks before the deadline to begin writing?

The answer, as with his roulette playing, seems to have been his need to feel that he was chosen, that he was a great and not an ordinary man. This, after all, is Raskolnikov's obsession in *Crime and Punishment*. If Dostoevsky won at roulette, if he finished his book in time, then God had chosen him, he had an identity. If not, then he could cease to struggle, he was nothing. The book he wrote, or rather, for speed's sake, dictated, was *The Gambler*, which is to say, the man who risks in order to become someone.

The narrator of *Notes* also dreams of being a writer. Once, in the past, he did actually write something, but the publishers turned it down. 'I was bitterly disappointed. – Sometimes my rage positively choked me.' Denied recognition, his dreams became vaguer: '. . . at that time I blindly believed that by some miracle . . . all *this* [his squalid life] would be drawn aside like a curtain, and a wide horizon would open out before me, a field of suitable activity, philanthropic, noble and above all ready-made . . . and I would emerge into God's sunlight, practically riding a white horse and crowned with laurel.'

But the great transformation never occurs. Unlike his creator, the narrator is not chosen and does not go on struggling to be so; denied 'God's sunlight', he remains underground, unknown, secret, multiple. The question that the second part of *Notes* poses is: in the world of individuals 'cut off from the soil', which is to say from the obvious roles offered by traditional communal relationships, what becomes of the proud and ambitious ego if denied the redemption of celebrity? 'I couldn't even conceive of playing a secondary part,' the narrator tells us, 'and that is why in actuality I quite contentedly filled the last of all. Either a hero or dirt, there was nothing in between.'

While the first part of *Notes* is all argument, the second is all narrative. The story is simple and schematic. Going back to a time when the narrator was twenty-four, we are given, one by one, his encounters with an anonymous army officer, with his boss, with his old school friends, with his servant and with a woman. In each case, our anti-hero tries to establish a relationship that would offer the gratification of recognition and identity, or, failing that, at least the exercise of power.

The army officer, a man of superior social status, casually shoves the narrator aside at a billiard table without paying him any attention. Insulted, the narrator pathetically and comically seeks to contrive a situation where he can bump into the man and force him to fight a duel, something that would amount to a recognition of equality. When he does finally pluck up the courage to bump into him, the officer still pays no attention. But at least our anonymous sufferer can pride himself on having acted in some way.

Unable to live in a completely solipsistic world 'for more than three months at a time', he goes to visit his boss who 'lived in four tiny low-ceilinged rooms, economically furnished and jaundiced-looking . . . The host usually sat in his study, on a leather sofa in front of the table, with one of his elderly guests . . . The talk was about excise duties, arguments in the Senate, salaries, promotion . . . I would sit there dumb, almost paralysed, and sometimes breaking into a sweat; but it did me good. Returning home, I was able to lay aside for a time my desire to embrace all mankind.'

This is barely more satisfactory than the encounter with the officer. But the narrator has an old school acquaintance, Simonov, whom he sees and occasionally borrows money from. One day at Simonov's he meets two other schoolmates, who are arranging a small farewell dinner party at a hotel for a fourth acquaintance, Zverkov. Irritated that he hasn't been invited, the narrator insists on inviting himself.

The evening is a comic masterpiece and, for the narrator, an unmitigated disaster. Zverkov, in his small way, is a celebrity, an army officer with a modest fortune. Despite his mediocrity, his three friends worship him. He is someone. Immediately, the only relation that the narrator of *Notes* can imagine with Zverkov is one of competition; he must force his friends to grant him the same status. He gets drunk, insults them, challenges Zverkov to a duel and is laughed at and finally ignored. When the others set off to end the evening in a brothel, the narrator borrows money to chase after them, alternating fantasies of self-abasement in which he begs forgiveness, with equally crazy plans to slap Zverkov's face and force him to a fight. Arriving at the brothel, he finds that his friends have disappeared. At once it is clear that this development was just an excuse to bring our narrator into the presence of a woman.

One day, recounts Leonid Grossman in his biography of the author, while Dostoevsky was dictating *The Gambler* to his young copyist, he told her that he was at a crossroads in life and had three choices: 'to go east, to Constantinople or Jerusalem and remain there forever; to go abroad for roulette and give himself up entirely to gambling; or to seek happiness in a second marriage. Anna advised him to take the last course.' Not long afterwards Dostoevsky proposed to the girl.

What do these three choices signify? 'Constantinople or Jerusalem' would appear to be the way of renunciation, sainthood; gambling abroad, the way of debauchery. But in the middle, for the man who, however hard he struggles, can choose neither of those extremes, lay a form of salvation, another way of being chosen and achieving identity: the love of a woman.

As *Notes* approaches its climax, the reader now witnesses a distressing instance of the right ideas coming from the wrong mouth. Waking from a drunken stupor beside the girl he has paid for and used, the narrator proceeds to persuade her that she must leave the brothel at once. She is beautiful, she could have love and respect and marriage and children. Instead, what awaits her as a prostitute are contempt, disease, poverty, death by consumption. Using trite words that 'sound just like a book', he creates a heartbreaking picture that soon has the girl sobbing with regret. This is precisely the result he was aiming for. With no intention of helping, he has demonstrated his power to wound, something he couldn't do to his less vulnerable friends. 'It was the game that carried me along, the game itself.' However, he then adds: 'but not only the game . . .'

Here is the key to the whole book. Dostoevsky is interested in the way ready-made visions adhere, or fail to adhere, or worst of all, *half* adhere to the mind. The narrator plays a hideous trick on the young prostitute. But his 'game' is only successful because he starts to believe in it. He is attracted to the girl. The hackneyed idea of saving a prostitute has got the better of him. His rhetoric becomes more convincing and dangerous. He gives her his address . . . Somebody is now in a position to step into his solipsistic world and make it real.

The denouement is as painful as it is farcical. Some days later the narrator is engaged in a comic argument with his servant when Liza arrives. He is refusing to pay the servant his salary, trying to force him to recognise a relationship of subservience that goes beyond the exchange of cash. The servant is having none of it. He will only work if paid. Into the room steps the woman who has been selling herself for money, but is now asking for a recognition that goes beyond money. Terrified by this reality, the narrator tells her he was only joking in the brothel. He breaks down in hysterics. Despite his disgraceful behaviour, the girl responds to his suffering. She comforts him. She is offering love. He has been *chosen*. This is his moment, his chance to come out from the autism of the underground. But he is not equal to the responsibilities involved. He has sex with the girl then thrusts money into her hand, pushes her out. She rejects the money and leaves. Totally confused, he runs after her to beg forgiveness. 'Never before had I endured so much suffering and repentance; but could there have been even the slightest doubt, as I went running out of the apartment, that I would turn back halfway?'

In any event, Liza has gone. Without a self, the narrator is left with a few roubles in his hand and a mind doomed to raking these moments back and forth for decades to come. In a distinctly Beckettian conclusion he tells us he has had enough, he must stop his pointless reflections. In his authorial voice Dostoevsky adds the postscript: 'This is not the end, however, of the notes of this paradoxical writer. He could not help going on . . .'

But if the narrator of *Notes* is in an ugly, perverse and potentially dangerous relation to the fantasies and the rhetoric he practises on others, what about Dostoevsky himself? His wife died of consumption in the apartment the couple shared while he was writing the second part of *Notes*. What were his thoughts as he penned the following passage where the narrator is terrifying Liza with the vision of her inevitable destiny in the brothel?

No, Liza, it will be lucky, lucky for you if you die quickly of consumption, someplace in a corner, in a basement . . . In a hospital, you say? If they take you there, fine, but what if your madam still needs you? Consumption is that sort of illness; it's not a fever. A person goes on hoping till the last moment, saying he's well. It's just self-indulgence. But there's profit in it for the madam. Don't worry, it's true; you've sold your soul, you owe money besides, so you don't dare make a peep. And when you're dying, they'll all abandon you, they'll all turn away from you – because what good are you then? They'll even reproach you for uselessly taking up space and not dying quickly enough. You'll have a hard time getting a drink of water, they'll give it to you with a curse: 'Hurry up and croak, you slut; you're moaning, people can't sleep, the clients are disgusted.' It's true; I've overheard such words myself. They'll shove you, on the point of croaking, into the stinkingest corner of the basement – dark, damp: what will you go over in your mind then, lying there alone? You'll die – they'll lay you out hurriedly, strangers' hands, grumblingly, impatiently – and no one will bless you, no one will sigh over you, all they'll think is how to get you off their backs quickly.

'I'm in a frightening state,' Dostoevsky wrote to his brother, six days before Maria Dimitrievna coughed her last, 'nervous, morally ill.' He then goes on to outline the story of these last chapters of the *Notes* . . .

Is there a sense in which writing fiction, for Dostoevsky, allowing himself to be carried away by such rhetoric and to describe all sorts of ugliness, involved a perverse indulgence and hence was experienced as a sin? Or was it rather a form of expiation? 'I've felt ashamed all the while I've been writing this story' the narrator of *Notes* tells us on the penultimate page: 'so it's no longer literature, but corrective punishment.' Or could it even be that Dostoevsky was unable to make up his mind what it was, crime or punishment, or even, given its implied moral condemnation of the narrator's perversions, a moral act perhaps? In any event, the reader is bound to feel something of the same ambiguity about his own engagement with fiction that flaunts negative behaviour, that is dense, as Turgenev put it, with 'smelly self-laceration'. There are few works that combine laughter and disgust as powerfully as *Notes from Underground*.

If the nineteenth century was the time when it became clear that any political future lay in the collective choice of the people, it naturally became necessary to discover who these people really were. This was the great task of realism and the novels of the period. Yet the more the modern individual was losing, in the impersonal throng of the industrialised city, those traditional roles imposed by the old rural, communal life, the more the suspicion arose that perhaps character was not so easily defined, that perhaps it was infinitely malleable. From the rented tenement rooms of the big European and American cities the most disturbing texts began to appear. In Berlin in 1844 Max Stirner wrote *The Ego and his Own*, in which he taught that there was no need to be morally bound by old promises you no longer wished to adhere to, nor rules you didn't agree with: the only thing that mattered was how much power you had to do as you wanted, now and now and now. In 1853 Melville invented a character who took a strange form of power by simply responding to every order and invitation with the refrain 'I would prefer not to.' In 1868 the nadir of negativity was attained when Lautréamont published his *Chants de Maldoror* which celebrates with utter complacency the atrocious crimes of a serial killer. Like *Notes from Underground* the text is disconcerting for its juxtapositions of quite different styles, so that it becomes hard to sense a consistent identity behind the overall production. This was *Pulp Fiction* over a century before Tarantino.

But it was in the monologue Dostoevsky created for *Notes from Underground* (1864) that the characterless character found his proper literary form, the man who talks endlessly of himself because there is no self, who imagines his listeners because he has none, internalising the whole world and fantasising impossible successes from the safety of complete non-engagement. Imitations, adaptations and ambitious developments of this voice produced some of the finest works of the twentieth century from Celine to Beckett and Bernhard. But at the time *Notes* was written few were impressed.

There is a reflection to be made here on a profound split in modern consciousness. To take on board the implications of *Notes from Underground* is to undermine any political debate predicated on the existence of people with stable selves who can make responsible decisions. Officially, ideas such as those Dostoevsky advanced in *Notes* must never be accepted. In reality, the amount of money spent pushing people from one political camp to another with inane slogans and meaningless manifestos suggests that those who enjoy power know all too well that identity is unstable at best. In any event, we can take the date of the publication of *Notes* as the moment when ready-made visions and packaged ideals are declared absolutely necessary, but only as a means of manipulation, or a form of mental comfort:

Even then I comforted myself with these ideas, as I do still. That's why we have so many generous spirits who even in the last degradation never lose their ideals; and although they won't lift a finger for their ideals, although they are declared thieves and gangsters, they are still tearfully devoted to their original ideals and extraordinarily pure of heart.

If a world of the 'pure of heart' who behave exactly as they choose is in any way recognisable to the modern reader then the polarities that tense Dostoevsky's narratives are still very much with us, even if the struggle against this state of affairs was long ago abandoned.

The Illusionist

[Benito Mussolini]

From the three great architects of the Italian Risorgimento in the mid-nineteenth century – Mazzini, Garibaldi, Cavour – to the rule of Mussolini from 1922 to 1943, it would be hard to find a single figure in Italian politics whose biography is in print in English today, this despite the country's colonial expansion in Libya and participation in World War One. A fluid parliamentary system of shifting alliances between fragmented parties largely in thrall to the whims of an interfering and mediocre monarchy meant that those who held power did so only by dint of interminable compromise and ad hoc administration. Much the same, minus the monarchy, could be said of Italian leaders since World War Two, at least until Berlusconi. Biographers find it difficult to have such men emerge from an elusive and very Italian context.

With Mussolini, on the other hand, the literature is extensive and the reader spoilt for choice. It is the nature of a totalitarian dictatorship that the psychology of a single, usually charismatic, individual is superimposed over a nation's destiny for an extended period. Thus it may seem that the story can be grasped without too much context. Then in Mussolini's case the psychology in question was neither simple nor stable. Indeed, we might say that for every action and declaration of Il Duce, as he liked to be called, there was, as it were, a shadow action or declaration which complicated or straightforwardly contradicted the first. As a result, regardless of the damage he did to Italian democracy and the ruin he brought upon Italy through his alliance with Hitler, historians can continue to argue about what his real intentions and achievements were.

Here was a man who both saved Jews from Hitler's Holocaust yet passed anti-Semitic laws in Italy, who talked about modernising his country and, simultaneously, of returning to the mentality of Roman imperialism, who fomented a European war then desperately sought to postpone it, who spoke of wishing to be hated and feared while giving money anonymously to charitable organisations.

Aside from the fascination one is bound to feel for a life at once so contradictory and eventful, there is the growing conviction as one reads recent biographies of Mussolini that the conflicting codes of behaviour between which he oscillated are still in competition for our minds today. In a nutshell: while most politicians will do everything to present themselves as 'good' and above all peace-loving, though often behaving in ways that seem to us tainted with self-interest if not downright evil, Mussolini was determined to appear warlike and ruthless while frequently finding it difficult to carry through his threats. No published photo, he ordered, must show him smiling. It was better, he felt, that the Italians be known for torturing their prisoners than for their mandolin-playing. But when a dangerous political opponent was murdered by Fascist henchmen, a shamed Duce was quick to give a generous pension to his family. There is room here for considerable controversy.

Born in 1883 near the provincial town of Forlì, son of a black-smith, a man known for his militant socialism and heavy drinking, young Benito soon had a reputation for turbulent behaviour. At school there were knife fights. He was expelled three times. But between these crises there were also long periods of quiet diligence and excellent exam results. Benito's mother was a schoolteacher, much admired for her exemplary piety, and in his late teens it was her vocation that he chose. He taught languages in primary school and in later years, often at moments of great drama, he would with-draw from his duties to immerse himself in some literary or historical translation, as if an alternative and contemplative way of life were still available to him. The works of Plato were always on his desk, together with a revolver.

In his early twenties the young Mussolini liked to take a woman by brute force, rape almost, then become romantically attached, then move on to another town. His father kept a mistress. Dismissed from his first school where, unlike his mother, he had been unable to control the children ('some of them were incorrigible and dangerous urchins' he complained), he wandered poverty-stricken around Switzerland, until involvement with the Socialist Party led to the discovery of a genius for inflammatory journalism. He was expelled from various Swiss towns and finally from the country. Back in Italy, he was sacked from other teaching jobs for blasphemy in the classroom, philandering, running up debts and political agitation. It was as if his mother's job had been given to someone with his father's qualities; but his mother was dead now, killed by meningitis in 1905. Brief periods were spent in gaol.

All the same, Mussolini was still hard-working and evidently talented. In 1909 he was given control of the socialist newspaper in Austrian-held Trento, where he engaged in a fierce battle of words with future Italian leader, the very Catholic Alcide De Gasperi. 'The church was a corpse' Mussolini wrote. The notions of loving your neighbour and turning the other cheek were pathetic and pernicious. Violence was the necessary and moral response to capitalist injustice. Once again he was expelled. But in 1912, with a view to imminent revolution, the Socialist Party decided to make use of his capacity for stirring up conflict and appointed him head of their national newspaper, *Avanti*, based in Milan. It was the breakthrough from minor agitator to major player.

The pattern of this early part of Mussolini's life, then, is one of kicking against all forms of authority while at the same time seeking both power and approval for himself, first with schoolchildren and lovers, then in the Socialist Party and its newspapers. Even his marriage in 1910, swiftly followed by the birth of his first child Edda, involved a breach of authority, if not taboo. Seventeen-year-old Rachele Guidi was the daughter of his father's long-time mistress. Both Benito's father and Rachele's mother were sternly set against the union. To get his way, Mussolini threatened suicide. Of peasant stock, uninterested in politics, regularly producing children and always supporting family values, Rachele gradually got a hold on her man and saw off a series of mistresses. One of her strategies was to challenge him really to play the macho part he advocated. His first supporter and goad, she invariably insisted that he be harder on opponents. Years afterwards, observers would remark that Mussolini appeared to be afraid of his wife. Whether or not that is true, he clearly experienced relationships of whatever kind as power struggles in which one side must eventually assert authority and take control. This psychological make-up, rationalised by an acceptance of Darwinian determinism, would ultimately be fatal in his dealings with Hitler.

The Italian Socialist Party of the early twentieth century was internationalist: capitalism was an international phenomenon and the workers as a class must respond with an international revolution. The socialists thus opposed wars between nation states as merely furthering the ends of capitalist manufacturers. As editor of the socialist newspaper, therefore, Mussolini vigorously opposed the idea of Italian intervention at the beginning of the First War. But his position rapidly shifted and in October 1914, without consulting his colleagues, he published a leading article claiming that Italy could not stand on the sidelines while such great events were going on.

There were various considerations behind this dramatic volte-face, not least the calculation that war might create a situation favourable to revolution. But with Mussolini the drive to take action and play a leading role – something to which he attached positive moral value – together with the attendant fear of being seen to be weak, was almost always decisive. In any event, he collected another expulsion, this time from the Socialist Party, and opened his own newspaper, *Il Popolo d'Italia*, telling the readers 'From now on we are Italians and nothing but Italians.' The move from international socialism to Fascism, or National Socialism as a similar phenomenon would elsewhere be called, had begun.

It was characteristic of Mussolini that he always assumed that wars would be short and victorious. 'The winner of the war will be whoever wants to win it', he felt, declaring a faith in the power of human will over material reality that would remain with him till the end. Conscripted into the army in 1915, he was wounded by a hand grenade in exercises behind the lines in July 1917 and thus back at the newspaper in Milan before the terrible collapse at Caporetto in October of that year which saw 300,000 Italians taken prisoner and the Austro-German army on the brink of capturing the Northern Italian plain. Eventual victory with Allied help brought a huge sense of national achievement but not the territorial gains that Britain and France had originally offered when encouraging Italy to join the war. With half a million dead, half a million injured, a weak government, a weak economy and a general sense that the country had been cheated, Italy was now fertile ground for political agitation. In particular, the rapidly growing Socialist Party had before it the example of the Russian Revolution.

It is in telling the next part of the story, the three years that brought Mussolini to power, that recent biographies declare their differences most powerfully. What is at stake is our attitude to democracy and to the use of violence in domestic politics. In 1919 Italy introduced universal male suffrage with a radical form of proportional representation. Every area of opinion would be faithfully represented in parliament, including the newly formed Partito Popolare Italiano which represented Catholic Italy and had the blessing of the Pope. The year's election thus returned a parliament where no one grouping had a majority and where neither the socialists nor the PPI would work with each other or with the older and now much diminished Liberal Party. The minority Liberal government eventually installed was faced with a dramatic wave of strikes organised by the socialists, who were evidently seeking to push the country to revolution.

Within this scenario of chronic fragmentation, a recurrent Italian nightmare, Mussolini had formed, in February 1919, the so-called Fasci di Combattimento (Combat Bands). Members were not obliged to relinquish membership of other parties. The idea was rather to ignore class differences and economic interests, insisting on solidarity, with all its advantages. At its simplest, one might say that Mussolini's Fascism, as it was soon being called, aimed to create, in peacetime, the embattled, nationalist solidarity he had experienced during the war. (A *fascio* is a bundle of things tied together.) So all differences of opinion would be subordinated to the principle of the good of the nation. In reality, this meant subordination to the principle of taking power over the nation. Every 'divisive' party, and in particular the socialists, would be attacked and denigrated until all parties were dissolved and the people bound together in the solidarity of Fascism. Expelled from every organisation he had been a member of, Mussolini would now absorb all organisations into his own.

Despite Mussolini's remarkable journalism and powerful public speaking, the new movement polled only 5,000 votes in the 1919 election. Very soon afterwards, however, it found a role in transforming widespread public resentment of socialist strikes into orchestrated punitive raids. While the police stood by, reluctant to intervene, groups of the Fasci di Combattimento set out in their black shirts and black lorries to break strikes, beat up opponents and burn down socialist headquarters. There were deaths on both sides.

Nicholas Farrell, in his *Mussolini: A New Life*, is sanguine about all this. Bolshevism was a real threat, he points out, and the socialists 'gave as good as they got'. He repeats this formula three times. Anyway, 'the Fascists', Farrell writes, 'opposed the bourgeoisie as much as they opposed the socialists because both exalted one class at the expense of the other. The Fascists exalted the nation, united not divided.'

This of course was the official line, but is difficult to square with the fact that in the early days Mussolini's newspaper and movement were funded primarily by land-owning and industrial interests. For the moment, resentment of the bourgeoisie, however heartfelt, went no further than rhetoric. The Socialist Party was the enemy that, largely because of its internationalism and relations with Russia, aroused the animosity that bound together Mussolini's variously assorted followers.

Farrell is likewise ready to endorse Mussolini's route to power. In 1921, new elections saw the Fascists gain thirty-five seats in parliament and take a place in government. But in 1922 when the socialists threatened a general strike and the government followed its normal line of non-intervention, Mussolini undertook his long-threatened March on Rome. Claiming to be more patriotic than the country's leaders, 30,000 of his followers converged on the city, for the most part travelling by train. For the good of Italy, the government must act or hand over power to those who would. The Fascists could easily have been dispersed given the army and police presence around the city. But the king was unwilling to call the marchers' bluff, perhaps afraid that widespread violence would ensue. Instead he invited Mussolini, who had barricaded himself in his office in Milan, to form a government. Mussolini thus took power legally, though only by threatening an illegal course of action.

Farrell, whose determination that we take a fresh look at Mussolini and Fascism is welcome, spoils his position by making enthusiastic claims such as: 'the king was in tune with what the majority of Italians wanted and felt they needed.' Certainly there was a desire to put an end to widespread strikes, but whether that meant people would have chosen Mussolini as their prime minister we have no way of knowing. King Victor Emmanuel will not go down in history as a man who knew or cared much about the will of his people. Farrell's repeated use of the disparaging expression 'chattering classes' to describe those who write off Mussolini without, as Farrell sees it, considering the consequences of a socialist revolution or the stalemate of Italian democracy, suggests that he is in fact using his book as a personal polemic against political correctness and liberal orthodoxies in general. As a result some of the excellent points he makes are less telling than they might be.

Presenting his new government to the Chamber of Deputies, Mussolini, now thirty-eight, told them: 'I could have turned this deaf and grey Chamber into a bivouac for my legions . . . I could have barred up parliament and formed a government only of Fascists. I could have, but I have not wanted to, at least not for the moment.' The speech is typical of the two contrasting attitudes that are always present in Mussolini's life and that characterise his relationship with the Italian people. On the one hand there is the arrogant, self-glorifying claim of the moral right to violence and destruction, on the other he looks for approval for not having done what he says he might have; for being, at the end of the day, benevolent. The concluding 'at least not for the moment' is both a real threat and an example of the way he learnt to keep competing moralities apart by reserving the more drastic manifestations of himself for some unspecified future occasion. For the moment he will deal with the king, the parliament and the Pope and accept their institutional roles; later, if he so desires, he may destroy them. Similarly, in the 1930s, Mussolini would speak frequently of the need for a European war to destroy the pernicious power of Britain and France, but this cataclysm was always to take place at some distant date. In this regard he was less drastic and ruthless than Hitler, who always wanted the future to arrive as rapidly as the German armaments industry could bring it about. One senses that Mussolini praised men of action and instinct so incessantly ('If I trust my instinct I never make a mistake' he claimed) because he actually pondered a great deal before taking action and more often than not found himself paralysed by indecision.

While Farrell often expresses his enthusiasm for Il Duce as an admirable example of effective authoritarian rule, R. J. B. Bosworth begins his *Mussolini* by declaring that he considers Mussolini a complete failure. He points out that the Liberal government's policy of non-intervention in socialist strikes had actually undermined and defused left-wing revolution. By 1922 Bolshevism was on the wane. Again and again he shows the inconsistencies in Mussolini's declarations and simultaneously acknowledges that the Fascist leader was not concerned with intellectual consistency but with finding a way to power. In this view, however, and partly as a result of Bosworth's heavy use of irony, Mussolini can seem merely cynical and opportunist, while the more visionary side of his personality appears only as a means to an end, or plain ridiculous. Bosworth uses the word 'rant' to characterise the aggressive rhetoric that Farrell admires.

In his more modest *Mussolini*, prepared for the Routledge Historical Biographies series, Peter Neville uses the word 'nonsense'. Neville drops various hints that he is not enamoured of his subject. He is a professional historian writing to order. But this does give him the advantage of having no axe to grind and no original research to show off. For anyone eager to get a succinct overview, at once well organised and easy to consult, his book is an excellent choice. What's more, his rather schoolmasterly determination 'to discern what really drove Mussolini and to assess the sincerity of his political opinions against his obvious desire to exercise great power' alerts us to an underlying problem with all these books. None of them offers a serious psychological study of this unusual mind and, despite all the lip service paid to context, and in Bosworth's case an admirable handling of background detail, none takes time to go back in history and consider how that mind may have meshed in exciting and dangerous ways with long-term cultural conditions in Italy.

As early as 1826 the poet Leopardi had suggested that Italy occupied a very special position in Europe as far as public debate and morality were concerned. In his *Discorso sopra lo stato presente dei costumi degl'italiani* he suggests that, faced with the collapse of traditional belief systems, England and France had been able to fall back on a well-developed aristocratic and moneyed society that had gradually substituted a morality based on metaphysics with one that rested entirely on custom and aesthetics, so that a man is 'ashamed to do harm in the same way that he would be ashamed to appear in a conversation with a stain on his clothes'.

Italy, on the other hand, divided as it then was, despotically governed and dominated by a religion people observed, as Leopardi saw it, mostly out of superstition and subservience, lacked such resources. Public debate was no more than a school for insults and people laughed at the idea of moral behaviour. A gesture of real nobility was unimaginable. What was required in these circumstances, Leopardi felt, was some kind of collective 'illusion', which, if it could never give life 'real substance or truth', might at least confer 'the appearance of the same, so that we might be able to think of it [life] as important.'

Other figures of the nineteenth and early twentieth centuries suggest a moral condition in line with Leopardi's description. Mazzini, the revolutionary ideologue behind the Risorgimento, found himself battling above all with the total indifference of the vast majority. To combat this he spoke of the need to encourage Italians to have a 'religious concept of their nation', an expression Mussolini would pick up.

Garibaldi, utterly scathing of the church and deeply pessimistic about the behaviour of his fellow Italians, nevertheless demonstrated how much could be achieved, at least in short-term military campaigns, by appealing to an exalted vision of the nation where solidarity and unity took precedence over any political colour. Like Mussolini, he frequently drew inspiration from the achievements of the Romans. Indeed it was precisely the abyss between past grandeur and present meanness that fed both despair and idealism. A convinced democrat, Garibaldi nevertheless decided that when you wanted anything done in Italy, you had to play dictator. Anti-Catholic as he was, he was worshiped as a saint, in much the same way that Mussolini would be. 'Incredible,' Mussolini remarked, 'the readiness of modern man to believe.'

Verga's splendid novellas of the late nineteenth century also present a world where all public and in particular Catholic morality is quite empty, its rhetoric no more than a weapon in a vicious Darwinian power game. His magnificent portrait of the violent young miner Rosso Malpelo is a description of a man waiting for his innate violence to be enlisted in some collective enterprise. D'Annunzio too, who pointed the way for Mussolini when he led a people's army into Yugoslav-held Fiume in 1920, had for many years been writing novels where an idealised rhetoric deployed by a Nietzschean superman imposes itself on and transforms grim reality into something noble.

'Now we have made Italy we must make the Italians.' So said ex-prime minister Massimo D'Azeglio shortly after national unification was achieved. Again the statement suggests both a pessimistic take on the present and a hope in moral regeneration. Clearly this was fertile territory for a man who combined a creative use of extravagant rhetoric with a tendency both to bully and then to seek approval for having bullied in a positive way, a man who, having spent his early twenties in a state, as he saw it, of moral collapse, had then urgently cast about for a mission that would harness his energies and bring self-esteem. Nobody could have been more contemptuous of the Italian character than Mussolini – 'a gesticulating, chatterbox, superficial, carnivalesque people' he called them – and nobody more determined to achieve the 'conversion of the Italians' through a powerful collective vision, for which, like Leopardi, Mussolini uses the word illusion. 'It is faith which moves mountains because it gives the illusion that mountains move. Illusion, is perhaps the only reality in life.'

How, most of us will wonder, can someone believe in and act upon something that he also (unlike the fundamentalist) stands back from and refers to as an illusion? Leopardi considered this *the* paradox for modern man. It required constant labour and energy, he felt, to sustain an illusion. Fascism, a movement with no real content beyond its nation-building vocation, 'constructs day by day', Mussolini claimed, 'the edifice of its will and passion.' Asked to define the phenomenon in a few words he said it meant that 'Life must not be taken easily.' He referred to himself as 'the national mule' carrying 'heavy burdens'. Fascist artwork would portray him as a builder, digging the foundations of Italian civilisation, on his own, with a spade. 'I am convinced', Mussolini told a conference of doctors in 1931, 'that our way of eating, dressing, working and sleeping, the whole complex of our daily habits, must be reformed.' It was a '*fatica grandiosa*', he remarked, using the word that describes the mythic labours of Hercules.

Behind all this, then – the distance between the Italians as they are perceived to be and the modern, united, industrious nation they might become – lies the heroism of the impossible task. 'The credo of Fascism is heroism, that of the bourgeoisie egoism.' It is as if, quite unlike Hitler, Mussolini was always half aware of being defeated before he started. Perhaps the most fascinating aspect of the Italian biographer Renzo De Felice's classic seven-volume study of Mussolini, and what most distinguishes it from English biographies, is not so much his supposed sympathy with Mussolini as his shared understanding of this reading of Italian life. The same cultural trait is observable with Berlusconi and his Forza Italia party today. What has to be grasped is the Italian willingness to subscribe to an ambitious project of transformation while actively disbelieving that it can succeed. This is why it is not a major setback when a leader fails to deliver. Certainly Il Duce had ceased believing in his project, De Felice remarks, before he was halfway through his time in power. He had 'dominated the masses like an artist', but he had failed to change them. On the contrary, his ostentatious shouldering of all responsibility encouraged irresponsibility in his adoring people. 'Fascism is nothing but a bluff' Mussolini's son Vittorio would tell his adolescent friends. 'Daddy hasn't managed to do anything he wanted to. The Italians . . . don't give a damn about the revolution.' All the biographies mention Mussolini's growing loneliness and melancholy as the hopelessness of his project emerged.

* * *

One thing, of course, that makes an illusion very hard to sustain is someone who reminds us of harsh reality, or supports a rival illusion. Having taken power, Mussolini became obsessed by propaganda and spent much of his time scouring the newspapers and reading police reports on friends and enemies. Neither he nor Fascism nor Italy must ever be presented as ridiculous. Having altered the electoral laws and deployed considerable thuggery to win a landslide victory in elections in 1924, he faced his first serious challenge in parliament. Socialist deputy Giacomo Matteotti accused him of widespread electoral fraud. Shortly afterwards, Matteotti was murdered. Having survived – only just – the ensuing scandal, Mussolini moved rapidly to turn his government into a dictatorship and the country into a one-party state. The lower house of parliament would eventually be closed and very tight control was taken of the press. 'Our totalitarian will', Mussolini declared in 1925, 'shall be declared with still greater ferocity.' Everything would be 'for the state, nothing outside the state, and no one against the state.' Throughout the 1920s the myth of a militaristic, modernising Fascism was slowly consolidated; its component parts included the Roman salute (the handshake was banned), paramilitary youth movements, after-hours workers' organisations, statues and bas-reliefs that recalled an imperial past and grandiose authoritarian architecture. Meanwhile police powers were considerably increased and thousands of communists and other agitators arrested.

But the illusion of totalitarian control was the greatest illusion of all. One thing, for example, that remained decisively outside state control was Mussolini's stomach. Shortly after having survived the Matteotti crisis, Il Duce coughed blood and was afflicted by crippling stomach pains. An ulcer was diagnosed and he was put on a diet of no meat, no alcohol and abundant milk, with which he continued for most of his life. The pains, however, would return with some frequency. The biographies in question, while all suspecting a psychosomatic element to the problem (a post-mortem decades later would reveal no trace of an ulcer), do not seek to establish a pattern between the attacks and the kind of decisions and circumstances Mussolini was facing. Matteotti's death was the first occasion when Mussolini himself was suspected of direct involvement in murder, when the criminal side of Fascism was seen by all for what it was, not a might-have-been or a figure of speech. Il Duce's decision to grant a generous pension to Matteotti's widow suggests he experienced a sense of guilt. Later, Mussolini would be especially afflicted by pain while involved in negotiating Italy's aggressive military pact with Germany. It remains for some diligent researcher to establish whether these pains occurred at moments when Mussolini found it most difficult to reconcile the poles of ruthlessness and accommodation between which his behaviour oscillated. In any event, for a man of action who liked to have himself photographed playing vigorous sports or cruising Rome in a convertible with a lioness called Italia, to find himself bent double in pain and reduced on occasion to writhing on the floor was a significant setback. Naturally, none of this could ever be spoken of in the press, just as years later newspapers were forbidden to mention Il Duce's age.

Also outside state control was the church. 'It is impossible to ignore reality, however sad' Mussolini had once written to D'Annunzio, and he was aware that it was unrealistic to imagine that the vision that was Fascism could ever entirely replace Catholicism. They would have to live together. Mussolini replaced the Christian calendar date 1922 with the Fascist date, Year I, but for the duration of his regime allowed the different dates to be printed side by side on official documents. It was a classic example of his habit of allowing contradictions to persist unresolved. For years Catholicism and Fascism fought each other over who would have the right to run youth groups and indoctrinate future generations, but in 1929 Mussolini and the Pope nevertheless settled the profound disagreement between church and state that had been going on since Italy seized Vatican territory in the Risorgimento: the Pope agreed to recognise Italian sovereignty over Rome in return for a series of generous concessions. It was an extraordinary coup and brought Mussolini considerable international acclaim.

In general, as Farrell is eager to remind us and Bosworth is obliged to admit, Mussolini enjoyed an excellent foreign press throughout the 1920s. Many – including influential names like Churchill and George Bernard Shaw – saw him exactly as he wanted to be seen: a strong leader who had restored public order and modernised his country with a programme of public works and a policy of intervention to protect workers' pay and conditions that had spared Italy the class conflict that dogged other nations. The sacrifice of freedom of speech and, by now it was clear, democracy, was overlooked. Bosworth, however, is interesting in suggesting how little the country was in fact modernised, how few were the members of the old establishment, particularly in the army, who were replaced, how much of the perceived change, in short, had to do with propaganda. The extent to which Italy still lagged behind would be dramatically revealed in wartime.

'He who does not feel the need to fight a bit of war', Mussolini remarked, 'is not in my opinion a complete man. War is the most important thing in the life of a man, like maternity in that of a woman.' The curious use of 'a bit' suggests Il Duce's eternal ambiguity. One cannot imagination Hitler having slipped in this qualification. G. Bruce Strang's *On the Fiery March* looks in meticulous detail at the dealings between the two men in the years that led to Germany's invasion of Poland in 1939 and Italy's declaration of war on an already desperate France in 1940. As in all these books, the story is fascinating if only because Mussolini's behaviour would appear to defy explanation. From 1922 to 1935, despite all its menacing rhetoric, Italy had hardly misbehaved on the international scene. Then in 1935 it invaded Ethiopia, in 1936 it intervened in the Spanish Civil War and was largely responsible for Franco's victory in 1939. In 1938 it invaded Albania and in 1939 it signed the Pact of Steel with Germany, an aggressive military alliance whereby if one signatory launched a war of expansion, the other was bound to join in. How far was all this the consequence of a long-term plan, of ideology or of opportunism? Or did it reflect a midlife crisis of both Fascism and Il Duce?

In Farrell's view, France and Britain were largely responsible for Mussolini's decision to side with Hitler. Italy was right to feel short-changed by the Treaty of Versailles and trapped inside the Mediterranean by British and French power, to challenge which it was understandable that it should seek to expand its colony in Libya and open a new one in Ethiopia. At the same time, Italy was a natural ally of Britain and France against German expansionism, in that an eventual *Anschluss* of Austria by Germany would threaten Italy's dubious claim to the predominantly German-speaking South Tyrol. There was also the fact that on first meeting, Mussolini despised Hitler and thought his anti-Semitic policy madness. The British and French thus behaved foolishly in pressing for US sanctions in reaction to the invasion of Ethiopia in 1935 (despite the 500,000 Ethiopians killed with nerve gas). Their opposition to Mussolini's involvement in the Spanish Civil War showed that they hadn't understood as profoundly as Mussolini the dangers of Bolshevism. In need of allies, Il Duce had to go to Hitler.

Strang refutes this interpretation. He shows how, despite Mussolini's initial hostility to Hitler, their dealings rapidly took on a quite different tone from his negotiations with the British and French as Il Duce began to see in the rise of the Reich a fulfilment of his Darwinian vision (and personal dream) of the vigorous, recently unified and now Fascist nations prevailing over the exhausted and decadent capitalist democracies of Britain and France. The decision for Mussolini was not, Strang shows, between opposing camps – he knew at once where he stood over that question – but whether the alliance with Hitler would be restricted to rhetorical support or arrive at full-scale military conflict.

All the same, precisely because Strang's approach is limited to a close examination of diplomatic exchanges, he cannot hide his consternation and puzzlement at the carelessness with which Mussolini and Galeazzo Ciano, his young foreign minister and son-in-law, accepted a German draft of the Pact of Steel without inserting the safeguards they had previously discussed, and this despite the fact that Hitler, with his sudden, unannounced invasions of Austria and Czechoslovakia, had already shown himself to be an extremely fickle ally. Neither opportunism nor ideology could explain the blindness with which Mussolini placed himself in Hitler's hands.

One clue to understanding Mussolini's behaviour is his introduction of the anti-Semitic Race Laws in 1938. Until that point, despite occasional anti-Semitic statements, Mussolini had denied the existence of a Jewish problem in Italy, criticised Hitler's anti-Semitism, allowed Jews to be members of the Fascist Party (thousands were enrolled) and encouraged his Jewish mistress Margherita Sarfatti to write an adulatory biography of himself. Now Jews were to be excluded from public life and forbidden to marry 'Aryan' Italians.

In his partial biography, *Mussolini: The Last 600 days of il Duce*, Ray Moseley declares himself puzzled and reaches the conclusion that the Race Laws were the merest opportunism, a cheap way for Il Duce to ingratiate himself with Hitler. Neville, likewise mystified, reaches the same conclusion as it were by default: if it isn't anything else, it must be opportunism. But this interpretation makes no sense. Hitler had put no pressure at all on Mussolini to introduce a Jewish policy similar to his own and these were days when Mussolini had no need to ingratiate Hitler, since Hitler's need of his Italian ally was urgent indeed if he was to pursue his adventurous policies in Czechoslovakia and Poland. On more than one occasion Mussolini had spoken of the folly of arousing the opposition of international Jewry.

Farrell has a different answer. The conquest of empire in Ethiopia had raised the question of racial consciousness, he claims. The Italians had to be fit to rule. To do this they must eliminate their sentimental and bourgeois tendencies. 'It was the Jewish psyche or spirit

– the epitome of the bourgeois spirit which he scorned as *la vita comoda* – that he wanted to stamp out, not the Jews.' This explains, Farrell says, the exemptions from the Race Laws extended to those Jews who had served loyally in the army or joined the Fascist Party before 1922. 'Mussolini's mission . . . was to transform the Italians into Italians. The Jews became victims of this bigger process.'

Aside from one's unease with Farrell's attempts to apologise for Mussolini (the terrible death toll in Ethiopia is partly excused by the fact that the Ethiopians were barbarous slave traders), this too makes no sense. If Mussolini wanted to stamp out the bourgeois lifestyle, he could have begun with those like Ciano who dressed expensively and played golf when they might more usefully have been working, or with the rich industrialists of Milan and Turin. He could have altered fiscal policy and limited the availability of consumer goods. As it was, he must have been aware that many of the Jews who would suffer from his laws were hardly bourgeois at all.

Bosworth comes closest to a convincing explanation. He notes that Mussolini's growing envy of Hitler and Nazism had intensified his frustration that 'he himself had not been an iron-hard engineer of human souls.' Aware, particularly after his visit to Berlin in 1937, of the mobilising power of racism, Mussolini returned to Italy where from now on he would be 'trying very hard to be wicked'. In this scenario, the anti-Jewish policy was, yes, as Farrell would have it, aimed at toughening up the Italians (they must become 'tough, implacable, hateful'), but more out of desperate emulation than because of any beliefs about the nature of the Jewish spirit.

The irony, if one accepts this explanation, is that Mussolini was indeed only trying to be wicked, for as Bosworth points out, until the German occupation of 1943, although Italian Jews were now 'persecuted in ways which they had not imagined when, in considerable majority, they approved Fascism: they were not, however, killed.' Mussolini spoke of setting up concentration camps, but did not do so. Nor did he punish those, including his own family, who protected Jews, nor even those members of the Italian army and bureaucracy who, after the war had begun, saved Jews from Nazi persecution in France and Croatia. What was going on?

On 29 November 1938, after Race Laws were announced, the Jewish publisher and Fascist Angelo Fortunato Formiggini jumped to his death from the cathedral campanile in Modena. In a letter to Mussolini he wrote: 'Dear Duce . . . You have gone mad . . . deep down you pain me, because you have fallen into a trap placed for you by destiny.'

Let us try to give a prosaic sense to this most pertinent observation. Until 1935, in a Fascism that, beyond restoring law and order through repression, was largely a matter of image and propaganda, Mussolini had found a strategy that kept the contradictory impulses of his personality in equilibrium: portrayed as heroically implacable, he was popular because, after all, for most ordinary people not much had changed and not much was required of them. The emergence of Nazi Germany, partly through the real opportunities it offered for altering the status quo, but above all through the person of Hitler, upset that equilibrium. Here was a man who really was ruthless and implacable, who really hurried history onward to its cruellest Darwinian convulsions.

Returning from Berlin in 1937, greatly impressed by the Nazi parades he had witnessed, Mussolini introduced the goose step to Italy. At the same time he suffered a severe attack of his stomach problems; they would continue to assail him throughout his many attempts to emulate Hitler in 1938 and 1939. He also suffered from acute indecision. Clearly the more accommodating side of his personality was still active. And indeed, however demeaning and humiliating the Race Laws were, there was no Kristallnacht in Italy. Impelled to transform himself and his compatriots into ruthless empire builders, history's winners, Mussolini at some deep level could not want, or at least not want close to home, or not for sustained periods, the evil such ruthlessness required.

Once Mussolini had joined the war (at a moment when he felt Hitler could not lose and hence was convinced as ever of a rapid victory), there was one last attempt to equal the man who had somehow stripped him of his self-respect. Nothing else can explain the strategically, politically and ideologically absurd invasion of Greece. When that failed, abjectly, Mussolini handed more or less complete control of the war to Hitler in the same way he expected underlings to cede control to him; he recognised, that is, that in this particular relationship he must take the subaltern position. Hence Moseley's account of Mussolini's last days presents us with the pathetic picture of a man who seems relieved to have renounced the struggle with himself and is secretly pleased every time Hitler is beaten, despite the fact that such defeats could only bring his own demise nearer.

Two reflections in particular remain after reading these five books: that we would all stand to gain if, from time to time, historians could put aside their reluctance to draw on the disciplines of psychology and anthropology. So many of Bosworth's intuitions are marvellously acute, but he does not bring them together in a coherent argument. We are overwhelmed with information that can only add up in ways the author doesn't discuss.

Second, that the best answer to Farrell's enthusiasm for dictatorship is that no psychology can be guaranteed as stable over the long run. Referring to difficulties forming a coalition government in 1922, Farrell speaks of 'Italianesque government by imbroglio'. Few coalitions, however, could have been as muddled, indecisive and internally divided as the mind of Mussolini in 1939.

Fear is the Key

'What has Providence done to Mr Hardy', wrote a reviewer of the Victorian writer's novel *Jude the Obscure* (1895), 'that he should rise up in the arable land of Wessex and shake his fist at his Creator?' The reviewer was referring to the long and painful series of misfortunes that befall Jude, culminating in the moment when his eldest child, aged twelve, is found to have hanged his younger brother and sister and then himself. So harrowing is the scene, and so apparently gratuitous, that the reviewer's cry for some explanation from the author's experience is understandable. The new biography of Hardy by Claire Tomalin would seem to be the place for today's reader to get an answer, but she declines to offer one. 'Neither Hardy nor anyone else', she tells us, 'has explained where his black view of life came from.' Most of his time, after all, was spent working at his desk. Tomalin does suggest, however, that 'part of the answer might be that he was writing at a time when Britain seemed to be permanently and bitterly divided into a nation of the rich and a nation of the poor.' Elsewhere she mentions the author's loss of Christian faith. But while it is true that Hardy's novels contain scathing criticism of the English class system and that he himself had been on the receiving end of much snobbery and elitism, still, for many of his contemporaries, even from his own background, even agnostics, this was a period of progress and confidence.

Another question about Hardy that remains largely unanswered is why he stopped writing novels relatively early in his long career. He was fifty-five when *Jude* was published. It was his fourteenth novel. He was at the height of his powers. Yet in the thirty-two years that remained to him he would never write another. Tomalin accepts Hardy's explanation that he had always thought of himself as a poet and that having now made sufficient money he could afford to withdraw from the pressures and compromises involved in writing serialised fiction and concentrate on his verse. Yet a certain mystery remains. Was there some relation between the intensity of the negative vision in *Jude* and the decision to stop writing? Why was poetry more congenial to Hardy and what is the relation between the two sides to his work?

Hardy was born more dead than alive in the small village of Bockhampton, Dorset, south-west England, on 2 June 1840, less than six months after his parents married. His father, a small-time builder, named the boy Thomas after both himself and his own father, giving no second name to distinguish the newborn. He was just another generation. His mother, Jemima, a servant and cook, had reached the relatively mature age of twenty-six without marrying, had had no desire to do so before this unwanted pregnancy, and would always warn her children against the move. Jemima's own mother had married in the last month of a pregnancy (her second) and brought up seven children in extreme poverty. Jemima would have three more after Thomas.

Frail, not expected to survive, Hardy was kept at home till age eight, learning to read and play the fiddle from his parents. Throughout her long life his mother would always refer to him as 'her rather delicate "boy"' while in his memoirs Hardy recalls that when asked what he wished to do as a grown-up he would protest that 'he did not want at all to be a man, or to possess things, but to remain as he was, in the same spot, and to know no more people than he already knew.' As late as 1917 he was describing himself at his first school as a still unfledged bird, 'Pink, tiny, crisp-curled'.

The desire to be spared adult experience is repeated in *Jude the Obscure*: 'If only he could prevent himself growing up!' Jude thinks, 'He did not want to be a man!' All Hardy's major novels, in fact, present us with a child, or childish adult, who is, as it were, thrust out into the world before he or she is ready for experience. Orphans abound and even where parents are present the question of shelter and protection is always to the fore. Of Tess and her six younger brothers and sisters in *Tess of the D'Urbervilles* (1891) we hear: 'All these young souls were passengers in the Durbeyfield ship – entirely dependent on the judgement of the two Durbeyfield adults for their pleasure, their necessities, their health, even their existence.' In the event, Tess is sent off into service dressed (by her mother) in such a way that 'might cause her to be estimated as a woman when she was not much more than a child'. The consequences are disastrous.

But what was so hard about growing up? One of the childhood anecdotes in Hardy's memoirs tells us how he fell in love with his first schoolteacher Mrs Martin. He recalls sitting on her lap, the rustle of her skirts, her smell. His mother, however, having decided to travel to Hertfordshire to assist her sister with the arrival of a fifth child, took Thomas away with her 'for protection . . . being then an attractive and still young woman'. This was clearly a family obsession. What protection could a nine-year-old offer a woman in her mid-thirties? Presumably what we are really talking about is her determination to protect him. The young Thomas was upset about losing his beloved teacher and even more so when, on returning to Bockhampton, he found he was to be sent to another school further afield. Desperate to see Mrs Martin now, he escaped from home to attend a harvest supper dance at which she would be present. There was a brief emotional meeting, after which he was abandoned and, tired and afraid, had to wait outside in the dark till three in the morning to be brought home and scolded.

The scene reads very much like something in a Hardy novel: it is a mindset where desire and fear battle for the upper hand in the absence of any moral content. Throughout his life, perhaps influenced by his parents' shotgun wedding, Hardy would be awed by the consequences of romantic and above all sexual experience. As a boy he hated to be touched. Years later he would visit the widowed Mrs Martin at her London home and even in his memoirs he would be reflecting that their love might have been 'in the order of things' if only he had got back to her earlier. In line with his general anxiety about exposing himself to criticism and derision, Hardy removed these lines from the manuscript to be sent to the publishers.

What was 'in the order of things' for the boy now was a three-mile walk to school in Dorchester, the nearest town. Thomas didn't like going so far from home. He complained of being sent when he was ill. All the same, 'born bookworm' as he was, he became a prize pupil. Deeming their son too delicate for building work, his parents seized on this intellectual success and had him articled to an architect, again in Dorchester. He was sixteen ('still a child' he later remarked). Upwardly mobile, he rose in his parents' esteem and, of course, architects and builders might one day hope to work together. At the same time he became different from the rest of the family and there were the embarrassments of moving in a class which might despise his manners and accent. Apparently it was impossible to have a positive thing without a negative.

Aged twenty, Hardy received his first salary and was able to rent a room in town, returning home at the weekends. It was the beginning of a long habit of oscillation between separate worlds, between bold independence and the safe protection of home, that would remain with Hardy all his life. In Dorchester he met the influential and intellectual Moule family who directed his reading and gave him encouragement with his first attempts at writing. Back home he went with his father to play the fiddle at village festivals, not so much the carouser as the one who provides the music, in the reassuring company of a parent. What romantic crushes there were at this stage were unconsummated; often Thomas flirted with his many female cousins, as if it might somehow be safer to keep love in the family. Then in 1862 this cautious young man suddenly decided to be brave, quit his job and set off to London.

One of Hardy's finest novels is entitled *The Return of the Native* (1878), and the expression might aptly be applied to many moments in the writer's own life. For after five years in London, years in which he fell on his feet, found a job with an architects' firm, won two Architectural Association prizes, immersed himself in the life of the capital, made friends and courted girls, in 1867, again rather suddenly, Hardy 'fell ill', 'felt weak' and, nothing diagnosed, abandoned all he had achieved to return home. In *The Return of the Native*, nothing is less convincing than the motives given by the handsome young Clym for his return to his tiny village after five successful years in the jewellery business in Paris. He claims to have grown tired of worldly ways, says he wishes to offer instruction to local village children. But clearly the most important person in Clym's life is his beloved mother; the passionate young Eustacia, who destroys his relationship with Mother, is portrayed in a most ambiguous if not negative light.

Aside from his 'health', Hardy's ostensible reason for abandoning London was that his lowly origins made it difficult for him to start an architect's practice of his own, or at least would involve 'pushing his way into influential sets'. Whether this was really such an obstacle is hard to say. In any event, what saved the retreat to Dorset from feeling like complete failure was that Hardy brought back with him more than 400 pages of a novel-in-progress. Hence while resuming part-time architect's work in Dorchester he was able to get on with the book at home. Mother's protection in Bockhampton was thus combined with aspirations that would be fulfilled in the big city.

It is usually said of *The Poor Man and the Lady* that it was rejected for publication and much is made of Hardy's sufferings as an aspiring man from a poor background seeking space for himself in the literary world. The circumstances are complicated. Since the manuscript was destroyed we have little idea what was in the novel, but he himself described it as a 'dramatic satire of the squirearchy and nobility, London society, the vulgarity of the middle class, modern Christianity, church restoration and political and domestic morals in general . . . the tendency of the writing being socialistic, not to say revolutionary.'

No doubt this was hard for London publishers to swallow, especially if the writer was still unaccomplished. But one publisher, Chapman, said it would do the novel if Hardy were willing to make corrections and pay £20 against losses. Chapman's reader, however, George Meredith, himself a novelist from a humble background, warned Hardy that publication of such inflammatory material might compromise his future. It would be better to write something else. Later, yet another publisher, Tinsley Brothers, offered publication if Hardy would guarantee the company against losses, not an unusual arrangement. He declined, complaining he couldn't afford it, though only a year later he would make a contract with Tinsley for his second attempt, *Desperate Remedies*, which involved handing over to them the very large sum of £75 against possible losses.

Perhaps, then, rather than this being a case of outright rejection, Hardy, cautious as he was, had taken Meredith's advice. He would also describe *The Poor Man and the Lady* as telling 'the life of an isolated student cast upon the billows of London with no protection but his brains'. Isolation, lack of protection, are so often the key with Hardy. This was how he thought of himself. A book that set the world against him was not what he had in mind. In any event, this first venture into publishing suggests how ambiguous, in his mature novels, is the relationship between social criticism and the misfortunes and defeats of his characters: snobbery, injustice, discrimination there may be, but these horrors can also offer the insecure child-adult an excuse to give up and return home, or they may confirm a preconception that life away from the parental hearth is unspeakably dangerous.

Despite his lowly origins, Hardy eventually published his first (now determinedly innocuous) novel at thirty-one and his second at thirty-two, at which point, with a contract signed to write a third, this time serialised, novel, he was already able to dedicate himself entirely to writing. Even today such an achievement would be remarkable. The London literary world was not after all so hostile to a country boy.

Meantime his last years in an architect's office were to bring Hardy to an even more momentous initiation than that of big-city life or publication. Having always specialised in church restoration, he was sent to Cornwall to assess the condition of a church in the tiny hamlet of St Juliot where he fell in love with Emma Gifford, sister-in-law of the incumbent clergyman. She was interested in literature and a bold horsewoman, something that a man with his history of frailty was bound to admire. In this poem, dated 1870, St Juliot is renamed Lyonnesse, a mythical land in Cornish legend:

> When I set out for Lyonnesse,
> A hundred miles away,
> The rime was on the spray,
> And starlight lit my lonesomeness
> When I set out for Lyonnesse
> A hundred miles away.
>
> What would bechance at Lyonnesse
> While I should sojourn there
> No prophet durst declare,
> Nor did the wisest wizard guess
> What would bechance at Lyonnesse
> While I should sojourn there.
>
> When I came back from Lyonnesse
> With magic in my eyes,
> All marked with mute surmise
> My radiance rare and fathomless,
> When I came back from Lyonnesse
> With magic in my eyes!

Typical of Hardy is the presentation of a before and after, with, elided in the middle, an experience that transforms someone absolutely, but cannot be spoken. In this case the transformation is positive; more often, and particularly where sexual, rather than romantic, experience is involved, it will be negative. After the beautiful young Tess has been deflowered by the rake into whose service she was so carelessly dispatched, we hear: 'An immeasurable chasm was to divide our heroine's personality thereafter from that previous self of hers who stepped from her mother's door to try her fortune at Trantridge poultry farm.'

In love, Hardy did not hurry to marriage. His mother was against it. Emma was a middle-class woman, and hence marriage to her would complete Hardy's move away from his kinfolk. She was also penniless. It was the worst of both worlds. Emma's father too was against her marrying into a lower class. In short, there was good reason for hesitating and enjoying an exciting romantic correspondence which Hardy later compared to that between Browning and Elizabeth Barrett, though they of course had thrown caution to the winds and eloped. Again and again in Hardy's novels, which are above all stories of attempted and usually failed partnerships, one partner will prefer 'perpetual betrothal' to consummation. Sexual experience, when it comes, will be all-determining, fatal even. Or will it? It is on this question, the fatal quality, or otherwise, of experience, that all Hardy's fiction turns.

In *Far From the Madding Crowd* (1874), Hardy's fourth novel and first major success, comedy prevails. Written while Emma was still at a safe distance in Cornwall, the novel reads like an extended betrothal. Independent shepherd Gabriel Oak proposes to orphan girl Bathsheba. Bold and beautiful, she rejects him, but not outright. He loses his flock in an accident. She inherits a farm from an uncle where he finds salaried work. Socially above him now, she unwisely attracts the attention of proud local landowner Boldwood who bullies her toward marriage. Courageous in running her farm,

Bathsheba is a child when it comes to romance. Before she can succumb to Boldwood, the disreputable Sergeant Troy seduces her with a dazzling display of swordsmanship that involves having his blade flash all around her body as she stands frightened and adoring. Desire and fear are fused. Later we discover that she married Troy because she was afraid that he had found someone else, afraid that her reputation was already compromised.

But in this early work the mistake is not allowed to be fatal. Exposed as a rake, Troy is murdered by Boldwood. With both pretenders out of the way, humble, hard-working Gabriel who has done everything to protect Bathsheba and her farm from ruin finally claims his prize. His loyal friendship has been more worthy than their passions, another constant theme in Hardy.

Following the author's marriage, however, there would be no more happy endings. Having tied the knot in 1874 Hardy began to move his wife back and forth from the suburbs of London, a short distance from where his career was developing, to the country round Dorchester, a short distance from his family. Seven moves in eight years. The family the couple wanted for themselves did not arrive. Allowed to help with his writing during betrothal, the childless Emma was now slowly frozen out. She did not mix well in London, where she preferred to live, or at all in Dorchester, which he preferred.

In 1880 Hardy managed to revamp the relationship by falling ill, confining himself to his bed for many months and allowing Emma to run his life. The recurring mystery illness, vaguely described years later as a bladder inflammation, did not prevent the writer from meeting the demanding deadlines of serialised novel publishing. On his recovery, Emma was sufficiently reassured about her role in the partnership to agree to the building of a permanent home not far from Dorchester.

Designed by Hardy himself, Max Gate, as the house was called, was small, unimaginative and surrounded by a protective belt of trees which he would never allow anyone to prune. To guarantee even greater security, the house was built by members of his family:

his younger brother Henry and his now ageing father. Guests complained it was gloomy and suffocating. No sooner were they installed there in 1882 than Tom and Emma began to rent accommodation in London for the summer season. The marriage sank into its previous torpor. Hardy was approaching that age when, as Emma would say, 'a man's feelings too often take a new course altogether. Eastern ideas of matrimony secretly pervade his thoughts, and he wearies of the most perfect, and suitable wife chosen in his earlier life.' In short, Hardy had adultery in mind. It was an exciting and anxious period, out of which he produced two of the finest novels in the English language, *Tess* and *Jude*.

Returning pregnant to her family after her catastrophic period in service, Tess gives birth to a baby that promptly dies. There are many dead babies in Hardy's work. The dead child is ever the sign that it would have been better never to have got involved in love. Vowing never to marry, Tess goes to serve as a milkmaid in a farm far enough away for her shame not to be known. Here she meets the perfect man, Angel Clare, trainee gentleman farmer. The scene is set for Hardy's characteristically tantalising mix of desire and trepidation. To sharpen our sense of anxiety, both characters and their possible but difficult union are made enormously attractive. Here is Tess after an afternoon nap, viewed by Clare:

> She had not heard him enter and hardly realised his presence there. She was yawning, and he saw the red interior of her mouth as if it had been a snake's. She had stretched one arm so high above her coiled-up cable of hair that he could see its satin delicacy above the sunburn; her face was flushed with sleep, and her eyelids hung heavy over their pupils. The brimfulness of her nature breathed from her. It was a moment when a woman's soul is more incarnate than at any other time; when the most spiritual beauty bespeaks itself flesh, and sex takes the outside place in the presentation.

Then those eyes flashed brightly through their filmy heaviness, before the remainder of her face was well awake. With an oddly compounded look of gladness, shyness and surprise, she exclaimed –

'O Mr Clare! How you frightened me . . .'

Hardy wished, he said, 'to demolish the doll of English fiction', to present woman's real sexuality. He is rightly given credit for doing so. But there was no question, as some critics imagine, of any campaign for female emancipation. What mattered was the freedom to evoke the lure and terror of sexual experience. Who but Hardy would have compared the interior of a girl's mouth to a snake's? Not only threatening in her beauty, woman is also frightened herself. And her fear too is unnerving. Here, somewhat earlier, is the couple's first conversation alone:

'What makes you draw off in that way, Tess?' said he. 'Are you afraid?'

'Oh no, sir . . . not of outdoor things; especially just now when the apple-blooth is falling, and everything so green.'

'But you have your indoor fears – eh?'

'Well – yes, sir.'

'What of?'

'I couldn't quite say.'

'The milk turning sour?'

'No.'

'Life in general?'

'Yes, sir.'

'Ah – so am I, very often. This hobble of being alive is rather serious, don't you think so?'

Two 'tremulous lives' move toward consummation. Will Tess be forgiven her early deflowering and dead child? Will Angel overcome class divisions to marry her? In short, is life a tragedy or a comedy? All kinds of hints suggest the latter. In the farmhouse where milkmaids and farmhands get together comic stories of infidelity are told. Hilariously and charmingly, three other milkmaids are also swooning over Clare. It is a world fizzing with fun and farce. Yet when finally Angel kisses Tess and she responds with 'unreflecting inevitableness' to 'the necessity of loving him', we are told that 'the pivot of the universe for their two natures' has shifted.

Against her mother's advice, Tess finds the courage to write a letter to Clare about her earlier misadventure. She puts it under his bedroom door but there is a carpet on the other side, underneath which the note is invisible to him. Hardy is frequently accused of introducing too many coincidences into his work, almost always at the expense of his characters' happiness. But they have the effect of confusing the issue of responsibility, begging the question of fatality, while also giving the disquieting impression that a chance meeting or a mislaid letter can be quite as devastating to an individual destiny as class discrimination or moral hypocrisy. There are simply so many things to be afraid of.

Tess's secret still untold, the couple get married. At last they are alone. No one can interfere. The sexual experience towards which a hundred and more very lush pages have been leading is imminent. Clare, however, chooses this of all moments to confess to a sin, some years before, of 'eight and forty hours dissipation with a stranger'. Tess instantly forgives him and responds with her own sad history. Angel instantly rejects her. There will be no lovemaking.

The scene is an extraordinary one. Suddenly both lovers' fears are entirely confirmed. For Angel, Tess is a different person, the decision to marry a girl from the lower classes has proved a terrible error: 'I repeat, the woman I have been loving is not you.' With 'terror upon her white face', Tess feels all the weight of Victorian morals and class division come down upon her. Meantime the reader cannot help but feel that both partners were all too ready to see 'the terrifying bliss' of sexual love thwarted. Sooner than expected, 'Having nothing more to fear', Tess falls asleep. Two days later, of her own accord, she returns home.

On a much lower key Hardy's poems suggest that his own life was beset by similar anxieties to those of his more melodramatic characters. A few years before *Tess*, in a poem entitled 'He Abjures Love', the poet announces that he will no longer make the mistake of idealising women: 'No more will now rate I/The common rare'. Was Angel right then when he abruptly retreated from his romantic vision of Tess? Three years later, writing a poem to a woman he had hoped would become a lover, Hardy speaks of a moment when they were trapped by the pouring rain 'snug and warm' together in a hansom cab that stood motionless at its destination. As so often, fear of sexual experience is at once hinted at and disguised behind coincidence:

> Then the downpour ceased, to my sharp sad pain,
> And the glass that had screened our forms before
> Flew up, and out she sprang to her door:
> I should have kissed her if the rain
> Had lasted a minute more.

Such frustrations, alleviated by a sense of relief, more or less sum up Hardy's midlife flirtations. The famous author would not become an adulterer. The obstacle was not a moral one.

Meanwhile *Tess of the D'Urbervilles* was enthralling and dividing its Victorian public. 'Dinner parties had to be rearranged', Tomalin tells us, 'to take account of the warring opinions.' Was Tess as the book's subtitle provocatively claimed 'A Pure Woman', or, as many suspected, a 'little harlot', heroine of 'a coarse and disagreeable story', told in 'a coarse and disagreeable manner'? Readers were used to thinking of sexuality in terms of morals, of good and bad behaviour. They expected to see the characters of a novel rewarded accordingly. But Hardy had other polarities in mind. His characters are bold or afraid, generous or mean, strong or weak. He insists on Tess's innocence. To make matters worse, Victorian justice *is* nevertheless done; Tess dies on the gallows after murdering the man who first deflowered her and now returns to ruin her life again. But this is so extreme as to be a travesty of justice, a horror story. Poring over the conundrum, Victorians were invited to suspect that the moral rhetoric in which they smothered sexual mores was a pathetic cover for deep underlying phobia. It was far more disquieting than any straightforward attack on moral hypocrisy could have been.

If Hardy's lush lingering over budding womanhood was a problem for Victorians and even for some critics today, when the same treatment was given to the English countryside he could only be applauded. Indeed, there are many for whom Hardy's representation of landscape and country life, his creation, through a series of novels, of an imaginative world he calls Wessex, roughly corresponding to Dorset, remains his great achievement. Certainly the richness of the evocation of fields, flowers and farming life in all its varied seasonal activities offers welcome relief to the dashed hopes of his young characters. I can think of no other author whose descriptions give such pleasure. I speak as one who usually wearies after only three or four lines of description. Yet Hardy's treatment of the landscape, the weather and the peasant community from which his characters emerge is more than a backdrop or compensation. It is essential to his preoccupations.

Far From the Madding Crowd begins with a shepherd tending his flock on Norcombe Hill:

> . . . one of the spots which suggest to a passer-by that he is in the presence of a shape approaching the indestructible as nearly as any to be found on earth. It was a featureless convexity of chalk and soil – an ordinary specimen of those smoothly outlined

protuberances of the globe which may remain undisturbed on
some great day of confusion when far grander heights and dizzy
granite precipices topple down.

This is Hardy's most profound attraction to his Dorset landscape.
It is supremely resilient. Through lavish and loving description of
it he hoped perhaps to accrue to his anxious self something of this
longed-for quality.

Almost all of *The Return of the Native* takes place on the wild
Egdon Heath ('civilisation was its enemy'), much of it at night.
One early chapter is entitled 'The figure against the sky'. A woman
is described standing on an ancient burial barrow that commands
the flat dark landscape beneath. 'Her extraordinary fixity, her
conspicuous loneliness, her heedlessness of night, betokened among
other things an utter absence of fear.'

Silhouetted above the landscape, passionate Eustacia is looking
for her lover. This bold detachment from both landscape and
community is a position of maximum vulnerability, and glamour.
How magnificent and unwise of her not to be afraid. By the end
of the novel, Eustacia's defeat and mental torment will be such
that, far from wishing to stand out, she seeks relief by sinking into
the landscape, drowning herself in the weir. Hardy's suicides almost
always seek death by drowning, by immersion in the imperturbability of the physical world. Jude seeks to drown himself standing
on the thin ice of a pond. Tess threatens to drown herself in the
river. In *The Mayor of Casterbridge* the main character Henchard
chooses, like Eustacia, the weir.

Fortunately, it is possible in Hardy's view to alleviate suffering
through partial rather than final merging with the natural world.
Alone in a wood at night, for example, 'the plight of being alive
becomes attenuated to its least possible dimensions'. So in happier
moments Tess's 'flexuous and stealthy figure became an integral
part of the scene'.

This yearning for absorption into nature is as much Hardy's as his characters'. How he relishes describing characters covered with seed spores and cobwebs, surrounded by buzzing insects, ankle-deep in leaves, butterflies on their breath, grasshoppers tumbling over their feet, dew on their hair, rabbits at their feet, rain on their lips. What a pleasure for pen and personalities to fuse themselves in beautiful impersonal natural phenomena. What a pity such restful retreats from adult life cannot last, or not until, as Tess reassures herself at one point, we will all at last be 'grassed down and forgotten'.

A powerful death wish drives Hardy's writing. In a letter in 1888 he remarked: 'if there is any way of getting a melancholy satis-faction out of life it lies in dying, so to speak, before one is out of the flesh; by which I mean putting on the manners of ghosts, wandering in their haunts, and taking their view of surrounding things. To think of life as passing away is a sadness, to think of it as past is at least tolerable. Hence even when I enter into a room to pay a simple morning call, I have unconsciously the habit of regarding the scene as if I were a spectre not solid enough to influ-ence my environment.'

The desire to remain a child and be spared life, the desire to be a ghost and beyond life are intimately related. In between, terrible in its intensity, lies adult life, narrative. One could usefully think of Hardy the narrator as a ghost within his own fiction, accompanying his wonderful, fearful child-adults through the initiations that will lead them to wish they were dead and indeed to die, if not through suicide, at least without much resistance. The word 'haunt' recurs with remarkable frequency. The archaic vocabulary and sentence structures frequently suggest a story whose melodrama is long over, ready to sink away into some ancient collective memory. Reading a magnificent description of the wind singing in the trees, or following a charmingly comic conversation of village rustics (another timeless world in which Hardy loves to submerge himself), it is all too easy to forget that this is the man who wrote to a friend on the occasion of the death of his son that 'the death of a child is never really to be regretted, when one reflects on what he has escaped.' His is a strong, shocking and above all defeatist vision. A ghostly existence is preferable because a ghost cannot influence his environment, which is a good thing because action in the world always leads to trouble.

But if Hardy hoped that a writer too might be spared influence in the real world, he was mistaken. He had forgotten Meredith's warning of years before. In the Victorian age a novel could cause a great stir and where *Tess* in 1891 might have charmed as much as it shocked, *Jude* four years later simply raised hell. 'Jude the obscene', 'a shameful nightmare', critics wrote.

Renouncing the reassuring descriptions of country life, the pleasing chorus of village rustics, with *Jude* Hardy arrives at the core of his vision. A poor orphan trying to hide from life in scholarship has a rude awakening when seduced by a raw country girl. Married and separated in a matter of pages, he falls in love with a refined cousin, Sue, a girl so terrified by sex that when she marries a much older man to escape Jude she denies him consummation, returns to Jude in the hope that he will be willing to live with her without sex, then gives herself to him only when she fears that physical need will drive him back to his wife. This was not easy material for Victorians. Coincidences and misfortunes abound. When the child got from Jude's wife kills the children got from Sue and then himself, it is the death of hope *tout court*, the proof that all attempts to achieve happiness will end in disaster. It would surely have been better never to have tried. To provoke his Victorian readers further, Hardy again offered an ending mockingly in line with their moral convictions: appalled by the death of her children, Sue gets religion and returns to her husband while Jude is seduced by his wife and returns to her shortly before his death. The shape of Victorian justice is thus again in place, as a nightmare, a terrible constriction of human potential.

* * *

A 'pale gentle frightened little man' Robert Louis Stevenson had described Hardy in 1885. On receiving a bad review for the novel *A Pair of Blue Eyes* in 1878, Hardy had written in his diary, 'Woke before it was light. Felt that I had not enough staying power to hold my own in the world.' Not unexpectedly, then, the storm of criticism over *Jude* shook him deeply. His wife loathed the book and said so in public. The bad news even reached the rustics in Bockhampton. To the extent to which all his novels had been a melodramatic exploration of his own dilemmas, to which all his characters, as he himself said, 'express mainly the author', it must have been clear that with his emotional life absolutely stalled any further work of fiction could only be deeply disturbing to write and very uncomfortable to publish. As a poet on the other hand he might more easily play the cryptic and inconsequential ghost. It was a medium that spared him too much narrative, too much contact with the sufferers who were his characters. Tomalin accepts Hardy's claim that poetry would require fewer compromises than serialised fiction. But there is nothing in terms of content that Hardy put in his poetry that he could not have put in a novel, nor is there much sign of compromise in *Jude*. Rather the contrary. It had been an act of enormous courage and artistic integrity to write such a book. By comparison, the huge and tedious patriotic poem *The Dynasts* (1904) looks far more like an appeal for public approval than a decision to be uncompromising. Perhaps the truth is that the decision to stop writing narrative went hand in hand with a decision to struggle with his problems no more. He would no longer seek to change his life.

By 1889 Tom and Emma were sleeping in separate beds. She had begun to write furious attacks on him in her diary. Hardy continued his sterile flirtations and never missed attending a funeral. In the mid-1890s they took up bicycling together. It offered a circumscribed adventure, a tolerable togetherness. Then in 1905 the twenty-six-year-old Florence Dugdale appeared on the exhausted scene, flattered both partners and soon became part of their lives. When Emma died in 1912, Florence was well placed to kick out the relatives, take over the author's life and eventually marry him. Afraid as always of the world's censure, the ageing author insisted the wedding take place in great secrecy.

Hardy had always gone out of his way to avoid conflict. Despite the social criticism in his novels he never made political statements, was extremely careful not to argue with relations. Yet his writing had always caused offence. The natives of Dorset felt farming people had been portrayed as simpletons. Emma complained that he had betrayed their marriage and the church. Now, no sooner was he married again than he offended his second wife, with a handful of poems about the first. They were among the finest he ever wrote.

The formula was simple: the ageing widower is allowed a glimpse of his wife as she was when they first met so long ago. So we have the moment of first love and, simultaneously, the sad relief of afterwards, with nothing in between but a poignant forty-year gap. Here is 'The Voice':

> Woman much missed, how you call to me, call to me,
> Saying that now you are not as you were
> When you had changed from the one who was all to me
> But as at first, when our day was fair.
>
> Can it be you that I hear? Let me view you, then,
> Standing as when I drew near to the town
> Where you would wait for me: yes, as I knew you then,
> Even to the original air-blue gown!
>
> Or is it only the breeze, in its listlessness
> Travelling across the wet mead to me here,
> You being ever dissolved to wan wistlessness,
> Heard no more again far or near?

> Thus I; faltering forward,
> Leaves around me falling,
> Wind oozing thin through the thorn from norward
> And the woman calling.

Real ghost and would-be ghost dissolve together into mist and verse. Florence was furious. 'I expect the idea of the general reader will be that T. H.'s second marriage is a most disastrous one and that his sole wish is to find refuge in the grave with her with whom he found happiness.' Once again Hardy had taken revenge on those whose protection he needed. Once again he could protest it was only art, spectral, inconsequential. What reality could one ever ascribe to such a beautiful word as 'wistlessness'?

Any biographer of Hardy faces the problem that he lived long after there was anything to report. It is hard to interest the reader in a list of public honours and the many titles of his fine poetry collections. Still, his death in 1928 affords a good anecdote. Hardy's wish was to be buried in the local churchyard at Stinsford: home. His literary friends wanted him at Westminster Abbey: town. In life he had been able to go back and forth between the two, but for a corpse this was impossible. The problem was solved with a gruesome bit of surgery: his heart was buried at Stinsford and his body cremated and interred in the Abbey. The decision as to which part should go where was definitely right, but it was a compromise that left everyone dissatisfied.

And afterwards? Hardy had had the epitaph ready for decades. It is a poem in which he imagines himself being remembered as a man attentive to the most subtle phenomena of nature. Thus he takes refuge simultaneously in the collective memory and in landscape, indeed he links the two. These are verses from which all the turmoils of narrative are scrupulously absent, as if, in his long life he had had the great good fortune never to have been involved in action of any kind, the only positive effort mentioned being a failed attempt to help small defenceless animals. Most of all, there are no women.

Afterwards

When the Present has latched its postern behind my
    tremulous stay,
  And the May month flaps its glad green leaves like wings,
Delicate-filmed as new-spun silk, will the neighbours say,
    'He was a man who used to notice such things'?

If it be in the dusk when, like an eyelid's soundless blink,
  The dewfall-hawk comes crossing the shades to alight
Upon the wind-warped upland thorn, a gazer may think,
    'To him this must have been a familiar sight.'

If I pass during some nocturnal blackness, mothy and
    warm,
  When the hedgehog travels furtively over the lawn,
One may say, 'He strove that such innocent creatures
    should come to no harm,
    But he could do little for them; and now he is gone.'

If, when hearing that I have been stilled at last, they stand
    at the door,
  Watching the full-starred heavens that winter sees,
Will this thought rise on those who will meet my face no
    more,
    'He was one who had an eye for such mysteries'?

And will any say when my bell of quittance is heard in the
    gloom,
  And a crossing breeze cuts a pause in its outrollings,
Till they swell again, as they were a new bell's boom,
    'He hears it not now, but used to notice such things'?

The Disenchantment of Translation

[A lecture delivered to Katha Utsah in Delhi, India]

What a strange moment when I opened the invitation to come here to Katha and saw the title of the session I was to lead: 'The Disenchantment of Translation'. Only a week before, I had given a talk on translation entitled 'Translating Enchantment'. As so often, one realises that far from being a lonely individual mind exploring new ideas, one is part of a larger, shared endeavour, even if it is not always clear what one's relationship with the collective mind behind that endeavour might be.

Enchantment, disenchantment. What do we mean by these most unscientific words? Why are they particularly appropriate to the practice of translation, its rewards and frustrations?

I think we'd all agree that the word disenchantment has negative connotations. It suggests a disappointment, a loss of pleasure. And yet the positive word enchantment is not one widely used in the West. As I said, it seems anti-scientific. More and more it is spoken and written with a certain embarrassment. Its use is restricted, for example, to refer to moments of childish innocence, pleasures that depend on ingenuousness. We use 'enchantment' or 'enchanting' to enthuse about such things as a white Christmas, a fairy story for children (and so much Western literature is for children, or rather, for the infantile). Or in Verona, where I live, the word enchantment might be used when speaking of the tradition of Santa Lucia, a blind martyr of many centuries ago, who, on the night before 13 December, is supposed to bring the local children their seasonal presents. If they have been well behaved, that is. If not, she brings them only a piece of coal. By the time they are seven or eight years old most children have started asking their parents why Santa Lucia only operates in the Verona area, while Father Christmas is more ubiquitous. With their growing curiosity, the period of disenchantment has begun.

At most, enchantment might stretch to first love, or the word is used in tourist brochures to describe the pleasures of some exotic location, deploying a rhetoric that no one is really expected to believe. In short, 'enchantment' is not considered part of serious life. Hence disenchantment becomes simply a necessary part of growing up. We might almost say that disenchantment is synonymous with enlightenment, a word that has an extremely positive connotation. Childish reassurance and rapture are put aside to confront the so-called real world.

But surely, when we talk of the disenchantment of translation we are not suggesting that a translation is something more realistic, less childish, more enlightening than the original.

Let us concentrate for a moment on this curiosity: we have two words, that would appear to share, at least to some extent, the same meaning – disenchantment, enlightenment – but one with a negative connotation and one with a positive, one stressing a loss, the other a gain. To grasp what we mean when we speak of the disenchantment of translation, we must try to understand this curiosity a little better.

The narrower and ever more superficial use of the word enchantment in English and other Western languages, as indeed the devaluing of the word myth (*mitico* is a common and almost meaningless expression of approbation among Italian youngsters), tells us a lot about the modern world and its uneasiness with the language it has inherited from the past. It suggests a desire to repress and deny an area of experience. Or rather, that experience is admitted – the word, like the experience, won't go away – but within a hierarchy of values where it is decidedly on one of the lower levels. 'Enchantment' is allowed to exist, but must not intrude into 'reality' – science and economics and politics, the territory of enlightenment. In short, it is allowed to exist in art, in books, paintings, sculptures, Disney films. Art becomes a ghetto where all kinds of things with which our modern world is uncomfortable are allowed a sort of shadowy existence.

Let us try to understand why this process of relegation and trivialisation was necessary with 'enchantment'. The answer of course is that the word refers to something that threatens our modern view of the world. Here we need to look closely at the roots of the word. This is easier perhaps in Italian. *In-canto*, the Italians say. In song. An enchantment is an entering into song. I could give two very literal examples in my own life.

I grew up in an extremely evangelical household. I sang in a choir. I sang a part. I was part of a whole larger than myself. The hymns came from the English Wesleyan tradition, or there were anthems from the tradition of German sacred music. The individual accepted the yoke of the community. The en-chantment happens within a group. It is not something you experience alone. And it is not just the contemporary community you become part of but one that stretches back into the past. My youthful enthusiasm was harnessed by something older and larger than myself. Many of the words were archaic, the devotion ancient. I entered into song.

This was very beautiful until my parents became involved in the so-called charismatic movement. I was in my early teens. There was speaking in tongues, prophesy, ecstatic singing, with arms raised to God, etc. To enter into song now meant a much greater sacrifice of self. The reasoning mind had to be sacrificed entirely and constantly.

It's interesting that the English use the word chant, en-chant-ment, rather than the word song. The chant is rhythmical, repetitive, captivating, coercive. To be enchanted is to lose a little control. It is to subject the mind to the community, to the past. Individual curiosity is replaced by collective devotion. I left the group when the charismatic movement became too coercive. From then on, group singing was always a problem for me, I felt its attraction and pleasures, the pleasures of belonging to a tight community, and I felt resistance to it. In short, I experienced what is a very modern state of mind, the nostalgia for community and the fear of being defined and possessed by it.

I didn't accept another enchantment of this simple form until years later I became a regular supporter of my local football club in Verona. Here too there is a strong sense of community. Here too, in the frenetic atmosphere of the stadium, you throw your weight behind the collective chant to urge on your team. Here too the past is present. Many of the chants name old stars whom most of those in the stadium never saw. But there is something different now. The whole experience is undercut and controlled by a pervasive irony. We sing about battles and victories and hatreds and loves, but we know that when we leave the stadium we will return to our disenchanted lives. We are playing with enchantment. We believe in our community and we don't believe in it. It satisfies our nostalgia for collective delirium without demanding our souls. We have a pleasurable loss of control, for carefully controlled periods.

Much of modern literature in the West could be characterised in terms of its ambiguous relationship to enchantment, to the submergence of the individual mind in the collective. Inevitably, this is reflected in the relationship of each individual style to the community's collective use of language. And this is where the relationship between translation and enchantment comes in. The translator of modern literature is above all involved in capturing and seeking to reproduce the complicity and tension between the writer and his language.

In my religious childhood, enchantment didn't just mean the moment of maximum collective ecstasy, the hymn. It also meant the rhythmic cadences of the liturgy, the prayers (morning and evening), the gospel stories, the life my parents expected me to live. All of this was enshrined in the language we used, and above all in the language of the 1666 prayer book, the Authorised Version of the Bible.

In a novel I wrote about this period of my life, I tried to express my love of that language, and my eagerness to be free of its enchantment. When the novel was translated into Italian it became clear that to a large extent that enchantment didn't exist in this other language; the Italians have an entirely different relationship with the Bible. Their liturgical and Christian rhetoric draws on other lexical sources and is not anchored to one particular historical period. Unable to evoke the spell of biblical language which was so important in the original they were then unable to convey the urgency of breaking that spell.

Here it might be objected that I am simply talking about problems of cultural specificity that inevitably arise in any translation. How can we describe English interior decorating in Italian, or vice versa? It's time to recall Wittgenstein's contention that philosophy was a battle against the 'bewitchment of our intelligence by means of language', and his more general concern that all thinking lies under 'the enchantments of language'. With this statement, our idea of enchantment is radically extended. And the whole presumption of the Enlightenment, that thinking is the instrument through which we dispense with such childish things as enchantment, is challenged. Now we have the troubling idea that *in order to think, we must be enchanted*. By what? By language, a language. The very word enlightenment, then, and all it stands for is actually part of a larger enchantment. Our clearest thinking lies under a linguistic spell. We are never outside language.

Let us then bring alongside this claim Paul Celan's bitter reflection on admitting defeat in his attempt to translate a poem by Baudelaire, that 'poetry is the fatal uniqueness of language'. As the highest expression of verbal art, poetry presents us with the most intense enchantment, a heady cocktail of meaning, emotion, beauty, that can only be generated by these words, this linguistic performance, and hence can only be experienced by speakers of this language.

If we accept this view of language and enchantment, then translation inevitably involves dis-enchantment; we must cast off the spell under which these thoughts were produced. One of the things I do with my students is to look at a lot of literary texts in English and Italian without telling them which is the original. Very quickly they learn, by considering the content, the relationship of content to style, the internal coherence of the two texts, semantic, and auditory too, to identify which is the original. Even the best translations lack the same level of cohesion, the meshing between the writer's mind and the language it moves in.

But of course, if our language is a form of enchantment, that must also mean that the translation, while at once a disenchantment, is also a re-enchantment. It is here that translation becomes truly fascinating. In a world where so much is now translated, where there is so much enthusiasm about pooling our different cultures, about achieving perhaps some international literary language (such claims have been made for English), what is the status of translation? Does reading mostly in translation change the nature of the reading experience?

One of the reasons I was invited to this conference is because I translated the book *Ka* by Roberto Calasso, a book, as you know, that retells the ancient myths of India and tries to explore their deepest meaning. Before working on *Ka* I had translated *The Marriage of Cadmus and Harmony*, a book that does much the same thing with the Greek myths. Very often in *The Marriage*, Calasso was obliged to settle on some Greek word, to quote it in the original language to reflect on its meaning, because there was no equivalent in Italian. Like the exposed tip of the iceberg, the word suggested a mass of submerged and unsuspected cultural differences. It is obvious that for a Greek of 3,000 years ago to listen to the stories which formed his world was a completely different experience than for a modern Italian to read about them. He understood the world only, wonderfully, in those terms; we savour the enchantment, while believing we remain outside it, a very modern state of mind.

The experience becomes different again, of course, when the

stories are translated from Italian into English, where layers and layers of culture have been built up through interpretation and appropriation of the classical world. Sometimes when Calasso quoted in Italian from the *Iliad* or the *Odyssey* I would go to an English translation to quote the same lines, only to find that the English version was so different that I was obliged to work from Calasso's Italian.

Yet the Greek stories made sense to me. It was as if one were exploring one's own subconscious. Chords were immediately struck. My own language had already had long dealings with those gods and ideas.

This was not true for me of *Ka*. The Indian myths seemed far stranger than any stories I had ever read. I was disorientated (a comic word to use for this experience, since this was probably as close to the Orient as I ever got). Once again Calasso settled on key words, in Sanskrit this time, words whose ambiguity or complexity of meaning made them touchstones. Once again he used quotations. Often there were no existing English translations to draw on, which was a relief. But whereas with the Greek myth I felt there was an existing rhetoric, an existing lexicon, a tradition, into which I could translate the stories, with *Ka* this was not the case.

More and more, then, I wondered about the intimate connection between the content of the story and the language of the culture that created it, more and more I felt the pull of the English to impose concepts linked to other traditions, above all the Christian. It is hard to use a word like sin, or repentance, in English, without imposing an alien, that is English, enchantment on a foreign text. More and more I was struggling to find neutral words. But the original stories were not written with neutral words. A story is not the same experience when told to a different audience in a different language in a different time. Why then does a writer go back to the stories of different times and cultures? What is the point?

I felt very strongly with both of Calasso's books that one of the underlying intentions of his work was to subvert contemporary Italian, or more generally Western, certainties by building up an alien pattern of thought that, at a certain point, would become recognisable to the reader as a plausible and indeed beautiful way of understanding experience. He might show us, for examples, how the ancient Greeks had offered an aesthetic justification of existence 2,500 years before Nietzsche formulated similar ideas. He might show how an ancient Indian *rsi* had elaborated thoughts which we consider the greatest achievements of our modern philosophy. The recuperation, that is, of the enchantment under which ancient India lived was an operation aimed to subvert the enchantment under which we live today and which, precisely because we are in its thrall, we never consider an enchantment at all. In this sense the introduction of a foreign word, rather than mystification, is an operation of demystification, it questions the way our language organises experience.

So Calasso is not telling these stories for the reasons they were originally told, but to challenge the stories we are always telling ourselves, and that perhaps we do not even think of as stories, but reality. In doing so he becomes part of a modern Western tradition which seeks to expose the enchantment we live in, to 'deconstruct' as the postmodernists say, while always aware that there is no disenchanted place to be. Curiously, it's a tradition that has simultaneously encouraged translation and made it impossible.

What I want to do now is to use a short text from a writer at the centre of that Western tradition to suggest the kind of antithetical impulses that run through much of modern literature – particularly with regard to the relationship between individual and community – and how problematic they are for translation. For if the intention of the original is to subvert the enchantment of its own language, to wake us up to the spell we lie under, how can the translation achieve this when the enchantment it translates into is different?

But here is Hemingway in 'The Snows of Kilimanjaro':

He thought about alone in Constantinople that time having quarrelled in Paris before he had gone out. He had whored the whole time and then, when that was over, and he had failed to kill his loneliness, but only made it worse, he had written her, the first one, the one who left him, a letter telling her how he had never been able to kill it. How when he thought he saw her outside the Regence one time it made him go all faint and sick inside, and that he would follow a woman who looked like her in some way, along the Boulevard, afraid to see it was not she, afraid to lose the feeling it gave him. How every one he had slept with had only made him miss her more.

The place names mentioned here are immediately a little disorientating. Where is most of the passage taking place, in Constantinople or Paris? The story seems to be one at once of promiscuity and loneliness. Cut free from the enchantment of an intense love, the man succumbs to the tawdry chronicle of a frenetic series of couplings. He tries to kill the love that has brought about his unease but then admits that he is afraid of losing this unease.

But what most surprises us when we read the passage is the position of that first 'alone': 'He thought about alone in Constantinople that time'. This is surely incorrect. One cannot put an adverb 'alone' after the expression 'thought about' which requires a noun or a gerund: He thought about love; he thought about being alone, or having been alone. The result is that the word 'alone' is heavily stressed precisely because it disorientates us. The rules of language, which are the rules of a community, are made to break up around this word 'alone', as if the experience of being alone threatened language, which is a shared thing.

Let me translate back into English the Italian translation of this first sentence to give you an impression of how it is experienced in the Italian:

He thought about that time when he was in Constantinople, alone, because they had quarrelled in Paris before his departure.

Here the aloneness is reintroduced into the community of language. While we notice in passing that the curiosity of the English 'gone out' has been eliminated by using the word 'departure' which now links Paris and Constantinople and gives us a feeling of security. We understand the narrator's movements.

I have asked many Italian translators if they could reproduce this English. They try out the phrase: *Pensò a solo* – literally 'He thought about alone' – then they shake their heads and tell me, No, no you can't do it. So why can it be done in English? In English, perhaps because the language has so few inflections, we have developed a habit of turning verbs and adjectives into nouns, as and when we choose, or nouns into verbs. We have: telephone, to telephone, to go, a go, and so on. Everyone knows this. So Hemingway can just about get away with it. It sounds 'wrong', it sounds 'unusual' but it sounds English, it is outside the usual community of speech, but still understood by speakers.

Let me give you another example from Lawrence. But I could quote hundreds. This is about a young woman who has just made love and is lying awake at night regretting it:

Gudrun lay wide awake, destroyed into perfect consciousness.

Well, in English we cannot say destroyed 'into'. Then it is standard in English to think of consciousness as a positive thing, not the result of a destruction. The word 'perfect' also seems provocative here. How can perfection be the product of the destruction of a person? Or if perfect is made in the sense of completed, in what way does it qualify consciousness? The Italian says: Gudrun remained awake, destroyed, in a state of perfect lucidity.

Again you could say, why does the Italian not keep the 'into' that links destruction and consciousness? Why is the word 'consciousness' not used? The second question is easily answered: the word *cosciente* in Italian has a different semantic range; *cosciente* can mean 'responsible' which would give the wrong idea.

As far as the 'into' is concerned, we must remember that there are many verbs in English which suggest a transformation using 'into' – transform into, change into, turn into. So the phrase doesn't sound so strange in English. Lawrence has taken a standard English structure and subverted it, but again, although surprising, it is recognisably English.

These sentences and the problem of translating them I hope tell us something about the nature of modern writing, of individualism and translation. The sentence from Lawrence comes from a book where two couples try to form non-traditional love relationships; they try to live outside society, but in the end, they find they can only define their position against the society they are rejecting and of which they are still inevitably a part.

Similarly, Lawrence can reject many of the values implied by English, and fight against them. But at the same time he cannot escape the overall enchantment and community of Englishness. Needless to say he was aware of this. We thus reach a situation where his text begins to have meaning only if we understand the context of the society he rebels against, and the broader context of the language. The meaning of 'she was destroyed into perfect consciousness' is very much that it is subversive of English and yet submissive to some of its more hidden mechanisms. The same was true of Hemingway's 'he thought about alone'.

A paradox follows. Imagining themselves as breaking free of society, as becoming individuals no longer defined by their culture (notoriously they go and live abroad), the modernists become attractive international figures, gurus whose work must be translated everywhere and immediately, because it is presumed to have universal significance. Yet at the same time, the breaking free in their work can only be understood in the tradition and context they are breaking free from. This is not to say that translation is pointless. But however beautifully one might write Lawrence into another language, it will always be a more reassuring text linguistically than it was in English. Above all, it will intersect with an alien tradition, the provocations its content may cause become entirely unpredictable.

Enchantments are constantly dissolving and re-forming. Translation can play all kinds of roles in that process. It may be that a country which reads in translations that domesticate every foreign text to its own values and usages will be able to preserve its own linguistic spell far longer than a language whose writers are always busy wrestling with their own culture.

It may also be that many people like reading translations because they are less dangerous than original texts. However challenging the content of a book may be, if the medium of the language is re-assuring then the reader perhaps can feel safe within his own world.

Alternatively, it can happen that a translation unleashes something quite new and strange into a culture. As I hope is the case with Calasso's *Ka*.

In particular though, it seems to me that one of the lessons one learns from looking at a lot of translations is that the difference between experiencing a foreign culture and experiencing one's own is a very great difference, and is greater still if we cannot know the foreign culture in the language of origin. These are truisms.

But they should alert us to two things. That we must cultivate our own language, however commercially unfashionable that may be. In the case of India, for example, many anthologies of Indian writing turn out to be written not in one of the country's native languages, but in English. Salman Rushdie in particular has spoken of English as being useful for allowing India to become known in the world. But is the purpose of literature to make ourselves known in the world? Isn't it rather to tell ourselves the stories that create the world we live in? And in so far as we live in a language then it is that language that is important to us.

Similarly, Kazuo Ishiguro has criticised some English writers for using words and expressions that are too complicated for translation and that prevent the books from being understood worldwide. Again, this seems to suggest an impoverishment of language for commercial ends, or for the creation of a global culture, which of course would mean the death of many traditions.

J. M. Coetzee takes an opposite position to Rushdie in his novel *Disgrace*. Of the black farmer Petrus, a man who is taking over the life and land of the hero, David's, daughter, we hear:

> Petrus is a man of his generation. Doubtless Petrus has been through a lot, doubtless he has a story to tell. He [David] would not mind hearing Petrus's story one day. But preferably not reduced to English. More and more he is convinced that English is an unfit medium for the truth of South Africa.

But David does not speak Petrus's language.

Walter Benjamin suggested that in each successive translation of a text, some mingling of languages was achieved, a process that ultimately and ideally, if the same text were translated over and over into all kinds of different languages, might lead us to rediscover the original sacred language lost with the destruction of the Tower of Babel. One wonders if such a language would bring the absolute enlightenment that certain philosophers of the early twentieth century hoped to achieve by expressing philosophical problems only in the terms of strict logic. Or would it create the ultimate universal enchantment, the exclusion of other influences in one single world-wide language?

Better, it seems to me, the Babel that defends us from a possibly totalitarian nightmare, that allows us if not to understand, then at least to be aware of the different ways we can enchant ourselves; and that keeps us constantly busy and perplexed with the exciting business of writing and rewriting each other's stories.

Still Stirring

[Samuel Beckett]

'Oh all to end.' Thus the Irish writer and Nobel Prize winner Samuel Beckett concluded his last work of fiction, *Stirrings Still*, making explicit once again, thirty years and more after Vladimir and Estragon first considered hanging themselves on the stage of *Waiting for Godot*, the powerful yearning behind so much of his work: for silence and extinction.

But while Beckett was granted his quietus in 1989, there is no closure for his readers and critics, nor would we want it; for if a death wish was central to his writing, no prose was ever livelier. So the hundredth anniversary of Beckett's birth on 13 April of this year [2006] will be an occasion for loud celebration and fresh reflection. There is a handsome four-volume re-edition of his works, edited by Paul Auster and with introductions from, among others, J. M. Coetzee and Salman Rushdie, a new collection of academic essays from Florida University Press (*Beckett After Beckett*), a fascinating and detailed memoir from Anne Atik, whose artist husband was the author's friend and drinking companion (*How It Was*), and a rich collection of memories taken from interviews with Beckett himself and with those who knew him (*Beckett Remembering, Remembering Beckett*).

The drift of many of those remembering Beckett is that admission to the literary canon isn't recognition enough for 'this *separate* man' as his friend the philosopher Emil Cioran called him.† There are hints of sanctification. 'Many have sensed', remarks Harvard

---

† Emil Cioran's sketch of Beckett in the book *Anathemas and Admirations* remains the most fascinating short memoir on the author.

professor Robert Scanlan, who visited Beckett on his deathbed in 1989, 'that Beckett's serenity towards the end resembled the patience of a saint.' The Polish writer Antoni Libera feels he owes the success of his own work 'to Beckett's "blessing" and to his spirit, which was watching over everything'. The German actor Horst Bollman considers that his 'encounter with Beckett is reward enough, in itself, for having been an actor all my life'. Many mention his 'legendary generosity' and love of children. Scanlan concludes his piece: 'Here's to you, Sam Beckett. God rest and bless your sweet and patient soul.'

How curiously this valediction rings, addressed as it is to a man who satirised every form of metaphysics and renounced any mental comfort that might subtract him from the exhausting experience of being alone with his conviction that the world was without meaning and expression futile, yet that he was all the same duty-bound to express the fact. But perhaps it is precisely in Beckett's repeated renunciations – of English for French, of a rich and traditional narrative facility for texts stripped of everything we would normally think of as plot or colour – that we can find a link between these sometimes sentimental centenary remembrances and the core of the author's work, his special position in the literature of the twentieth century. 'How easy', writes Cioran, 'to imagine him, some centuries back, in a naked cell, undisturbed by the least decoration, not even a crucifix.' With Beckett, it is the persistence of a 'religious' seriousness in the declared absence of any sustaining metaphysics that gives his work its special, for some saintly, pathos.

Born in 1906, Beckett was brought up in a well-to-do Protestant family in County Dublin. Educated at private schools, he excelled in both academic work and sport and, after graduating in French and Italian at Trinity College, Dublin, in 1927, went back and forth between teaching posts in Dublin and Paris, where he met James Joyce who was then writing *Finnegans Wake*. But Beckett soon decided he was not cut out for teaching and gave up his job, thus disappointing his parents. The ensuing and bitter arguments, with his mother in particular, plus what appear to have been a number of panic attacks, led to the decision to undergo psychoanalysis in London, where Beckett spent two years trying and failing to start a career as a literary reviewer. After an extended visit to Germany and another unhappy period in Dublin, he settled permanently in Paris in 1937.

In two essays written in his twenties Beckett declared his great admiration for Proust and Joyce, yet his first novel, *Murphy*, written shortly afterwards, suggests a different inspiration. While Proust and Joyce share a confident commitment to the evocation of complex psychological reality within a densely described world, Beckett seems embarrassed to present his story of a feckless, unemployed Irishman in London as 'real' at all. Despite, or perhaps because of, the novel's evident autobiographical content, all kinds of strategies are used to prevent the reader from becoming immersed in plot and character in the traditional fashion. The book opens with a tone of mockery:

> The sun shone, having no alternative, on the nothing new. Murphy sat out of it as though he were free, in a mew in West Brompton. Here for what might have been six months he had eaten, drunk, slept and put his clothes on and off, in a medium-sized cage of north-western aspect commanding an unbroken view of medium-sized cages of south-eastern aspect. Soon he would have to make other arrangements, for the mew had been condemned. Soon he would have to buckle to and start eating, drinking, sleeping, and putting his clothes on and off, in quite alien surroundings.[†]

The very etymology of 'novel' suggests that the form brings newness. Echoing Ecclesiastes, Beckett renounces the idea. The solar system

---

[†] Beckett's French translation of *Murphy* gives the 'mew' in West Brompton as '*l'impasse de l'Enfant Jésus*', introducing a Christian frame of reference into the city grid. In his illuminating book *Beckett's Dying Words*, the critic Christopher Ricks has pointed out that 'mew' rather than the more correct 'mews' is in fact an archaic word for 'cage'.

is a prison, ever the same, and the notion that Murphy might have achieved some freedom by sitting 'out of it' (out of the sunshine) is laughable. Nor is it the only prison. His room is a 'cage' in the rigid grid of London's terraced streets. Even the language aligns itself with this imprisoning environment as groups of words are repeated as though to form the walls that close Murphy in: 'eaten, drunk, slept and put his clothes on and off' is mirrored by 'eating, drinking, sleeping and putting his clothes on and off', while in between 'a medium-sized cage of north-western aspect' faces 'medium-sized cages of south-eastern aspect'. Those compound, hyphenated adjectives reinforce the sense of entrapment making the irony that Murphy's room might 'command' a view even heavier.

In Joyce Beckett had admired the fusion of word and sense. 'When the idea is sleep, the words go to sleep', he remarks, and he speaks of his compatriot as the heir to Shakespeare and Dickens in this regard, great masters of onomatopoeia and evocation. But a letter written to his friend Axel Kaun a year before the publication of *Murphy* suggests that Beckett's sense of what could be achieved with language was changing radically:

It is indeed becoming more and more difficult, even senseless for me to write an official English. And more and more my own language appears to me like a veil that must be torn apart in order to get at the things (or the Nothingness) behind it. Grammar and Style. To me they seem to have become as irrelevant as a Victorian bathing suit or the imperturbability of a true gentleman. A mask. Let us hope the time will come . . . when language is most efficiently used where it is most efficiently misused. As we cannot eliminate language all at once, we should at least leave nothing undone that might contribute to its falling into disrepute. To bore one hole after another in it, until what lurks behind it – be it something or nothing – begins to seep through; I cannot imagine a higher goal for a writer today.

And he adds:

> With such a programme in my opinion the latest work of Joyce
> has nothing whatever to do.

Interesting here is the way what at first seems the dissatisfaction of
any adventurous young artist with current conventions is drastically
extended to the whole of language, which, in the name of honesty,
is to be attacked with 'a mocking attitude towards the word through
words'. The stance explains those odd slippages in the opening
sentences of *Murphy* where first we hear of clothes being put 'on
and off', rather than put on and taken off, and then more comically of having to 'buckle to' not to finding a new apartment or a
job, but to 'eating, drinking, sleeping', three activities not usually
considered onerous. Throughout the book Beckett misses no opportunity to exploit certain automatisms in the language which lead it
to fall into error. It is as if he were warning us that his own verbal
brilliance is a matter of little import beside the threat of 'quite alien
surroundings'.

Murphy himself is implicated in the book's linguistic waywardness
when his girlfriend Celia remarks that his words 'went dead' as soon
as spoken, as if he didn't believe in them. It is not difficult here to
see a relation between the author's denial of a traditional realism
to his story and Murphy's problems with language, his problems
above all in taking seriously the world of employment in 1930s
London, something which might well reflect Beckett's own difficulty
in engaging with the very conventional expectations of his parents.

Despite the air of mockery that hangs over Murphy, reality of the
economic variety does impinge: if the hero is to make a living, and
above all to stop his beloved Celia from prostituting herself to pay
the rent, he will have to take the world of work seriously, even
though he can't. He simply cannot do it. But he must. It's an early
formulation of what would become Beckett's motto, 'I can't go on,
I'll go on.' This is not, as is sometimes supposed, a celebration of

human resilience, but simply the contrast of an emotive conviction on the one hand – I can't go on – and an inevitable fact on the other – willy-nilly life goes on. 'No future in this,' says the narrator of *Worstward Ho*, and continues: 'Alas yes.'

Needless to say, the only and ultimate solution to such a contradiction is death. At the end of the novel Murphy's ashes will be kicked around the floor of a London pub, then 'swept away with the sand, the beer, the butts, the glass, the matches, the spits, the vomit.' If Beckett later chose to end his novels and plays without anything so clear-cut as his main character's demise, nevertheless his works always point in that direction, to the release of silence and non-being. There thus emerges a complicity between the plots he creates and his attitude to language. So far as either leads to a resolution or final truth it lies not so much within the text as in the silence after its end.

Much is made in the academic world, and rightly so, of Beckett's 'deconstruction' of traditional realism, his constant undermining, that is, of the premises of conventional fiction. 'He veritably hunted realism to death' says Paul Davies with evident satisfaction in *Beckett After Beckett*. And indeed the writer's second novel, *Watt*, makes fun of traditional narrative in all sorts of wonderful ways. In the following passage, for example, the bleakest possible pessimism is framed in a nursery-rhyme sequence of rhyming anapaests formed entirely with monosyllabic words:

> Personally of course I regret everything. Not a word, not a deed, not a thought, not a need, not a grief, not a joy, not a girl, not a boy, not a doubt, not a trust, not a scorn, not a lust, not a hope, not a fear, not a smile, not a tear, not a name, not a face, no time, no place, that I do not regret, exceedingly. An ordure from beginning to end.

Reading this, it is genuinely hard for the reader to respond to the unhappiness of the speaker, since his attention is captured by the trite ordering of experience into so many opposites – girl boy, tear joy – and in general by the bizarre manner of the expression, a manner that exposes language's inevitable tendency, as Beckett would see it, to mask reality.

Yet for all these aggressive experiments, one is struck on rereading Beckett that he did not dispense with traditional realism *tout court*. Throughout his work we come across passages of haunting descriptive power in which we cannot help feeling the author has a considerable emotional investment. Deciding to fill the empty days before his death by telling himself stories, the character Malone, in *Malone Dies*, casually invents a family of ignorant farmers. After some high comedy with Mr Lambert's pig-sticking activities, we have this:

> Then Mrs Lambert was alone in the kitchen. She sat down by the window and turned down the wick of the lamp, as she always did before blowing it out, for she did not like to blow out a lamp that was still hot. When she thought the chimney and shade had cooled sufficiently she got up and blew down the chimney. She stood a moment irresolute, bowed forward with her hands on the table, before she sat down again. Her day of toil over, day dawned on other toils within her, on the crass tenacity of life and its diligent pains. Sitting, moving about, she bore them better than in bed . . . Often she stood up and moved about the room, or out and round the ruinous old house, five years now it had been going on, five or six, not more. She told herself she had a woman's disease, but half-heartedly. Night seemed less night in the kitchen pervaded with the everyday tribulations, day less dead. It helped her, when things were bad, to cling with her fingers to the worn table at which her family would soon be united, waiting for her to serve them, and to feel about her, ready for use, the lifelong pots and pans.

'Mortal tedium' announces Malone dismissively, after constructing this description. But mortal tedium is more the experience he has so effectively evoked than the reader's reaction on reading it. Albeit with the small rhetorical flourishes that remind us of Malone's self-conscious, creative efforts, the passage is as convincing and moving as anything in conventional fiction.

What is new in Beckett, however, is the way these powerful moments of conventional realism are never allowed to extend right across a novel or play, creating, as in a traditional work, a fully imagined and consistent world that the reader is invited to consider reality. Rather they appear as brief fragments, the vagaries of an idle mind, their intensities contrasted with the inertia of the moribund narrator who produces them; or they emerge as unreliable, fleeting memories to which no date or place can be attached, 'after images' S. E. Gontarski and Anthony Uhlmann call them in their introduction to *Beckett After Beckett*, a book largely concerned with the many different relationships between Beckett's narrators and the images they half remember, half invent.

The consequence of Beckett's strategy is that we are never allowed to relax into the determined forward movement of the traditional story or the encyclopedically complete worlds of Joyce and Proust. Rather, something is given, then immediately taken away, as the mind tracks back and forth between engagement and disengagement, or, in Malone's case, memories of life and the more urgent reality of dying.

Beckett Remembering includes a few pages of notes that Patrick Bowles made of his conversations with Beckett while undertaking the translation of *Molloy*. Written immediately after the war, this was Beckett's third full-length novel, the first written in French and the first of what would become the trilogy (*Molloy*, *Malone Dies*, *The Unnameable*) in which, as the work proceeds, we have the impression that each narrating voice – the bedridden Molloy, the detective Moran, the dying Malone – turns out to be no more than an invention or earlier manifestation of the next, until finally we arrive at the 'unnameable', the voice behind and beyond all the others, unsure of anything except the interminable chattering of language in the mind.

In his notes Bowles recounts a conversation in which Beckett insisted that in order to represent the meaninglessness of the world it was necessary to allow chaos into the text and break down form, to declare the maker of the work as 'blindly immersed' in 'chance' rather than standing outside it. At the same time, all mere details of history or social context must be stripped out of the work, so as to arrive at the ultimate reality of consciousness and being. We understand that it was partly in response to these convictions that Beckett decided to work in French, renouncing the greater control and facility he had in English, together with the powerful associations a mother tongue inevitably brings with it.

However, in the same conversation it is clear that author and translator take very great pains over the exact choice of the words in the English version of *Molloy*. Similarly, Richard Seaver, who translated the short story 'La Fin', recalls Beckett's meticulous work on the English text. Reflecting on the sentence 'They dressed me and gave me some money', Beckett suggested 'what would you think if we used the word "clothed" instead of "dressed"? "They clothed me and gave me money." Do you like the ring of that better?' 'Yes,' replies Seaver, '"clothed" was the better word.'

So although facility must be shunned, form broken down, the creator shown to be subject to chance, nothing was actually left to chance when it came to the ring of a word. 'It was as far apart from machine translation as one could imagine' writes Bowles.

Beckett was aware of course of the contradiction in his position, that it is inconsistent, if not masochistic, to talk, as he does to Anne Atik, of writing being a 'sin against speechlessness' and then go on writing, perverse to apply such meticulous control in texts that seek to demonstrate the impossibility of control. Given this state of affairs, honesty (and sanity) demanded that he bring the contradiction to his readers' attention, use its colliding energies – the yearning for expression and the conviction of its futility – to give his work pathos, and, in the end, realism, since it was this contradiction that lay at the core not only of Beckett's experience, but of a whole strand of Western thought that declares the world without sense, but then finds that to go on living one is obliged to behave as if the opposite were the case. Looking for a voice for this modern mindset, Beckett produced a style in which, with all its developments over his long career, lyricism and parody, affirmation and denial, are always fused in such a way that each intensifies the other. Here are three examples.

Watt was written during the war but not published until 1953. The eponymous hero of the book has spent many pages trying and failing to explain the world – at once elaborately structured and utterly incomprehensible – in which he finds himself at the house of Mr Knott. Leaving, as he had arrived, in obedience to mechanisms beyond his ken, Watt is mistreated at the railway station, where, after his departure, the abusive station workers look out across the countryside:

> The sun was now well above the visible horizon. Mr Gorman, Mr Case and Mr Nolan turned their faces towards it, as men will, in the early morning, without heeding. The road lay still, at this hour, leaden, deserted, between its hedges, and its ditches. From one of these latter a goat emerged, dragging its pale and chain. The goat hesitated, in the middle of the road, then turned away. The clatter came fainter and fainter, down the still air, and came still faintly when the pale had disappeared, beyond the rise. The trembling sea could not but be admired. The leaves quivered, or gave the impression of doing so, and the grasses also, beneath the drops, or beads, of gaily expiring dew. The long summer's day had made an excellent start. If it continued in the same manner, its close would be worth coming to see.

Irrelevant to the progress of the book's plot, the passage is a complex mix of lyricism and caprice, tease and satire, though as so often with

Beckett it's not immediately clear what the object of that satire might be. At the centre of the piece there is the goat – free, but not enjoying the fruits of freedom, disappearing, but, like so much in Beckett, never quite gone. There are the men, distinguished only by their undistinguished names, unconscious of being locked into the mechanisms of the universe where the day is described as a magnificent frame – dawn and dusk – but without reference to any content in between. And there is the language, a constant mingling of beauty and fatuity, including as it does the pretty play with 'latter' and 'clatter', 'still air' and 'still faintly', then the pomposity of 'could not but be admired' followed by the disturbing absurdity of 'gaily expiring dew'. The genius of the passage is that the more the tone of address seems wayward, random, uncommitted, the more closely it resembles the goat cut free from wherever he was chained but dragging himself melancholically about, not unlike the book's hero, Watt, who, now freed from his duties at Mr Knott's house, asks for a train ticket to 'the end of the line' and when asked which end replies, 'the nearer end'. 'No symbols where none intended' Beckett wrote at the end of *Watt*. The object of his satire, it would seem, is our futile desire to attribute meaning to his prose.

Some years later, in *Malone Dies*, Beckett had now settled on the technique of dramatising the act of narration and indeed speech in general as a stratagem for killing time, filling silence. Here, Malone has been trying to tell himself the tale of a young boy, Sapo, who, ill-adapted to the world of his anxious middle-class parents, wanders alone about the countryside. Malone is finding it hard to keep up his interest . . .

> The market. The inadequacy of the exchanges between rural and urban areas had not escaped the excellent youth. He had mustered, on this subject, the following considerations, some perhaps close to, others no doubt far from, the truth.
>
> In his country the problem – no, I can't do it.

The peasants. His visits to. I can't. Assembled in the farmyard they watched him depart, on stumbling, wavering feet, as though they scarcely felt the ground. Often he stopped, stood tottering a moment, then suddenly was off again, in a new direction. So he went, limp, drifting, as though tossed by the earth. And when, after a halt, he started off again, it was like a big thistledown plucked by the wind from the place where it had settled. There is a choice of images.

Only when Malone drops all the social considerations and finds a parallel between Sapo's uncertain style of perambulation and his own narrative hesitations is he able to go on. At once the tone shifts from comedy to lyricism, as we sense Malone's engagement grow. Ironically this can only happen when he ceases to believe in the story he was telling himself and turns back, however indirectly, on his own fragility and unease.

A hierarchy of reality thus begins to emerge in Beckett's work. Centre stage is the purgatorial presence of the moribund narrator, the decrepit Krapp of the play *Krapp's Last Tape* being perhaps the most famous example. Any ultimate reality lies in the future with death and silence. Meantime, all vigour and purpose lost, the mind wanders oneirically over a past drained of substance or sense, except in those moments when it can be understood as foreshadowing the narrator's present state. Intriguingly, the original French of this passage from Malone does not include the final distancing remark, 'There is a choice of images.' It is as if, when he came to translate the piece, Beckett was uncomfortable with its poignancy and decided to add his characteristic gesture of denial.

Having renounced the extended and coherent plot, and reduced his characters to larvae, one of the problems Beckett faced after the trilogy was a difficulty sustaining the length of text we are used to in a novel. So the later works get shorter and shorter, and the form towards which they aspire is now the rhythm of breathing; it was as close as one could get, on the page, to a representation of being.

In *Company* (1980) a consciousness in the dark speaks of another voice that it hears intermittently declaring a few spare facts which may or may not be memories. Any notion of identity, time or place is gone; we have only voices speaking in darkness; nor is it clear whether these voices belong to the same person or to separate people. Yet even in this state of extreme deprivation, lyricism occasionally flowers, attended as always by bathos and comedy.

> You are an old man plodding along a narrow country road. You have been out since break of day and now it is evening. Sole sound in the silence your footfalls. Rather sole sounds for they vary from one to the next. You listen to each one and add it in your mind to the growing sum of those that went before. You halt with bowed head on the verge of the ditch and convert into yards. On the basis now of two steps per yard. So many since dawn to add to yesterday's. To yesteryear's. To yesteryears'. Days other than today and so akin. The giant tot in miles. In leagues. How often round the earth already. Halted too at your elbow during these computations your father's shade. In his old tramping rags. Finally on side by side from nought anew.

Once again we have dawn and evening and nothing in between but footfalls, ditches. Deathly and always tending to arrange themselves in enclosing grids, ditches are as omnipresent in Beckett as in Dante's *Inferno*. Irony and pathos are delivered simultaneously in the pun 'sole sounds' or in the suggestion of 'aching' behind 'akin' ('Days other than today and so akin'), or again in the comic possibilities of 'the giant tot'. There is the typically Beckettian satire of the futile pursuit of descriptive precision ('Rather sole sounds for they vary from one to the next') and in the vain search for some kind of control in computation, the count of the footsteps being soon baffled by the sheer enormity of 'yesteryear's, yesteryears'', whose lyricism then calls up the deceased father's shade, not in his winding sheet, but his 'tramping rags'. The rhetorical flourish of

'Finally on . . . from nought anew', a refrain repeated throughout *Company*, is one of those wry gestures to an elegance, at once archaic and compressed, which lend the speaker the illusion of a stoic dignity, while at the same time reminding us of the narrator's counting obsessions. If language falsifies, we nevertheless indulge in its consolations and comic possibilities.

For those of us who were long ago enchanted by this prose and believe it second to none, there will always be a certain sadness in the reflection that Beckett achieved fame through the theatre and will be remembered by a wider public only for his plays. Yet there are obvious reasons why Beckett's peculiar aesthetic was more immediately effective on stage. Some of the most intriguing pages of *Beckett Remembering* come from actors who recall the author travelling to theatres all over Europe to assist with productions of *Waiting for Godot, Endgame, Krapp's Last Tape* and *Happy Days*, telling them not to play their parts realistically, never to enquire about the characters' lives beyond the text, and, in general, to deliver their lines so far as possible in a flat monotone. 'Too much colour' was his frequent, head-shaking objection during rehearsals. Once again he was uneasy with the potential for sentimentality in what he had written.

Yet the actors often felt he was quite wrong and that the plays worked better with a lively, realistic delivery, a position to which Beckett himself eventually began to come round. The fact is that the flesh-and-blood presence of the actors on stage creates for the spectators a sense of reality and identification which the absurd plots and dialogues then undermine, so that the tension behind all of Beckett's work between affirmation and denial is dramatised for us in the contrast between the believable actor and the inexplicable, disorienting world he inhabits. At the same time, the conventions of the theatre which trap us respectfully together in an intimate space for a pre-established time make it far more likely that the sceptical will follow a major Beckett work from start to finish and have time to be enchanted by the rhythms of his writing. If few get through *The Unnameable* or *How It Is*, almost everybody can watch *Godot* to the final curtain.

But most importantly of all, the theatre allows both silence and physical movement to come to the fore, in a way they cannot on the page. A blank space between paragraphs simply does not deliver the anxiety of a hiatus in a stage dialogue. Only in the theatre, as the audience waits in collective apprehension for the conversational ball – between Didi and Gogo, Hamm and Clov – to start rolling again, could Beckett's sense of the truth as being that something, or nothing, beyond speech come across with great immediacy. Likewise the actors' interminable and pointless movement back and forth across the stage is a more immediate statement than the words of a page-bound narrator telling us of his aimless daily wanderings. When we watch the plays, the impotence of language to explain the characters' experience is compellingly evident. Conversation serves above all to pass the time, which of course 'would have passed in any case'.

Exploding, with his multiple internal voices, the old fiction of individual identity, Beckett created one of the most identifiable and individual literary voices of the twentieth century. Shunning enquiries into his life, he lived to see it given a well-defined shape in the public mind, raised to the status of myth almost: the mother obsession, the attachment to Joyce, the service in the French Resistance, the years of determined toil on the trilogy, the sudden celebrity after *Godot*, the Nobel Prize, and, finally, the years when everyone who was anyone wanted to be able to say they had spent an evening in a Parisian café drinking with 'Sam' – the 'Sammists' as one old friend ironically dubbed these late arrivals.

Beckett rarely denied himself to them. For the truth that emerges from the biographies, and again now from *Beckett Remembering* and Atik's very lively *How It Was*, is that although everybody liked to see him as a solitary and even saintly man, 'a withdrawn being who pursues an endless and implacable labour', as Emil Cioran put it, Beckett in fact loved company, particularly drinking company, and far from living alone spent most of his adult life with his partner and finally wife, Suzanne Deschevaux-Dumesnil. Her voice is conspicuous for its absence in *Beckett Remembering*, indeed she is hardly mentioned at all, as if there were some collective denial on the part of Beckett worshippers that their unworldly hero might have had a conjugal life at all. But in a breach of the general discretion, charming because unique, we hear this from the theatre designer Jocelyn Herbert:

> I think a lot of [Sam's relationship] with Suzanne . . . was gratitude and loyalty and I think that he felt remorse for the fact that he had so many friends whom he got drunk with. She didn't drink. And he had after all endless other women. And when people say to me he was a saint I say: 'Oh no he wasn't a saint at all. And thank God he wasn't.'

How interesting that God is invoked even here where sanctity is denied. Beckett would have appreciated one more demonstration of meaningless linguistic inertia. Still, it is cheering to think that during all those trips to direct his own plays, urging the actors to avoid all colour, Beckett was in fact – in another of the contradictions that make his work so real – actually seeking to add a little colour to his own life. Certainly, Jocelyn Herbert seems very sure of what she is talking about; and those three words of hers, 'after all endless', have a decidedly Beckettian ring to them.

Genius of Bad News

[Thomas Bernhard]

The many novels and plays of Thomas Bernhard, at his death in 1989 Austria's most prominent and controversial writer, achieve their full impact and are properly understood only within the context, or confines, of the author's native culture and language. Such is the persuasive argument of Gitta Honegger's biography, *Thomas Bernhard: The Making of an Austrian*. But where does this assessment leave those of us whose grasp of Austrian history is shaky at best, those who, though we have read Bernhard in various languages, are unable to tackle the original German? Is our sense of his importance to us the fruit of a misunderstanding?

To warn us of her unorthodox, largely non-chronological approach, Honegger opens with a typically provocative remark from Bernhard himself: 'I hate books and articles that begin with a date of birth. Altogether, I hate books and articles that adopt a biographical and chronological approach; that strikes me as the most tasteless and at the same time the most unintellectual procedure.'

Explaining that her work is as much a cultural history of post-war Austria as a biography of Bernhard, Honneger goes on: 'The process of [Bernhard's] self-invention reveals more about him and the world he lived in . . . than a chronological account of his life and work could do.'

Such an attitude is no doubt in line with Bernhard's own tendency to introduce us *in medias res* to a mind in turmoil where events past and present, real or apocryphal, flash by in rapid succession without apparent order or hierarchy, where the voice speaking is so aware of its own performance as to raise doubts about its candour.

Yet notoriously every story does have its chronology and every life, between cradle and grave, its trajectory. To understand the significance of any 'self-invention' one must have a grip on the inescapable facts on which self feeds and from which invention diverges. The same is true of a nation. How are we to understand modern Austria's mendaciously sanitised image of itself without an account of its Nazi past? One of the pleasures of Bernhard's novels, after all, is the slow reconstruction of the sequence of events that underlies the present state of mind, and with that the exposure of the process of self-invention. Each book, and play, is, to a very great extent, a life. Ah yes, we say to ourselves towards the end of *The Lime Works*, so those were the circumstances in which, forty years before, Konrad married. Now I understand.

To be tastelessly chronological, then, perhaps the first thing we need to know about Bernhard is that his last name was an accident and something that would estrange the author from his family rather than unite him to it. In 1903, while still married to one Karl Bernhard, Thomas's grandmother, Anna, ran off with the struggling writer Johannes Freumbichler, by whom she was pregnant, later giving birth to a daughter, Herta, who, despite her natural father, was registered Herta Bernhard. In 1931, working as a maid in Holland, Herta gave birth to an illegitimate child, Thomas. The father denied paternity, disappeared and committed suicide before the law could catch up with him. In 1936 Herta married and became Frau Fabjan, bearing her husband first a son in 1938, then a daughter in 1940. Thomas was now the only member of the family with the name Bernhard. His stepfather refused to adopt the boy and allow him to become a Fabjan. In *The Lime Works* we hear of the central character Konrad that

> he suffered because his sister and his brother Francis were only one year apart in age . . . while he, years older than they . . . was separated from them by the difference in age between them and him, a separateness that hurt him to the roots of his being . . .

the misfortune of being six years older than his sister, seven years older than his brother Francis . . . led to his life of chronic isolation . . . All during his childhood he worried about losing touch with his siblings and his family in general because of their continuing instinctive rejection of him.

Whether or not this is autobiography, it is typical of Bernhard's habit of spinning out possible and invariably unhappy accounts of his own early life. Shifted back and forth between his grandparents' family and his mother's, between Austria and Bavaria, Thomas clearly had every chance to feel separate, isolated, rejected and displaced. One piece of information we find only in the chronology at the back of Honegger's book is that in 1941, soon after the birth of his half-sister and completion of the Fabjan family nucleus, Thomas was sent away to an institution for 'difficult children' in Thuringia. Later there would be a Catholic home for boys in Salzburg (during the Allied bombing).

In the autobiographical works he wrote in his forties, Bernhard makes it clear that the centre of the family, and the key emotional attachment for himself, was his grandfather. Dreamer, anarchist and bisexual, Johannes Freumbichler spent his whole life trying and failing to become a great writer. Unable or unwilling to hold down a job, moving frequently in search of a situation congenial to his writing, he depended economically on his wife and daughter, both of whom seemed willing to sacrifice their lives to his doomed ambition.

From his grandfather, Bernhard learned the nobility of artistic endeavour, but also the coercive and destructive nature of the artist's powerful influence on those around him. Indeed, his later objection to 'books and articles that begin with a date of birth' can probably be best understood in the light of his relationship with his grandfather; for as, in his early twenties, the charismatic Thomas began to exercise the powers of seduction that would overcome rejection by his family, or gain him a surrogate family, or earn him an honoured place in the larger family of Austrian society, he must have been aware that he was imitating his grandfather, borrowing a behaviour pattern that had begun well before his own conception. And he would also have been aware that Freumbichler himself was locked into a destructive relationship with past Austrian culture and romantic notions of artistic greatness, a relationship that both won him a devoted family and devastated its members. This awareness never prevented Bernhard from exercising that charisma and seeking devotion and greatness. But likewise he would never forget to expose the dark side of artistic ambitions. Almost all his writings offer us a monomaniac, achievement-obsessed central character. Whether he is an epitome of intellectual perfection, as the Wittgenstein figure in *Corrections*, or a paralysed failure, as Konrad in *The Lime Works*, he is always a catastrophe for those around him, and ultimately for himself.

Seeking redemption through art, grandfather Freumbichler wanted the same for his children and grandchildren. Daughter Herta was to become a ballerina. Thomas, having abandoned school at sixteen to work as an apprentice in a grocer's shop, took up private singing lessons. The family was living in Salzburg now. But hardly had he begun to dream of being an opera singer than he was overwhelmed by another experience that was to prove absolutely formative. In 1949, aged eighteen, he was hospitalised for pleurisy and then diagnosed with tuberculosis. In line with his conviction that every institution that admitted him, family, college or hospital, was secretly hostile and likely to destroy him, Bernhard believed that he actually caught tuberculosis at the Grossgmain sanatorium. There followed a series of hospitalisations that lasted some two years and saw the young man at death's door for long periods. During this time both his grandfather and his mother died. Bernhard learned of his mother's death from a newspaper announcement. In the autobiographical memoir *Breath: A Decision*, Bernhard describes his spell in intensive care thus:

> All the patients were on drips of some sort, and from the distance the tubes looked like strings, I had the constant impression that the patients lying in their beds were marionettes on strings . . . in most cases these strings . . . were their only remaining link to life.

Typical of Bernhard is the combination of feeling absolutely abandoned to one's self, yet at the same time absolutely dependent on the community, the institution, which remains, despite, or *because* of, the life-giving drips, absolutely sinister. It is not merely a question here of suffering the irritating presence of others – 'the purgatory of loneliness and the hell of togetherness' as he refers to it elsewhere – but rather that one's being is determined from outside. You are a marionette. Some years hence the lonely boy would be writing for the theatre, pulling all the strings himself, the actors obliged to imitate *his* voice. Unless that voice was his grandfather's, or Beckett's for that matter, or any of the endless other voices any author is obliged to imitate. Bernhard never forgot this. In the short story 'The Voice Imitator', the one voice the famous impressionist is unable to imitate is his own.

After a period of deep depression following his mother's death, Bernhard at last 'entertained the supreme ambition to return to full health.' He began to break hospital rules and visit a nearby village each evening and ultimately left the institution without an official discharge. Though Bernhard does not mention the fact in his autobiography, this step was only made possible with outside support. On his evening excursions he had met Hede Stavianicek. Twice widowed, wealthy heiress of a famous brand of chocolates, thirty-six years older than Bernhard, Frau Stavianicek became the writer's protectress, mentor and perhaps even lover. She believed in his genius, was prepared to finance him when necessary and able and willing to introduce him to influential figures in Vienna. It was with her support that in January 1951, frail, acne-scarred but determined, a twenty-year-old Bernhard plunged into the fray of Austrian society.

The question now was: how would Bernhard's very particular and powerful private experience mesh with the very particular and ambiguous situation in Salzburg and Vienna in the early 1950s? After having been close to death himself and bereaved of the most important members of his family, Bernhard was looking for a new home, a new identity in Frau Stavianicek's sophisticated world. After the disgraceful years of Nazism, the Austrian middle classes were casting about for a new respectability. Bernhard studied them. How could these two needs profitably come together?

From 1951 to 1955 the young man worked as a cultural journalist and court reporter for a Salzburg newspaper, taking in a wide range of modern theatre and collecting endless accounts of troubled lives. He published some poems and short stories, one under the pseudonym Thomas Fabjan, the name that had always been denied him. Then in 1954 came the first piece of writing to bear his distinctive voice: a vitriolic attack on the Salzburg Theatre. It was scathing, over the top, almost hysterical. It won him his first libel case. But oddly it didn't exclude him from the society he attacked, as his grandfather, working quietly away on his novels, had always been excluded. Rather, the papers began to talk about him. There would always be in Bernhard's plays and novels a journalistic element of scandalous topical attack aimed at recognisable and influential figures. So Bernhard would push his way into his Austrian home as a thorn in the flesh. A society wrestling with guilt cannot easily dismiss its accusers, indeed, a certain virtue may accrue to giving them space.

Speaking of the moment he left hospital, Bernhard remarked: 'I was no longer capable of starting work with a firm . . . I was revolted by any work, any job. I was appalled and horrified by the thought of working, of being employed by someone, just to be able to survive.' Throughout Bernhard's fiction, the minor and sometimes even the major characters are identified only by their occupation: the miller, the woodcutter, the miner, the stoneworker, the doctor. It is a reminder that they are marionettes, that society is a chorus of complicit roles orchestrated by tradition and necessity. 'I never wanted an occupation', Bernhard wrote, 'but to become myself.'

So it was unlikely that he would remain a salaried journalist for long. From 1955 to 1957, supported by Hede Stavianicek, he studied acting and directing at Salzburg's Mozarteum. Trying different parts, he found he was most successful at the cantankerous old man. He began to mingle with the Viennese avant-garde. Good at forming intimacies that never quite became stable relationships, he started to spend his summers in the bohemian community of Tonhoff, summer mountain residence of rich musicians and patrons Gerhard Lampersberg and his wife Maja. Both Lampersbergs fell in love with him. They weren't alone. Bernhard flirted, left and right, with men and women, put on his first three plays in the Tonhoff barn, then escaped to Frau Stavianicek when things got tense. By now he was calling her 'Auntie', as ill-defined a relationship as ever one could wish. It is intriguing that his ferocious attack on the Lampersbergs many years later in the novel *Woodcutters* accused them above all of cosy complicity with the establishment they pretended to oppose. Sued, as so often, for libel, Bernhard gave aggressive interviews in which he claimed that the entire bohemian community was state-subsidised, whereas he alone had always been independent. 'Only if you're really independent can you write really well . . . I always lived from my own initiative, never was subsidised, no one gave a damn about me, to this day. I am against all subsidies, all patronage . . .'

Honegger is no doubt right to suggest that the hyperbole and hypocrisy of Bernhard's position – for he had received many awards and was generously patronised – was an indication of his anxiety about his own inevitable involvement in Austrian culture. 'The past of the Habsburg Empire is what forms us' he said in another interview around the same time. 'In my case it is perhaps more visible

123

than in others. It manifests itself in a kind of love-hate for Austria that's the key to everything I write.'

By now an uneasy pattern of behaviour was all too evident: insecure, Bernhard craved intimacy and recognition. Yet his real admiration went for total independence, which, alas, he feared was impossible. He became a master of the on-off friendship, the unconsummated love affair. He would make friends with a married couple, insinuate himself into their family, monopolise the wife, then withdraw. The casualty list of those confused by his behaviour grew rapidly. Intense, yet distant, even with 'Auntie' he would switch back and forth from the intimate *du* to the formal *Sie*. But at least, he justified himself, he wouldn't make the mistake of marrying and destroying wife and children as his grandfather had. The genetic buck would stop with Thomas.

After his break with the Tonhoff community, Bernhard travelled widely, but as soon as he had financial success (with his first major play), he bought a farmhouse and began to reinvent himself as an Austrian country gentleman. Then he thought he really ought to sell it and distance himself. Then he decided to keep it after all. Remorselessly castigating the Establishment, he eagerly sought the company of the aristocracy. A picture of the emperor Franz Joseph was hung upon the wall.

But there is nothing like the permanent dilemma for creating great art. Honegger is excellent at showing how Bernhard's personal contradictions connected with the peculiarly Austrian genre of the *Heimatroman* and the very special role of the theatre in a suffocatingly tight-knit Austrian society. With the nation reduced, after the First War, to a fragment of its imperial, Austro-Hungarian glory, there had been a deliberate attempt to build up a national identity around narrative depictions of vigorous and morally commendable Austrian peasant life (the so-called *Heimatroman*). During the Nazi period, such literature had taken on a decidedly blood-and-soil flavour which afterward was repackaged, in many cases by the same writers, as a healthy, optimistic nativism, all too appealing to the Green Party and the tourist industry.

Johannes Freumbichler had enjoyed his only success, in 1937, with the unorthodox *Heimatroman*, *Philomena Ellenhub*, a book that ran against conventional Catholic morality by offering a sympathetic account of the vicissitudes of an independent, unmarried mother. Grandson Thomas went far further. His first novel, *Frost* (1963), presents a ferociously dystopian view of rural life. The narrator, a young medical student, has been instructed by a senior doctor to go to a remote mountain village to observe the doctor's brother, a painter, who has secluded himself in the place for many years in a state of near insanity. 'He lives, as they say, in his head. But he's terminally confused. Haunted by vice, shame, awe, reproach . . . my brother is a walker, a man in fear. And a misanthrope.'

The student records the painter's ravings which combine a deep inner anguish with an obsessive loathing for the shameless sensuality of the landlady of the inn where both he and the student live and the violent drunken men who revolve around her and her two daughters: 'The primitive is everywhere . . . Sex is what does for them all. Sex, the disease that kills by its nature . . . they live for sex, like most people, like all people . . . All of them live a sex life, and not a life.'

As the book progresses, we begin to fear for the sanity of the medical student as he is both seduced and overwhelmed by the intensity and negativity of the painter's vision. In particular he loses all confidence in his chosen profession. 'Helper of mankind, I thought. Helping and mankind, the distance between those two terms. I can't imagine myself ever helping anyone . . . I don't understand anything.'

Amras (1964), Bernhard's second long work of prose, actually manages to step up the intensity, reconstructing the history of a family induced to attempt collective suicide by the rapacious ugliness of the surrounding rural society. Again the despair of the intellectual narrator, one of the sons who survives the attempt, feeds misan-thropically on the utter spiritual emptiness of the ordinary world, but in such an exaggerated fashion that the reader is uncertain how to respond.

Gargoyles (1964), the third and by far the most accomplished of Bernhard's subversions of the *Heimatroman*, once again picks up the theme of medical science's inadequacy when confronted with extremes of intellectual despair on the one hand and blind appetite on the other. In this case the narrator, a young engineering student, accompanies his doctor father on a round of visits to sick patients in the dark woods, deep gorges and rocky mountains of the south-eastern province of Styria. The morning begins with a failed attempt to save an innkeeper's wife, victim of a mindless drunken assault, and proceeds from catastrophe to catastrophe as it penetrates an ever gloomier countryside. The doctor's denunciation of a dull and brutal provincial society could not be more radical or convincing:

> Crimes in the city are nothing in comparison with crimes in the country. The innkeeper, he added, is your typical violent man, your born delinquent. Everything *in him* and *about him* is violent and criminal. At every moment and in every situation he is the merest cattle trader, it's his job and he never transcends it. 'And if he is now weeping and desperate,' my father said, 'he's weeping because he's lost a valuable beast. For an innkeeper his wife is never anything more than a valuable beast.'

But it is characteristic of Bernhard that he doesn't stop there. Soon enough the doctor doing the denouncing is himself implicated in the general failure. His cures are always inadequate. He is unable to communicate with his son. He seems resigned to the idea that his daughter will eventually commit suicide. We discover that his wife too suffered from depression and neurosis which may well have been at the root of her illness and early death. The doctor, the intellectual, seems quite unable to improve the world.

Indeed, where there is intelligent life in *Gargoyles* it tends to isolate itself. Bloch, the doctor's only friend, is a successful estate agent, who keeps his intense intellectual life entirely separate from his commercial activities. More extreme, the (unnamed) writer/industrialist lives in complete segregation in a destructive, incestuous relationship with his sister. The doctor's final visit is reserved for the most brilliant and isolated character of them all: Prince Sarau, hereditary landowner of vast areas of gloomy forest, lives in the gothic castle of Hochgobernitz perched high above the doomed landscape we have crossed. A dying monomaniac who at once fears and fantasises the extinction of his family and everything it represents, the prince launches into a hundred-page monologue which entirely shifts the equilibrium of the book and marks a crucial turning point in Bernhard's career, as doctor, son and reader are spellbound by the obsessive and self-destructive power of the prince's delivery:

'If we succeed in becoming aware of the problematic nature of our existence *we believe we have philosophical minds.* We are constantly irritated by everything we touch, with the result that everything irritates us all the time. Those parts of our lives that are out of harmony with nature are particularly irritating. When the weather is bad (when visibility is poor!) we are warmly advised not to climb above a certain altitude, never mind the highest peaks. What's more we feel weary,' said the prince, 'when philosophical speculation has wearied us. Obviously we all defend ourselves saying: I've got nothing to do with that lot! and we have every right to do so. I too, in fact, am always saying that I have nothing to do with them, that *I don't belong to anything or anyone.* All the same, by pure chance, here we are together. We soon grow weary if we don't resort to lying. It's in the earth that foundations are laid, *in the deepest substratum*, we feel that without needing to think, and then fear besets us. Do we ask too much of others?' asked the prince. 'No,' he answered himself,

'I think not. I meet someone and think: *what are you thinking?* Can I, I wonder, walk a while with you inside your brain? The answer is: no! We can't walk a while together *in the one brain*. We force ourselves not to see our personal abyss. Yet all our lives long we do nothing but look down, at our physical and psychic abyss, without ever really seeing it. Our illnesses systematically destroy our lives, like handwriting that gets worse and worse until it destroys itself.' The prince said: 'Each of us argues interminably with himself saying: the "me" I'm talking to doesn't exist. Every concept implies in itself an infinite number of other concepts . . .'

As ever in Bernhard, the more isolated a character, the more chaotic the mind, and the more the world dissolves into a stream of words that might be either revelatory or meaningless.

In his next novel, *The Lime Works*, published in 1970, the characters who might normally be expected to appear in a *Heimatroman* are reduced to the few local people – the ex-works manager, a public safety inspector, the two managers of nearby estates – who give accounts of the life and ideas of the main character, Konrad, who, disgusted with the world and society, has withdrawn with his crippled wife to the absolute silence and segregation of the abandoned lime works where he hopes to write the definitive account of the faculty of hearing and, by implication perhaps, of the nature of communication.

Konrad's humiliation is total. Not only, in his perfectionism, is he unable to write so much of a word of his book, not only does he find isolation as detrimental as company, but when at the end he murders his wife and hides from the police in the cesspit, he becomes himself just another statistic in the country's long list of brutal domestic crimes. The ultimate defeat is that any valuable ideas he may have had are now passed on and modified, and indeed only exist, in the minds of the sort of people he despised and who, more conventional and more cautious than he, happily consume, along with the reader, his fascinating story. Inescapably, he is part of the local mental ecology. He was never separate at all. With wonderful irony, the various accounts of his downfall are gathered by an insurance agent struggling to sell life insurance policies in the local village inns. Konrad will serve as a cautionary tale.

Writing with immense power and the blackest of wit, Bernhard thus denies writing any power to alter the society it remorselessly criticises. On the contrary, the artist is implicated in the general freak show. Given that the wider Western world of today still likes to imagine creative authorship as a respectable branch of progressive liberal politics, such a negative vision was hardly the passport to international popularity. And indeed Bernhard has never achieved that. There remains, however, particularly for those of us who come to him through his novels rather than his plays, and that means most of his admirers outside the German-speaking world, the mystery of his success and notoriety on the Austrian and German stage, which was, after all, the source of his income. Herself trained in the theatre, Honegger is at her best here, and at her most confident in declaring Bernhard only partially comprehensible if read apart from his national setting.

Like so many of his characters, Bernhard loved to be alone, segregating himself behind the tall hedges surrounding his farmhouse, rapidly becoming part of local folklore, a misanthrope whose imagined malignant powers could be used to threaten a naughty village child. But he also loved, from time to time, to be the centre of attention. And since the theatre, as Honegger amply shows, has always played a central role in Austrian society – in particular the Burgtheater in the old imperial palace and the Salzburg Festival, Mecca of Austrian high culture, what better place for Bernhard to show himself? In one play, a character, who is herself an actress, remarks: 'I'm not really an actress at all/I just wanted to be among people/that was the reason . . . I didn't want to isolate myself.'

Borrowing from Beckett, Strindberg and other immediate pre-decessors, Bernhard's plays distinguish themselves for the virulence of their monologues attacking the middle-class Establishment. But who were in the audiences at the Salzburg Festival and the Burgtheater if not the middle-class Establishment? In the play *Am Ziel* (which might be translated *Arrived*) the nameless lead char-acter, who is simply designated The Writer, remarks of his successful play:

> I can't understand
> why they applauded
> we are talking about a play
> that exposes every one of them
> and in the meanest way
> admittedly with humor
> but nasty humor
> if not with malice
> true malice
> And all of a sudden they applaud.

The staging of a Bernhard play thus demonstrates two apparently contradictory truths: the power of the artist to get people to accept absolutely anything; and simultaneously the impotence of the artist to change anything at all. The same people come back, once again applaud savage criticism of themselves, but never change ('the Burgtheater', he wrote, 'could become a national mental institu-tion for those who have proved themselves incurable.') Honegger is fascinating when she describes how Bernhard used his casting to reinforce this idea of embattled stasis. Actors with a Nazi past would be cast in the role of Nazis, or even better in the role of a Jew whose rhetoric and neurosis is indistinguishable from a Nazi's. An actress from one play would be given a role that in some way was a comment on her previous part. Elements in each play might refer to controversies created by earlier plays. In short, the collective memory of the local audience was essential. People were constantly reminded that all was as it always had been.

In this regard a productive misunderstanding between Bernhard and the man who directed most of his plays galvanised the author's theatre career from beginning to end. *Enfant terrible* Claus Peymann came from the extreme left of the German political spectrum, openly sympathised with the terrorist Red Army Faction and insisted that the theatre was 'a place of opposition – in certain times to the point of subversion'. When Bernhard wrote a play like *Eve of Retirement* which features an ageing ex-SS officer, now a respectable judge, who puts on his old uniform and sleeps with his devoted sister once a year to celebrate Himmler's birthday, while the younger and crippled socialist sister is dressed up as a concentration-camp victim, Peymann no doubt saw this as grist for his political mill. Convinced of the positive value of shocking the audience, he did everything to create an atmosphere of scandal around Bernhard's work. This suited Bernhard, for whom scandal was the only way he could enjoy himself in public, since it combined intense attention with supposedly independent action.

Politically, however, the playwright was far more complex than his faithful director. Of *Eve of Retirement* Honegger astutely remarks: 'the outrage . . . was not the suggestion that the majority of Germans are incurable Nazis but the implication that fascism is just another symptom of an innate obsessiveness that also drives scholars, scientists and artists.' To which we might add that without such obsessiveness, life for Bernhard was unimaginable.

What is it then we are applauding when we enthuse over a writer who doubtless would have included each and every one of us in his scathing criticisms? The excellent Honegger with her sometimes jargon-bound academic prose and her research grant, as she properly acknowledges, from the Austrian Ministry of Culture and Education, would not have been exempt. Nor the writer of this review with his shamelessly biographical approach. In *Gargoyles*, the narrator's father speaks of a painting that is at once absolutely ugly and at the same time absolutely beautiful. Then he explains: 'It's beautiful because it's true.' The picture, we are told, shows two naked men standing back to back, but with their heads rotated, so that they are also face to face. It is a grotesque contradiction of isolation and intimacy.

As we read, in Bernhard's coercively rhythmic prose, of the dangers of being possessed by the rhythms of another's mind, as we put down one novel whose monomaniac narrator dreamt of being the last of his dynasty only to pick up another and find ourselves confronted with the man's spiritual successor, as we smile over those interminable superlatives that always suggest that even the supreme effort will not be enough, as we embark on huge sentences, never-ending paragraphs, that remind us that experience is seamless and that if we want to say one thing we must be prepared to say everything, which is of course impossible, in short, as we read and reread Thomas Bernhard we have the intense impression of being able to savour, briefly held together in the decidedly artificial space of these performances, a true picture of the grotesque contradictions that drive our lives. The world described is ugly, the reflections leave no space for optimism, but the mechanism invented for delivering the bad news is never less than exhilarating.

Writing more often than not about writer's block, Bernhard became one of the most prolific authors of his generation, producing seventeen full-length plays, a dozen novels, five works of autobiography. Insisting that all was parody and quotation, he created one of the most distinctive voices of the twentieth century. Awareness, in the last decade of his life, that he was terminally ill with lung and heart disease seemed only to accelerate his output. Denying the possibility of perfection, lamenting the false promise of genius, his own work got better and better. His last novels – *Concrete*, *The Loser*, *Woodcutters*, *Extinction*, *Old Masters* – are his finest.

In 1984 Hede Stavianicek died. Always discreet, never sharing the limelight, she had been his lifelong companion, his *Lebensmensch* as he put it. Bernhard was there at the end to care for her. 'Suddenly I gave my tears free rein' says the author's stand-in in the novel he wrote immediately afterwards. 'I wept and wept and wept and wept.' It is perhaps the only moment of cathartic release in all Bernhard's work. Five years later, having always declared that we are no better than marionettes, Bernhard nevertheless made the gesture of severing the fatal strings himself, taking a lethal overdose shortly before an inevitable death. And in a last, mad bid for independence from his native country, his will, revised two days before his death, prohibited all publications or productions of his work in Austria until the end of his copyright.

Bernhard must have known that this stipulation would not long be respected, that he would inevitably and rapidly be appropriated into the Austrian canon. But with Bernhard it was always the yearning for independence, the gesture of opposition, that served to confirm the deeper complicity between the artist and the world he works in. As the East German playwright Heiner Müller commented of the controversy surrounding Bernhard's plays: 'He writes as if he had been hired by the Austrian government to write against Austria . . . The disturbance can be articulated that loudly and clearly because it doesn't disturb.' And the reason it didn't disturb is because Bernhard always presents his criticisms in such a way that the critic, the author, Bernhard himself, seem just as unbalanced and guilty as the world they deplore. Nor does any alternative form of behaviour appear to be imaginable. Indeed, it was in his staging of the modern liberal individual's interminably lost battle with his origins and milieu, which is to say with the whole human condition, that Bernhard becomes such a powerful voice even outside the world to which he was so fatally attached.

Let Sleeping Beauties Lie

[Elfriede Jelinek]

In her avowedly autobiographical novel, *The Piano Teacher* (1983), the Austrian author Elfriede Jelinek has her alter ego Erika Kohut engage in a variety of voyeuristic activities. She pays to sit in a booth at a peep show, smells a tissue into which the man before her has masturbated and watches attentively as the girls on display feign sexual pleasure. On another occasion she takes greater risks spying on a couple having sex in a car and again on a 'turklike' 'man emitting foreign yelps [as he] screws his way into a woman' in the park at night. The descriptions are lengthy.

Despite this assumption of what is normally a male role, Erika herself does not masturbate. She does not remove her gloves. Loathing 'anything pertaining to bodies', a musician whose insistence on technical perfection is a scourge to her students, she seems eager to contemplate scenes so alien to her nature that she will then be happy to escape unscathed to the apartment where she sleeps in the same bed with her mother, wishing sometimes to 'creep into' the older woman 'and rock gently in the warm fluid of her womb'.

Reading the five novels that over twenty years Jelinek has published in English, each more determinedly and uniformly unlovely than the one before, all ferocious in their denunciation of a still patriarchal Austrian society, it is not hard to see those voyeuristic scenes of *The Piano Teacher* as a key to understanding the author's, or at least narrator's, relationship to the stories she tells: she dwells on what is repugnant in order to congratulate herself that she has steered well clear of the world. It is a strategy that invariably divides her readers into fiercely opposed camps. Many, particularly in academic circles, believe Jelinek has achieved a triumphant combination of avant-garde technique and progressive social criticism. In 2004 she was awarded the Nobel Prize, 'for her musical flow of voices and counter-voices in novels and plays that with extraordinary linguistic zeal reveal the absurdity of society's clichés and their subjugating power.' However, one member of the Nobel committee resigned over this decision, describing Jelinek's work as 'whining, unenjoyable public pornography' and 'a mass of text shovelled together without artistic structure'. Newspaper reviewers have frequently agreed.

Born in 1946, an only child of Jewish origin, Jelinek was educated in a convent school and pushed by her mother towards a musical education, taking an organist's diploma at the celebrated Vienna Conservatory. A university course in drama, however, had to be interrupted when an anxiety disorder led to the young woman's being unable to leave the family home for a year. Meanwhile, her father had been shut up in a mental asylum. Withdrawal from life or openness to it would become key themes in Jelinek's work, openness exposing one, and particularly women, to every kind of violence and degradation, withdrawal allowing for the sterile calm of a living death. A dramatic dialogue entitled *Sleeping Beauty* (2003) has the female sleeper reluctant to be woken and immediately in conflict with the presumptuous prince who has kissed her into life. 'Mine is a social intelligence that does not derive from knowledge and experience,' Jelinek explains in interview with the German writer Hans-Jürgen Heinrichs, 'but from avoiding them.'

Paradoxically, this apparent preference for isolation and withdrawal has always gone together with a reputation for vigorous political engagement. The earliest of her novels available in English, *Women as Lovers*, was written in 1975 shortly after Jelinek became a member of the Austrian Communist Party, then a fringe movement with Stalinist leanings. In an aggressive, rhythmically repetitive prose the book presents a group of young characters uncritically adopting the shallow, money-driven conventions that, as Jelinek sees it, regulate sex and marriage in provincial Austria. The tone is one of sardonic, even comic-strip Marxism where love is an empty word whose coercive repetition mostly serves to get a girl out of the factory where she is 'replaceable and unnecessary' and into a home paid for by her husband.

> i need you and I love you, says brigitte, her hair shines in the sun like ripe polished chestnuts, love is the feeling that one person needs the other. i need you, says brigitte, so that i no longer have to go to the factory, because really i don't need the factory at all, what i need is you and being near you. i love you and i need you.

The pay-off for her young man Heinz who, as an apprentice electrician, is learning a trade that 'one day will put the whole world at his feet', is sex, which, in Jelinek's work, is never coloured by sentiment:

> Unbuttoning and into brigitte only takes a moment and today we can announce, that something has clicked at last between these two young people [i.e. she is pregnant] . . . and so brigitte will not after all have to end her life in cold and loneliness, which otherwise she would have had to do.

Meantime, Brigitte's friend Paula seeks a man thus:

> paula sometimes goes onto the dance floor, if there's a party. sometimes paula is led away into the woods again by a drunk dance-floor visitor, which no one must see, because that would immediately cause her market value to go through the floor.
>
> in the woods then paula is grabbed by her breasts or at worst between the legs or by the arse.

> paula has been taught to assess who is grabbing her there between the legs. Is it someone with or without a future.
>
> is it someone with a future or a work horse.
>
> if it is a work horse, then he cannot become paula's fate. paula's brain has learned to work like a computer in such cases. here's the printout: married, two children.

This technique of stringing together clichés to expose the shallowness of the character's lives and 'the subjugating power of language' is sustained for nigh on 200 pages.

Five years later in *Wonderful Wonderful Times* (1980), Jelinek gives us a more sophisticated group of 1950s Viennese youngsters who bend the jargon of revolutionary dissent to justify violent street crime and hence satisfy selfish appetites, all this under the depressing influence of their war-damaged parents. The prose is more flexible now and there is more psychological development but the peremptory irony and resolute rejection of emotional engagement remains, while the sex grows more unpleasant. Here is the father of two of the youngsters, an ex-SS concentration-camp guard, who, having lost a leg, is now obliged to transform his bestiality into 'art' by taking pornographic photos of his long-suffering wife. Shouting at her as he does so, he is reminded of the joys of killing, thus drawing a parallel between Nazi war crimes and man's violence towards women:

> You have to look afraid. It's always a terrific feeling to smash down resistance, I smashed resistance quite often myself in the War and liquidated numerous persons all on my own. Nowadays I have this wretched leg to contend with, but back then the women couldn't get enough of me, it was the magical attraction of the uniform that did it. That smart uniform. I remember how we were often up to the ankles of our riding-boots in blood in Polish villages. Look, thrust your pelvis further forward, you slut, where's your pussy got to again? Ah, there it is.

Favourable reviews of *Wonderful Wonderful Times* praised the novel's political commitment and withering criticism of a post-war Austrian society that had never come to terms with its Nazi past. Jelinek, however, embraces only the negative, denunciatory energies of left-wing politics and shares none of its constructive optimism. There are no positive experiences to relate and nothing to hope for. In particular, victims are as unattractive and perverse as their persecutors and can thus be dispatched without regret. Of a woman and the man who regularly beats her in the later novel *Greed* (2000), the narrator remarks, 'She can throw him alive into boiling water, for all I care, and jump in after him . . .' At another point she wonders: 'Why do I always only see the negative?' The answer, perhaps, is that such a consistently dark view of life confirms the decision to 'avoid experience'.

The extremity of Jelinek's tirades soon won her comparisons with the novels of Thomas Bernhard who had also remorselessly attacked the residual fascism of modern Austria. Seeking, in an interview with Gitta Honegger, respected theatre critic and biographer of Bernhard, to distinguish her approach from his, Jelinek claimed that as a man Bernhard 'could claim a position of authority', projecting an identity with which readers could relate and giving a coherent, rhetorically convincing account of Austrian society, whereas, being a woman, even this form of 'positive' approach was denied her; a woman working in a man's world and language could not present a coherent identity (a play of Jelinek's has the female parts mouthing words that are actually spoken by male voices, as if women could not really possess the language). Starting from this position of 'speechlessness', a woman writer could only work by subversion, undermining the language's prejudices, showing its crassness and attacking its perverse and mindless momentum. As the narrator puts it in *Wonderful Wonderful Times*, 'everything that's said is a cue for something else.'

However, one hardly need resort to feminist theories of language to see more obvious differences between the two writers. Bernhard's

139

narrators are firmly placed within the stories they tell and a certain pathos attaches to the damage they do themselves with their constant negativity. In many of Bernhard's works (*Frost* for example, or the later *Correction*) we see a narrator drawn into the orbit of a compellingly negative figure and are invited to feel all the danger of his being seduced and destroyed by the other's despairing vision. There is never, that is, any complacency about what it means to see the world so darkly nor a conviction that withdrawal is any solution.

Jelinek's narrator may constantly make her presence felt, addressing the reader directly and voicing the fiercest invectives, yet she remains resolutely outside the story, invulnerable in her sardonic detachment, her avoidance of experience. This separation is occasionally reinforced by reminding us that her characters are 'only' creations, something Bernhard never does. 'It's a frequent reproach', we are told in the opening pages of *Greed*, 'that I stand around looking stupid and drop my characters before I even have them, because to be honest I pretty quickly find them dull.' Or again, 'I for example have nothing to say faced with the figures I create, bring on the stock phrases and some more, and another and another, until they squirm beneath me with pain.' 'My characters are only coat-hangers on which I hang the language' Jelinek explains in interview. Only in *The Piano Teacher* is this static relationship between narrator and story excitingly threatened, no doubt because this is the only novel where we have a fully imagined, Jelinek-like figure *inside* the narrative, a woman torn between withdrawal from the world and openness to it.

With a wealth of detail we don't find in her other books, *The Piano Teacher* sets up an unusual triangular power struggle. Despite dwindling energies, an ageing mother tries to keep her pianist daughter away from men, her ambition having always been 'to squeeze money out of [her daughter's] arduously achieved perfection'. Herself approaching middle age, 'an insect encased in amber', Erika, the piano teacher, is as it were hypnotised by the sexual experience that has passed her by. She dresses in unsuitably youthful clothes and stays out late after her lessons, but perhaps only to provoke her mother and cultivate the illusion of a freedom she doesn't have or even truly want. Into this stale scenario steps a handsome young student, Klemmer, determined to add his teacher to a list of conquests.

The book is full of telling set pieces. A violent opening scene that has mother and daughter clawing at each other over a dress Erika has bought swiftly establishes the relationship between them. At a drawing-room concert we see how the piano teacher uses her music, not to give or communicate, but to separate herself from others in icy technical perfection. Later, disgracefully, she puts broken glass in the jacket pocket of a promising girl student who has also attracted Klemmer's promiscuous eye.

In particular, the novel has two scenes of great dramatic effect where action, dialogue, description and reflection work powerfully together. The first is in the school bathrooms where the vigorous, sporty Klemmer boldly kisses his ageing sleeping beauty into life; Erika enjoys a moment of abandonment, then transforms this opportunity for passion into a frustrating masturbation scene in which the man, as if being taught a lesson, is brought almost to orgasm then forced to recompose himself.

Some days later, back home, Erika barricades herself in her room with Klemmer and, while her mother bangs hysterically on the door, forces him to read a letter in which she begs him to mistreat her, beat her, tie her up, sodomise her and so on (the list is long). The letter inhibits Klemmer from showing any ordinary desire, prompting him either to leave her or to use violence as asked. Either way Erika, who is actually afraid of violence, will have controlled the situation.

Such an account of the book suggests a familiar kind of unhappy psychological drama, but Jelinek's prose has now abandoned the transparency of the conventional novel. The sardonic, even facetious voice is stronger than ever, likewise the ironic use of cliché and allusion, but, as though these old habits were no longer sufficient to prevent emotional engagement with material so dangerously close to home, a barrage of new techniques ensures that the mind is never allowed to settle on the drama: frequent and flippant puns for example: 'She belittles herself in front of his dick which stays little'; 'Now he has to live with a charge that he could not discharge'; 'Klemmer drifts along on his own head waters, he is never in over his head.'

Very often, the narration is as it were derailed by some odd association (a word picked up and used in another sense) and heads off in a different direction, or into some extravagant metaphor. Metaphors, it should be said, are frequently mixed and collide oddly with both the story and each other creating unsettling shifts of register. Rather than clarifying the action or giving it emotional colour, they muddle and distract. Here, for example, are Erika and Klemmer at the point where he tracks her down in the women's bathroom and climbs to look over the toilet door as she urinates. No sooner has this dramatic event been described than the narrative voice steps back:

These two lead performers intend to put on a love scene, completely private, no extras, no walk-ons, only one lead under the leaden heaviness of the other lead.

In accordance with the occasion, Erika instantly gives herself up as a person. A present wrapped in a slightly dusty tissue paper, on a white tablecloth. As long as the guest is present, his present is lovingly turned and twisted; but as soon as he leaves, the present is shoved aside ... and everyone hurries to supper. The present cannot go away by itself, but for a while it is comforted by the fact that it is not alone. Plates and cups clatter, silverware scrapes on porcelain. But then the package notices that these noises are produced by a cassette player on the table. Applause and the clinking of glasses – everything on tape! Someone comes and takes the package. Erika can relax in this new security: she is being taken care of. She waits for instructions or orders. She has been studying for years – not toward her concert, but toward this day.

Klemmer has the option of putting her back unused in order to punish her. It's up to him, he can utilise her or not. He can even toss her around mischievously. But he can also polish her and place her in a showcase. Maybe he'll never wash her, but just keep pouring fluids into her; and her edge would be sticky and greasy from all the mouthprints. A day-old coat of sugar on the bottom.

Walter Klemmer pulls Erika out of the toilet stall. He yanks her. For openers, he presses a long kiss on her mouth . . .

To watch the same scene in the film (*The Piano Teacher*, directed by Michael Haneke, 2001) is to appreciate the work that Jelinek's style is doing here. On screen, told in a direct, traditional fashion, the story invites ordinary identification and excitement, however brilliant Isabelle Huppert (Erika) may be at repelling our sympathy. In the book, the drama of the plot is distanced but also strangely intensified by another, greater drama that threatens to overwhelm it: that of a narrator who seems afraid to confront her story head on and is constantly taking refuge from it in sophisticated literary games and bizarre digressions. Always unpleasant and frequently irritating, *The Piano Teacher* is nevertheless a powerful and convincing achievement.

A strongly individualistic style 'easily moves into a parody of itself', Jelinek tells us. In her case, *Lust* (1989) is the novel where this development is most evident. A ruthless industrialist imposes his love of music on factory workers, son and wife, thus transforming the art form most frequently associated with Austria into a means of perpetrating violence. The workers must sing in the factory choir if they want to keep their jobs, the son must sweat over his violin lessons, the wife must listen to music while her husband, promiscuous by nature but concerned about AIDS, forces her to submit, 'passive as a toilet', to his violent and inexhaustible sex drive:

> he wants a crack at her. He's cancelled two appointments in order to have it. The woman opens her mouth to cancel *this* appointment, she thinks of his strength and shuts her mouth again. This Man would play his tune even in the bosom of the mountains, his violin stroke would echo off the rocks, he'd stroke his rocks off. Time and again the same old song. This resounding banging tune . . . She's threatened with a beating. Her head is still full of music, Johann Sebastian Bach . . . going round and round in circles on the record player, chasing its tail. The Man is chasing his tail too, or his tail is chasing and he is following.

This sexual domination is explicitly compared to his treatment of his factory workers:

> The Direktor's weight keeps the woman down. All he needs to keep down the workers, as they joyfully return from their labour to their leisure, is a signature, he doesn't have to lie on them.

Or again:

> He'll screw the ass off her, it's all he wants in life, except to screw the rest of the world and draw his massive salary.

Remarkable throughout *Lust* is the torrent of angry energy that fizzes up in metaphor after metaphor, some crass, some brilliant, but always in the total absence of any convincing presentation of character or society. The absence of an Erika Kohut figure who might put us in an interesting relation to the unpleasantness described leaves the novel drifting, albeit with admirable panache, into mannerism. Thus, having started out by observing how cliché possesses and oppresses the minds of ordinary people, Jelinek now allows her own work to be driven by a simplistic, ever predictable polemic that many readers will find decidedly dated. Preaching only to the converted, *Lust* cannot encourage constructive reflection, rather it polarises debate, dividing readers into those who can still subscribe to a radical and embattled 1970s feminism and those who always suspected the feminists of overstating their case. Nowhere is there any trace of nuance: every man is violent, every woman a victim. At the end of the book, finding life irretrievably ugly, the industrialist's wife chooses a withdrawal from which there is no return, killing her son and herself.

Jelinek has a habit of using interviews to anticipate or pre-empt criticism. 'The men are really malicious', she tells Honegger, complaining that an editor with the magazine *Spiegel* has attacked her on his website, though it then turns out she hasn't read the criticism. Readers who don't respond to her style are people who have no background in music, she explains to Hans-Jürgen Heinrichs. The controversy over her winning the Nobel has merely confirmed her opinion that women are treated with condescension, she says, and the world is indeed as she describes it.

The effect of all this is like a distant echo of the letter Erika Kohut wrote to her would-be lover inviting him to mistreat her; we are in a no-win situation. If we react angrily to her work, we confirm Jelinek's view that a patriarchal society is hostile to women; alternatively, we can confirm that view by agreeing and applauding. It is extraordinary how consistently critics move to positive or negative extremes when reviewing Jelinek, the academics (who perhaps share an inclination to withdraw from the ugly realities of society and see their analytical powers flattered and stimulated) being positive, the journalists (who see their clichés ridiculed and tend to feel the author's approach is pathetically simplistic) negative. This is the force field Jelinek invariably creates around herself. Hence, as a male critic coming to her most recent, most ambitious and most difficult novel, *Greed*, I am aware that any reaction of mine has been foreseen and discounted and in some cases even incorporated in the book: 'I know, I know, you've heard it all before' the narrator taunts the reader at one point. 'But consider this: there are nevertheless unbelievably few of you worldwide.'

The plot of *Greed* takes up perhaps five per cent of the book's 330 dense, often impenetrable pages. Rather than coat-hangers for suits of language, the characters are intermittent and precarious stepping stones in a flood of sardonic generalisations about life's awfulness: 'Every poor man wants to be rich, that is just as natural a phenomenon as the fact that one can introduce all kinds of things into one's asshole, both small and surprisingly large objects.' Many readers will feel that neither phenomenon is natural and Jelinek's 'wit' here more coercive than illuminating or amusing.

Superficially, there are reminders of *The Piano Teacher*. Gerti, a middle-aged woman who has been both pianist and translator, lives alone in the country with her dog, a situation similar to Jelinek's. Having 'for a long time behaved with excessive reserve', she now 'can't stop herself busily and tirelessly' chasing a policeman who pulled her up for a minor traffic offence. So we have the same oscillation between withdrawal and involvement. Typical of Jelinek's men, Kurt Janisch, the policeman and hence figure of patriarchal authority, is violent, insatiable, promiscuous and an eager sportsman, sport being invariably seen negatively as a manifestation of male aggression and desire for domination. Kurt, who goes about sex with Gerti in much the same way as the industrialist in *Lust* did with his wife, really only wants to get hold of Gerti's property; this is the ultimate object of his greed, and the book insistently superimposes the image of the house with the image of the body. At one point we even hear that Kurt has tried to 'build on' his erect cock.

To complicate matters, the policeman begins to bring a sixteen-year-old girl, Gabi, to Gerti's house, locking Gerti out while he has sex with the girl. In the car one day he kills Gabi by pressing on her carotid nerve while she is giving him a blow job. He then dumps her body in a sterile man-made lake created to exploit hydroelectric power. Nodding back to Bernhard's negative transformation of the Austrian tradition of the *Heimatroman* (the novel of the Austrian homeland), Jelinek parallels greedy exploitation of the Alpine environment with man's violence to woman, the two coming together in this deathly lake, which, in a rant lasting a dozen pages, becomes the book's central image of a ubiquitous ugliness that will ultimately prompt Gerti's again terminal withdrawal: she kills herself after signing over her property to Kurt, thus confirming man's triumph over woman, over both women.

Unpromising as all this sounds, the book might just have worked had Jelinek dedicated any energy at all to creating the dramatic encounters and characterisation that make *The Piano Teacher* such a strong novel, or alternatively if her ruminations were sufficiently coherent and convincing for us to take them seriously. I quote a typical paragraph where the narrator is denouncing the way a mountain has been tunnelled into and hollowed out as part of the hydroelectric project which produced the lifeless lake. The engineering work has led to landslides and since there are houses on the lower slopes a catastrophe seems imminent:

So, how can we help up to its feet this ground, which is just rushing down towards us, down the mountain flank, and promptly landing on its nose, not on ours please? This nice, comradely mountain – also a face which has fallen and no one wants to help up. The mountain has dropped its mask. Now it already looks different from how it did a little while ago, when it was still whole. Perhaps houses will even have to be evacuated? Watch out, that could mean loss of homeland and lead to critical situations! I wish I could plan an early warning system, but would need help, so that the life of these people here could be maintained to the same high standards they are used to inclusive of the deep-freeze cabinet, into which at least one whole deer would fit if it were foolish enough to go into it. And also inclusive of a glazed conservatory, in which things could very well be a bit more exotic, if we had been sent the appropriate catalog, which we ordered on the phone.

What is one to make of such clumsy bludgeoning prose, such a wayward use of metaphor? And what is one to think of the fact that *Greed* was Jelinek's most recent novel when she was awarded the Nobel Prize and hence the work most immediately before the Swedish committee? We are used to the idea that the Nobel usually goes to writers engaged in an anti-establishment polemic with their cultures of origin. It is hard to keep politics out of international prizes and the rebel from another land is an attractive figure. Jelinek had been vociferous in her opposition to Jorg Haider's extreme right-wing Freedom Party which caused concern in the European Community when it became part of Austria's government in 1999. The Swedish judges also seem sensitive to the national literary awards that a writer has received, and perhaps precisely this continuing awareness that the Austrian Establishment has never confronted its Nazi past prompts the country's liberal intelligentsia to reward those who speak out courageously on the matter. Jelinek has received every major Austrian and German prize. That said, the social criticism she offers seems simplistic, rancorous and wilfully unhelpful, while *Greed* itself is unreadable: I recall not a single moment of pleasure turning its pages, not a single insight that impressed. Jelinek's selection for the Nobel, said resigning jury member Knut Ahnlund, 'has not only done irreparable damage to all progressive forces, it has also confused the general view of literature as an art.'

Perhaps part of our difficulty, at least with the English version of *Greed*, lies in the limits of translation. Any serious quarrel with our culture of origin is also and inevitably a quarrel about language, the values it enshrines and thought patterns it tends to impose. Jelinek, who herself translated Pynchon's *Gravity's Rainbow*, has often observed that she does not see how her writing can be successfully translated, depending as it does on an intensive use of wordplay and intertextual allusion that only an Austrian or German could understand. Readers of this review will already have wondered, for example, how closely the puns I quoted in the English translations can have matched the original German. Indeed, comparing the German texts of *The Piano Teacher* and *Greed* with both English and Italian translations, one finds that puns turn up in different places, create different effects, and often come at the expense of clarity and fluency. Here, in *Greed*, is a moment when a young woman goes to church leaving an elderly, incontinent, bedridden woman alone with no one to change her nappy:

> The old dear can just lie there in her own shit until evening, or until she rusts, we're going to evening Mass now, she has to stand firm until it's time to go to bed, the old dear, not the Church, it has already stood firm for much longer and doesn't need nappies either.

'*Durchhalten*' is standard German for 'holding on' in the sense of not moving one's bowels. It's hard to imagine anyone using 'stand firm' for this in English. The expression is there only to prepare the pun. This feeling that a wrong note has been struck is constant throughout the translation and robs the work of the linguistic conviction it presumably has in the German. If there was the music that both Jelinek and the Nobel committee speak of, it has disappeared.

How far the translation problem contributes to the book's failure in the English edition is hard to say. In any event, the comedy remains that Jelinek, locked as she is into a very specific cultural and linguistic context, was the least likely of candidates for international canonisation. 'I'm a provincial phenomenon' she tells us. 'Just as I can't take my body anywhere [Jelinek finds it impossible to travel] so my language can't be moved around either. My language and I watch TV together of an evening since we can't go anywhere else.' Readers of *Greed* may wish it had stayed that way.

A Polished Pessimism

[Emil Cioran]

'For all their merits,' writes Emil Cioran, opening an essay 'On Sickness', 'the healthy always disappoint.'

I quote the line from memory, not because I have an excellent memory, or made any effort to memorise it, but simply because this Romanian thinker and philosopher is so memorable. Every sentence is at once eloquent and provocative, and, as his vision of the world gradually takes shape, dreadfully pertinent.

Here is another train of thought that I just haven't been able to forget, though I read it a good year ago. Remarking, in a piece entitled 'A Portrait of the Civilised Man', on our determination to convert all to our likeness, Cioran declines to defend the cannibals ('theirs is perhaps not the best humanity has produced'), but then takes his stand on behalf of the great masses of the world's illiterate, 'whom we pursue with a virulence that nothing can justify: is it such a great evil not to know how to read and write? In all frankness, I cannot think so. Indeed I will go further and say for certain that when the last illiterate has disappeared from the planet, we may dress in mourning for mankind.'

Based in Paris after abandoning his native country to communism, Cioran published a dozen collections of essays and aphorisms. His subject is consciousness, or rather the impasse of consciousness, the irony that our greatest achievement, an increasingly refined self-awareness, has only made life more difficult. In this scenario the healthy and the illiterate of the two quotations above have something in common: they share the good fortune of a lower level of consciousness. And if we pursue the illiterate it is because, like the healthy person, they too 'cannot help but disappoint'. 'Do you devote yourselves to another's conversion? You are not doing it to save him, but to oblige him to suffer like yourselves . . . No one saves anyone: one saves only oneself and there is no better way to do that than to clothe in convictions the unhappiness one wishes to lavish on others.' 'Better an innate vice', the author concludes, 'than a virtue acquired . . .'

To say this is to offer only a crude introduction to the general drift of Cioran's thought. For it is the resourcefulness and insistence with which this extraordinary thinker explores his subject, his ability to come at it from all angles, turn it inside out, wed wit and despair, find image after image for the paradoxes that beset us, that is so remarkable and so convincing. The essays included in the collection *History and Utopia*, perhaps the easiest of Cioran's books with which to start, are no exception. The underlying thesis here is most succinctly (and fancifully) put as follows: 'Man, once expelled from paradise, in order not to think about it, in order not to suffer from it, is given in compensation the faculty of will, of aspiring to action, of foundering there with enthusiasm, with brio . . .'

Thus history begins: a will to action contaminated by a persistent nostalgia. Cioran's observations in this regard win our immediate recognition: 'Nothing shows more clearly the metaphysical meaning of our nostalgia than its incapacity to coincide with any moment of time whatever; hence it seeks consolation in a remote, immemorial past . . . somehow anterior to becoming.' Paradise. And so man girds up his will to recreate paradise, to establish Utopia, the end of suffering, the end of time. But in order to do this he must cultivate illusion, for 'the very notion of an ideal city is a torment to reason, an enterprise that does honour to the heart and disqualifies the intellect.' Thus develops what Cioran wryly calls 'the obligatory optimism' of modern political thought, its invention of Progress and again of the Meaning of History, since the fact 'that history just unfolds, independently of a specified direction, of a goal, no one is willing to admit'.

Likewise, few would be ready to accept, as Cioran does in an essay entitled 'Odyssey of Rancour', that it is this unsung sentiment which most galvanises action and ambition: 'Let us beware of those who subscribe to a reassuring philosophy, who believe in the Good and willingly erect it into an idol; they could not have done so if, honestly peering into themselves, they had sounded their own depths or their miasmas . . .'

But it is precisely at this point of his consummately pessimistic analysis that Cioran becomes most interesting, most attractive. For he is not simply a reactionary and a cynic. By no means. Driven as he is to dissolve illusion, he nevertheless sees that nothing can be done without it. And wishes that it were not illusion. For putting ourselves – disillusioned, unable to act – outside history would be a greater horror than engaging with it. Nor does he suggest that he has himself overcome all illusion, since one of the things that one cannot do without some sort of credulity is write. 'We depend, in order to create, upon the opinion of our neighbours, we solicit, we implore their homage, we mercilessly pursue those among them who offer us nuanced or even equitable judgements . . .' In short, one writes for admiration, for the illusion of success, and 'all measured praise' is 'identified with injustice'.

By implicating himself in this way, both with illusion and rancour, by keeping us constantly aware, partly through the sheer pungency of his prose, of the complexity of his own motivations, Cioran offers us the most lucid anatomy of our own perplexities with regard to any engagement in public life, any judgement of another's engagement. Decidedly post-Nietzschean, clearly committed to continuing the 'transvaluation of all values', he thus brings us to see the sense of such propositions as 'since we are unable to overcome our ills, we must cultivate them and take pleasure in them'; or again, 'We should bless the man who stirs our rancour, stirs us to action.'

Yet even as we warm to Cioran, to his strenuous provocation, his enviable eloquence, he introduces a worm of doubt into our enthusiasm: 'Admiration,' he says, 'by eroding our substance, depresses and ultimately demoralises us; hence we turn against the admired – anyone guilty of having inflicted upon us the task of raising ourselves to his level.'

All of which might make me hesitate to confess, in conclusion, that Cioran is the most brilliant thinker and essayist I have come across in many years, one of the few who make thought exciting to the point of intoxication. Were it not for the fact that he is now dead, and, as he wrote in 'Odyssey of Rancour', while 'we resent everyone who has "chosen" to live in the same epoch as ourselves, those who . . . hamper our stride or leave us behind . . . we resign ourselves to the superiority of the dead man . . .' Thus resigned, I am presently progressing through Cioran's recently published diary with only occasional fits of envy and anxiety.

True Scandal

[Niccolò Machiavelli]

He is still a scandal. Yet to read Machiavelli is also and always to take a very deep breath of fresh air, and that despite the almost 500 years that have elapsed since he wrote *The Prince*. How can these conflicting reactions coincide? The fresh and bracing air blows, no doubt, from our immediate sense that this man is telling the truth about realities normally sugared over with rhetoric. The scandal lies in the fact that Machiavelli himself is not scandalised by the bitter truth he tells.

The very idea behind *The Prince* overturns any official hierarchy of values, whether ancient or modern. Machiavelli decides to give us a manual not of how a prince, or political leader, *should* behave, but how he *must* behave *if he wishes to hold on to power*. Every action will be judged with reference to that one goal. Power thus becomes, at least for the prince, an absolute value. There is no talk of man's soul. There is no question of power's being sought in order to carry out some benevolent programme of reform. The good of the people is not an issue, or even a side issue. The prince must hold on to power . . . *e basta*.

Societies and military strategies, individual and collective psychologies are rapidly and efficiently analysed. A wide variety of possible circumstances are established and enquired into. Examples are given from classical literature and recent history. The aim is never to savour the *achievements* of a given culture, to assess the attractions or otherwise of this or that political system, the balance of weal and woe under this or that regime: what we need to know is how, in each specific situation, a prince can best consolidate his

155

authority and security. The underlying assumption is that, whatever may have been written in the past, political leaders have always put power first and foremost, and indeed that any other form of behaviour would be folly.

The scandal of the book is not felt in its famous general statements: that the end justifies the means; that nothing is so self-defeating as generosity; that men must be pampered or crushed; that there is no surer way of keeping possession of a territory than by devastation. It is easy to imagine these formulations arising from the transgressive glee of the talented writer who simply enjoys turning the world upside down.

No, it is when Machiavelli gives concrete examples and then moves on rapidly without comment that we begin to gasp: the Venetians find that their mercenary leader Carmagnola is not really fighting hard any more, but they are afraid that if they dismiss him he will walk off with some of the territory he previously captured for them: 'So for safety's sake, they were forced to kill him.'

Hiero of Syracuse, when given command of his country's army, 'realised that the mercenaries they had were useless . . . It seemed to him impossible either to keep them or to disband them, so he had them all cut to pieces.'

Cesare Borgia, having tamed and unified the Romagna with the help of the cruel minister Remirro De Orco, decides to deflect the people's hatred by putting the blame on the minister and then doing away with him: 'one morning, Remirro's body was found cut in two pieces on the piazza at Cesena with a block of wood and a bloody knife beside it. The brutality of this spectacle kept the people of the Romagna for a time appeased and stupefied.'

Borgia then consolidates his position by 'destroying all the families of the rulers he had despoiled'. 'I cannot possibly censure him', Machiavelli concludes, because 'he could not have conducted himself other than the way he did.'

This sense of coercion, of there being simply no alternative to brutal and murderous behaviour, is central to Machiavelli's at once pessimistic yet strangely gung-ho vision. It involves the admission that there is a profound mismatch between the qualities that we actually appreciate in a person – generosity, loyalty, compassion, modesty – and the qualities that bring political success – calculation and ruthlessness. As Machiavelli sees it, this mismatch occurs because people in general are greedy, short-sighted and impressionable and must be treated accordingly if a leader is to survive. 'I know everyone will agree', he concedes, 'that it would be most laudable if a prince possessed all the qualities deemed to be good among those I have enumerated, but, because of conditions in the world, princes cannot possess those qualities . . .'

Since the modern English reader of Machiavelli has largely been brought up on a rationalist, utilitarian philosophy which ties itself in knots to demonstrate that, given the right kind of government, self-interest, collective interest *and* Christian values can all be reconciled, it is something of a relief to come across a writer who wastes no time with such utopian nonsense. Yet though Machiavelli never actually welcomes the world's awfulness and certainly never rejoices in cruelty, our own upbringing prompts us to feel that he should at least have *seemed* to be a little shocked by it all.

Seeming is an important issue in *The Prince*. Given that moral qualities are no longer to be taken as guides for correct behaviour, what then is their importance? They become no more than attractions. It is *attractive* when a man is compassionate, generous and modest. It is attractive when a man keeps his word and shows loyalty to friends. We are in the realm of aesthetics, not moral imperatives. And what is attractive, of course, can be manipulated as a tool of persuasion. So even if a prince is actually better off without certain moral qualities, he should *appear* to have them, because people will be impressed. In particular, he should appear to be devout in his religious beliefs. 'The common people are always impressed by appearances and results' Machiavelli tells us. But he leaves us in no doubt that if you have to choose between the two, what matters is the result.

One of the great pleasures of reading and rereading *The Prince* is the way it prompts us to assess contemporary politicians and the wars of our own time in the light of Machiavelli's precepts and examples. To read *The Prince* in the 1980s was to have Thatcher and Reagan very much on one's mind, to think about American interference in Nicaragua, about the British adventure in the Falklands, as Machiavelli might have thought of them. Returning to the book in 2006, the reader is struck by how many of his observations could be applied directly to the Anglo-American invasion of Iraq, or indeed to many other such enterprises. This for example would seem applicable to any post-invasion situation:

> a prince is always compelled to injure those who have made him the new ruler, subjecting them to the troops and imposing the endless other hardships which his new conquest entails. As a result you are opposed by all those you have injured . . . and you cannot keep the friendship of those who have put you there. You cannot satisfy them in the way they had taken for granted, yet you cannot use strong medicine on them as you are in their debt. For always, no matter how powerful one's armies, to enter a conquered territory one needs the good will of the inhabitants.

Future readers, no doubt, will have other wars to think of as they turn the pages of *The Prince*. That fact alone is a sad confirmation of Machiavelli's understanding of international politics. Yet after the obvious parallels have been made and we have marvelled at how applicable this Renaissance writer's precepts still are, the further surprise is our growing awareness that, like it or not, the way we judge the wars of our times is indeed 'Machiavellian'. Would we be so critical of Suez, of Vietnam, of Iraq, if those adventures had succeeded? Wouldn't we rather begin to think of them as we think about Korea, or the Falklands? We do not, that is, judge the action in and for itself on a moral basis, but for the consequences it produces. Which is the same as saying that for us, as for Machiavelli, the end justifies the means.

'The wish to acquire more', *The Prince* laconically reminds us, 'is admittedly a very natural and common thing; and when men succeed in this they are always praised rather than condemned. But when they lack the ability to do so and yet want to acquire more at all costs, they deserve condemnation for their mistakes.'

If there is a difference between ourselves and Machiavelli in this regard, it is that he remembers to condemn the adventurers for their *mistakes*, while most of us prefer the comfort of a moral high ground, imagining that we would have condemned the adventure even had it been successful.

Are we then simply to accept Machiavelli lock, stock and barrel? In many ways he presents us with the same problem as the lesser known but even more disturbing Max Stirner who in *The Ego and His Own* (1845) extended the amoral Machiavellian power struggle into the life of every individual, rejecting the notion that there could be any moral limitation on anyone's behaviour. For Stirner the only question a person must ask before doing what he wants or taking what he desires is: do I have the power to get away with this or not?

Certainly it would be foolish not to be warned by what Machiavelli has to tell us about politicians and politics in general. We must thank him for his clear-sightedness. Yet a charming ingenuity in *The Prince* allows us at least to imagine a response to what appears to be a closed and largely depressing system of thought. Why did Machiavelli publish the book?

Ostensibly written in the attempt to have Lorenzo de' Medici give him a position in the Florentine government, *The Prince* is obviously self-defeating. Who would ever employ as his minister a man who has gone on record as presenting politics as a matter of pure power? If Machiavelli himself remarked that leaders gain from appearing to have a refined moral sense and strong religious belief, why did he not at least hint at these qualities in himself, or find some moral camouflage for his work, or put the book in Lorenzo's hands for private consultation only?

The answer has to be that as he was writing Machiavelli allowed himself to be seduced by the desire to tell the truth come what may, a principle which thus, at least for him, in this text, takes on a higher value than the quest for power. And in exposing the amoral nature of politics he actually and rather ironically threatens the way the political game is played. If it has not been possible, for example, for our contemporary armed forces in the West simply to lay waste to the various countries they have recently invaded, that may, in some tiny measure, be due to the kind of awareness that Machiavelli stimulated with this book, not in princes, perhaps, but in their subjects.

A Model Anomaly

[Silvio Berlusconi and Italian Politics]

Over every debate about Italian politics hovers the tyranny of the model. Italy is out of line. 'The Funding of Political Parties and Control of the Media: Another Italian Anomaly', proclaims the title of one essay in an annual round-up of developments in the *bel paese* produced by the Istituto Cattaneo, a private political think tank in Bologna. 'The End of Italy's Referendum Anomaly?' enquires another. And yet another: 'Towards a New Political Economy for a "Normal country"?'

The model, or normality, that Italy falls short of has a moral value. It is the morality of the modern Western democracy. So anomaly is also scandal: 'In any other country of the European Union,' claims Elio Veltri in the introduction to *L'odore dei soldi* (The Smell of Money), a book written to show that Silvio Berlusconi is a crook, 'the facts we describe would lead to a political earthquake. At the very least those responsible would be forced to quit the political scene. But in Italy this is not the case.'

Fortunately, it turns out that our Western model is not merely abstract, or invented, but a state of affairs to which humanity, or history, naturally tends. Italy is thus frequently seen as being on the way to, or even on the brink of, normality (sometimes revealingly described, by the authoritative historian of Italy, Denis Mack Smith, for example, as 'maturity'). The decision of the Italian Communist Party, after the fall of the Berlin Wall, to change its name to the Partito Democratico della Sinistra (The Left-wing Democratic Party) and later just Democratici di sinistra (Democrats of the Left) could thus be interpreted as part of a process of 'normalisation'. The world

161

need no longer feel, as it had since 1948, that one of Italy's major political parties was unelectable. On the other hand, *Tangentopoli*, the network of political corruption whose unmasking in the early 1990s destroyed the main parties of the centre right, was a step back: no sooner had the left become legitimate than the parties traditionally opposed to it vanished. 'Italy's "exceptionalism",' comments the book *Social Identities and Political Cultures in Italy*, 'which had been thrown out by political analysts, was thus fully reinstated by sociologists, historians and social anthropologists' who put the blame on 'a persisting culture of familism and particularism'.

In this Hegelian interpretation of the world, the scandal of the anomaly is not, then, just its deviation from the proper model, but, more precisely, the extent to which it obstructs the beneficent historical process that will one day bestow on every country a parliamentary democracy with strong and morally admirable political groupings who alternate in honest government according to the sovereign will of the people. The most recent such spoke in history's wheels is Silvio Berlusconi. 'Berlusconi', wrote the respected journalist Indro Montanelli in *Corriere della Sera*, 'is the millstone that paralyses Italian politics.' 'Why Silvio Berlusconi is unfit to lead Italy' proclaimed *The Economist*'s cover headline shortly before the Italian elections of 2001. The leader article began: 'In any self-respecting democracy it would be unthinkable . . .' etc. etc.

After more than twenty-five years living in Italy – years in which we have interminably been told that the country is about to become normal – it seems to me that this way of approaching Italian politics, prevalent both in Italy and abroad and so seductive in its simplicity, is entirely unhelpful. It is thus reassuring to find that *Social Identities and Political Cultures in Italy*, the only one of the books under review that draws on interviews with voters in an attempt to understand the relationship between their voting choices and their lives, comes to the conclusion that 'Reassessing the degree of change (but also of continuity) in Italy's social identities and political cultures also means reassessing concepts of modernity and modernisation.' And again: 'Solutions which may appear ideally suited to the Italian case . . . can easily backfire.' There is, in short, no ideal model towards which history tends. Or not in Italy.

L'odore dei soldi was tossed like a hand grenade into the Italian election campaign of 2001, when, on 14 March, its author, Marco Travaglio, was interviewed on *Satyricon*, an 'experimental' programme produced by public TV and famous for having plumbed new depths of bad taste when a pretty model slipped her red panties from under her dress to offer them as a gift to the show's presenter, Daniele Luttazzi. On another occasion guests were given chocolates in the form of turds. Two months before election day, Travaglio claimed to have discovered a lost, indeed suppressed, TV interview with the murdered anti-mafia magistrate Paolo Borsellino which spoke of relations between Berlusconi and the mafia. The burden of Travaglio's book is that the Berlusconi fortune is based on dirty money and hence, quite apart from the problem of his ownership of three of the seven national TV channels, he is unelectable. 'You're a courageous man in this shit of a country,' Luttazzi told the writer.

In the days following the programme, *L'odore dei soldi* soared up the bestseller list. The Berlusconi camp claimed that this was further proof that the three public channels were biased towards the government and the left. There were calls to boycott the television tax that funds the public channels (despite the fact that these channels also carry advertising). The commission that assesses the fairness of TV programmes during an election campaign agreed that the rules had been broken and suspended *Satyricon* for a week. Despite the furore, there was almost no debate about the content of the book.

It is not hard to understand why. *L'odore dei soldi* opens with an attempt to establish that Berlusconi is connected to the Sicilian mafia. In the early 1970s, while still a young man embarked on a career of property development in Milan, he gave employment, on the advice of his Sicilian assistant Marcello Dell'Utri, to a certain Vittorio Mangano who was to be gardener at the Berlusconi villa and possibly a horse breeder (horse breeding is apparently mafia jargon for drug smuggling). Mangano was later fired when suspected of being responsible for a number of thefts and even of trying to organise the kidnap of a rich guest. Later still, it turned out he was a member of a mafia family.

Travaglio floats the idea that it was through the mafia and the person of Mangano that Berlusconi acquired the finance to start his business. There are long quotations from various *pentiti* (those mafia members who have decided to collaborate with the magistrates) that support this interpretation. At the end of the opening section we are given the interview, just four pages, with magistrate Borsellino, an interview that, far from being suppressed, was published in the popular magazine *Espresso* in April 1994 (shortly after Berlusconi entered the political arena) and shown on public television. It is unremarkable. To the key question 'It has been said that he [Mangano] worked for Berlusconi', Borsellino replies: 'I wouldn't know what to say about that . . . even if I must make clear that, as a magistrate, I'm reluctant to talk of things I'm not certain of . . .' 'There is an ongoing investigation though?' 'I do know that there is an ongoing investigation.'

There are some frequently used Italian words which may be useful here for conveying the effect of the stories told in Travaglio's book: *polverone* (a great cloud of dust) is the confusion generated by extravagant and hotly contested versions of the same ambiguous incident; *fantapolitica* refers to fantastic, scandalous, usually paranoid accounts of what is going on in political life; *dietrologia* (behind-the-scenes-ology) is the obsessive study or invention of *fantapolitica* and of the way life is *pilotata*, secretly and illegally manipulated (by one's enemies); *insabbiare* (to clog in the sand) describes the process by which an overwhelming quantity of red herrings (often provided by mafia *pentiti*) and/or red tape can lead to a criminal investigation's being *archiviato*, filed away and forgotten.

The sad comedy of a book like *L'odore dei soldi*, typical of much investigative journalism in Italy, is that the extravagance and sheer abundance of the claims made creates such bewilderment in the reader that any truly damaging content is lost and ignored. That Berlusconi's companies will have come into contact with the mafia when extending his TV stations to Sicily would hardly be surprising. That he was involved in the murder of Borsellino, as Travaglio vaguely hints, is about as believable as that the queen ordered the death of Princess Diana. Here is a typical paragraph: Travaglio has just quoted Berlusconi's assistant Marcello Dell'Utri as saying that he wasn't aware that a certain Gaetano Cinà was a mafioso:

> Strange. Because Tanino Cinà, born in Palermo in 1930, owner of a laundry and a sports shop in Palermo, together with an elementary school certificate, is reported by all the main *pentiti* to have been the man who . . . at least from 1980 onward and doubtless up until the murders of Falcone and Borsellino (1992), was supposed to have made substantial payments to the mafia on behalf of the Berlusconi group. Cinà obviously denies this. But arrested and questioned in 1996, he would be forced at least to admit having relatives and friends among some of the finest names of the honourable society, names including Mimmo Teresi, cousin and right-hand man to Stefano Bontate.

If the desperately dry *Social Identities and Political Cultures in Italy* was eager to document the persisting importance of the family and local community in the dynamics of Italian public life, it could usefully have quoted this account of Travaglio's where to be related to someone, or to have been part of a community, is to be presumed guilty and where the syntax deployed seems itself to embrace the complications of the extended family. Typical of this kind of journalism is the way an account of the facts gets mixed up with a complacent declaration of cultural superiority (the comment on

Cinà's level of education) which nevertheless doesn't exclude a certain residual populist romanticism about the very phenomenon condemned ('some of the finest names of the honourable society'). Clarity, whether intellectual or emotional, is not at a premium.

But Berlusconi himself is no stranger to the art of generating confusion. The most amusing part of Travaglio's book is the section where he describes the dizzying series of Chinese boxes which was Berlusconi's financial empire throughout the 1970s and 1980s. Aside from the umbrella finance company, Fininvest, and a variety of real estate and later TV companies, twenty-three holding companies were formed, officially owned by old and innocuous friends and relatives, and monotonously named Holding Italiana 1st, 2nd, 3rd, 4th, etc., as if in an attempt to defy distinction. Quoting the reports of various tax inspections, all launched, it has to be said, soon after Berlusconi's entry into politics in 1993, Travaglio describes how large sums of money of unknown origin were shunted back and forth between, for example, holdings 9, 10 and 11, or 2, 17 and 6, or 3, 18 and 22, to no apparent end.

Travaglio suggests that the company is laundering dirty money. Clearly something suspicious is going on. What he never mentions is that whenever a piece of real estate changes hands in Italy at least a third of the total value is paid under the table, usually in cash. I know of very few exceptions to this habit, at once illegal and tolerated, to the extent that when assessing a client for a mortgage the bank will politely enquire what price he is actually paying as opposed to the price he is declaring for tax purposes. Hence a company dealing in property on the vast scale that Berlusconi did would have needed all kinds of ways of bringing cash amounting to a third of its income into useful circulation. Travaglio, whose book is mainly an uncomfortable and inadequately explained weave of extended quotations from judicial sources, doesn't do the work that would be required to establish the relationship between these mysterious sums of money and the size of Berlusconi's operations overall. It thus becomes hard to understand what kind or degree of illegality we are talking about. While for the puritan this may hardly seem relevant, for the Italian voter it is crucial.

The same sort of ambiguity undermines the last and interminably long section of the book which offers, with no analysis, 170 pages of extracts from the trial, one of the various trials, of Marcello Dell'Utri, to which Berlusconi was called as prosecution witness. Questioned about a number of potentially illegal movements of huge sums of cash, Berlusconi again and again makes the same fascinating double gesture: on the one hand he assures the judges that backhanders and sweeteners are endemic in the world he moves in, but then insists that his companies are quite unique in never having been involved in such practices. He is clean. On the subject of tax evasion he gives the judges a little lecture straight from the campaign trail:

> You know well enough how our tax system works, you know that the present system of high tax rates, the highest in Europe, is such that there is a presumption of systematic elusion and possible evasion. Hence the citizen responds with a certain attitude, on a moral level too that, well . . . look, a state that doesn't give back in services what it takes in taxes and that has rates way above the general norm, above the level that our natural sense of justice tells us is right . . . When the state asks of a citizen and of the fruit of his toil more than a third of that fruit, then the citizen feels, well . . . morally at loggerheads with the state.

Having made these appeals, which curiously use exactly the rhetoric of norms and innate morality deployed by those who consider him a scandalous anomaly, Berlusconi then goes on to deny that he or his company have been involved in any wrongdoing. The magistrates could legitimately have picked on anyone but him. I'm reminded of a conversation I recently had with Giambattista Pastorello, the owner of Hellas Verona, a football club in Italy's Serie A. I asked him whether there wasn't a conflict of interests in his sons being the agents for some of the players he had bought. 'People are just jealous,' he remarked. 'The fact is that when an agent is your son he doesn't ask for $20,000 under the table when you buy a player.' 'Are you saying', I enquired, 'that other player transactions you have made involved illegal payments?' Pastorello smiled: 'Of course not.' One of the many trials Berlusconi is involved in has to do with his football team's purchase of the player Gianluigi Lentini. He is accused of false accounting. The general public is not interested.

The comedy of these exchanges between Berlusconi and his judges brings us close to what is not so much the anomaly – for there is no universal norm for public behaviour – as one of the main distinguishing features of Italian public life. That there be a gap between what is legal and what is common practice is not unusual anywhere. But a special psychology seems to govern people's handling of that gap in Italy, with the result that however constantly exposed and alluded to it never seems to be diminished. The irony of Travaglio's book is that many of its readers, while suspecting that Berlusconi is guilty as charged, will nevertheless feel a certain sympathy with the man. It is not, they sense, or not only, because he has broken the law that he is being put on trial. Behind this intuition lies all the Italian vocation for factionalism. However much one may appeal to national unity and the authority of the state, no institution, least of all the judiciary, is ultimately perceived as anything other than one more warring group in competition with one's own.

Social Identities and Political Cultures in Italy poses a dull and naive premise: in a 'traditional' society people vote ('passively') according to family and community allegiances; in a modern society the individual emerges from family and community and votes ('actively') according to 'rational choice'. The author Anna Cento Bull, who works at the University of Bath, sets out to analyse Italy's position in this presumed evolutionary process by conducting detailed surveys of voting habits in Sesto San Giovanni, an area of declining heavy industry in the suburbs of Milan that traditionally voted communist; and in Erba, a small town near Como that traditionally voted Christian Democrat. Both communities, like so many in Italy, have recently changed their voting patterns, with DS (the erstwhile Communist Party) losing their majority in Sesto and the Christian Democrats all but disappearing in Erba. Nevertheless, the author's findings, diligently collected and reviewed with an admirably open mind, do not indicate a move to the vision of the sovereign individual deciding how to vote on the basis of rational self-interest mediated by conscience. In particular, the huge vote for the Northern League in Erba in 1996 suggests a renewal of localism with people consistently voting in line with community and family. The phenomenon obliges the author to allow that the future of a sense of identity may not after all reside entirely with the freewheeling individual. On the contrary, where such an individual exists, he or she may actually choose to join the fold of a collective identity, which, far from being trapped in the past, can be dynamic and forward-looking. But such qualities do not necessarily mean that all is sweetness and light. Bull concludes with a consideration that gets closer than anything else I have read to what one senses is happening in Italian society:

> whereas traditionally the Catholic and communist subcultures exercised a pervasive influence upon and successfully appeared to encompass the entire territorial community, nowadays a political subculture . . . seems to represent the interests and needs of specific groups within a territory. The exclusionary aspect of a political subculture ('Us' versus the 'Others') has become more in evidence than its inclusionary one.

In the light, then, of what seems to be an exacerbation of factionalism, rather than the reverse, let us try understand the story of Berlusconi's party, Forza Italia, which is still, even after his government's defeat at the 2006 elections, the largest political party nationwide in Italy.

169

Born in 1936, son of a bank employee, the exemplary young Silvio pays for his university education by singing to tourists on summer cruise ships. In his early twenties he invests his father's retirement fund in a property development. In very short order he wins the right to develop Milano 2, a complex of 4,000 homes in an eastern suburb of Milan. Generous with space and greenery and including all possible services, the project is recognised as a model development. By the early 1970s Berlusconi's is the largest construction company in Italy. Father Luigi and brother Paolo are ever beside him. This is a clan in the making.

With the removal of the state monopoly on TV broadcasting in 1976, Berlusconi starts a cable TV channel for Milano 2 which is rapidly transformed into a local channel for the whole of Lombardy. Hindered by a state monopoly on national broadcasts, he purchases local channels across the country and has them broadcast pre-recorded programmes simultaneously. Taken to court for breaking the law on national broadcasting, he claims he is fighting a battle for liberty: the image of the modern entrepreneur embattled against the forces of an obtuse and entrenched status quo is born. Certainly the general public is on Berlusconi's side. Large contributions to the Socialist Party of Bettino Craxi, a key player in the coalition government of the time, guarantee Berlusconi protection and eventually lead to a made-to-measure law that legalises his position.

Exploiting a consumer-boom thirst for advertising space, Berlusconi's TV rapidly produces huge incomes. He establishes two more national channels and thus commands more than forty per cent of viewing time, with a near monopoly in the private sector. In 1991 he is able to offer the first national news programme that can compete with the public television channels, which are still largely following the dictates of the old political parties. Italy does not have a strong tradition of independent TV journalism.

Married with two children, Berlusconi falls in love with a young actress, divorces and remarries. This does not prevent him from presenting himself, ad nauseam, as a family man. Three more children, all of them enviably handsome, will follow. The older children take their places in the business. The younger attend a Steiner school which forbids them from watching TV. Meantime, Berlusconi purchases one of Italy's major book and magazine publishers, Mondadori, and one of the big five football teams, AC Milan. His commercial successes are endless, his largesse mythical. With 30,000 employees, he is now the second largest employer in Italy.

In 1992, the 'Clean Hands' investigation into *Tangentopoli* takes a heavy toll of Berlusconi's political connections, leaving him without protection. In particular, Craxi flees the country to avoid prison. When elections are announced for the spring of 1994, it seems inevitable that the left will at last take power. Berlusconi joins those who speak of the 'Clean Hands' operation as an example of one faction's use of the judicial process to destroy another, not an impartial application of the law. Apparently terrified by the prospect of a left-wing government, he does everything to persuade what players remain in the centre and right of Italian politics to form a coalition capable of winning with the country's new majority voting system. The various fragments will not agree. Advised to the contrary by his closest associates and family, Berlusconi nevertheless forms his own movement, Forza Italia, in February 1993. His instinct is to make it a centre party but his market research tells him to stay to the right: a liberal ticket of fewer taxes and radical deregulation is the thing. Bringing together an improbable coalition of the country's two political pariahs, the Northern League and National Alliance, he, amazingly, wins the elections of 28 March.

It is now that Berlusconi experiences his first spectacular failure. Ninety per cent of his party's deputies are new to parliament. They are inexperienced. The Northern League and the National Alliance are at loggerheads. Under fire for the obvious conflict of interests, Berlusconi is reluctant to let go of his TV channels. He is an empire builder, not a constitutionalist. A first package of laws to deregulate business practice is successful, but then the government turns to the problem of pensions. It is universally recognised that Italian pensions are ruinously generous. Berlusconi proposes a drastic reform that would bring the country in line with others and make Italy 'normal'. As a result, the hitherto divided left is at last given an issue to unite around. Nobody wants to surrender acquired pension rights, however abnormal they may be. There are huge demonstrations, larger than any in the history of the country. A man who loves to be seen as a benefactor, not a pruner, Berlusconi loses his nerve. His businesses are now under constant assault from the tax police. While presiding, in Palermo, over a United Nations conference on international crime, he is given formal notice that he himself is under investigation for corruption. The magistrates involved claim that this timing was not deliberate. They are not under oath. When the Northern League desert the coalition, Berlusconi resigns, imagining that new elections will be called. Instead, President Scalfaro gives a mandate to a government of 'technicians' supported by the fragments of the centre, the left and the League. At this low point many imagined that Berlusconi's love affair with politics was over, his virtual, TV-driven party would surely wilt as rapidly as it had blossomed.

More than seven years later, Gianfranco Pasquino, professor of political science at the University of Bologna and one of Italy's most respected political commentators, finds himself reviewing Berlusconi's pre-election manifesto book, *L'Italia che ho in mente* (The Italy I have in Mind). It is well known that Pasquino's sympathies are with the left. Nevertheless, he does not, like so many, write Berlusconi off as merely a corrupt tycoon and vulgar showman. On the contrary, the man has stayed the political course:

> For those like D'Alema [then secretary of DS] who think that these days it's enough to have 'TV and cash' to make it in politics, Berlusconi's books will hold many surprises: a speech to the first National Assembly of Forza Italia's Women Members . . . a speech to the first National Assembly of Senior Members, a speech to the National Congress of Young Members, a speech

to the Councillors of Lombardy . . . It would be interesting to know how many of the secretaries of traditional parties have worked the circuit so hard . . . The truth is, that if Forza Italia is no longer nor in any sense a tinsel party, it owes its transformation to the unflagging efforts of its founder and president. In short, the party's successful organisation is the result of much hard work and is well deserved.

These remarks echo Anna Bull's findings in *Social Identities*, which recognises the importance of traditional methods of creating a sense of community and drumming up support. How Berlusconi would gloat! For what emerges from the 300 and more pages of his book is not so much an acute political analysis, nor a coherent programme of reform, as the man's growing excitement with his own image, his chosen role as visionary political leader. Not for nothing does the volume come in the form of transcripts of speeches complete with italicised parentheses (*applausi*) (*applausi prolungati*). The man's unerring instinct, as when he sang on those cruise ships in his youth, is to play the seducer. He is determined to draw you into his clan. He actually *needs* you to succumb to him. He is charming. He will work night and day to have you believe in him. If you join him, he will sweat blood not to disappoint you. As he repeats over and over his sensible, laissez-faire policies for getting Italy's over-regulated economy moving again, it is hard to keep your attention on such dull issues. Rather one is fascinated, appalled, by the demon that condemns this talented tycoon to go on and on overachieving, swallowing up the whole world in his empire. Frequently he refers to Forza Italia as a large happy family with himself at the head.

But perhaps Berlusconi's obsession is not an unnatural reaction to endemic factionalism. The Istituto Cattaneo's annual reviews include at the outset a list of 'the main party acronyms used in this text'. There are thirty-one in the account of the events of 1997. Despite the introduction of a majority voting system, all kinds of laws encourage the existence of small parties. Any party with over one per cent of the vote receives €1.70 for every vote polled, this despite a referendum in which Italians clearly indicated that they did not want political parties to receive public funds. Even parties with minimal representation in parliament are granted equal time for party political broadcasts. Thus a fragmented coalition gets more free time than one of two or three larger parties. But that does not mean it will be more successful. Unlike the lobby, the small party is interested not in the achievement of any particular policy, but in the perpetuation of itself, the affirmation of its own group. As a result postures are frequently struck in perverse defiance of coalition partners in order to gain the limelight.

So complex is the resulting parliamentary situation, that a publication such as the Istituto Cattaneo's is absolutely essential for any kind of overview of the constantly shifting alliances that lie behind Italy's frequent if largely cosmetic changes of government. Between 1996, when, despite all his TV ownership, Berlusconi lost the general election, and 2001, when, despite a ban on party political TV commercials, he nevertheless won convincingly, there were five governments. In an attempt to overcome the inevitably weak executive that results from this state of affairs, the parliament set up a so-called Bicameral Commission to discuss major constitutional reforms. To read, in the Istituto Cattaneo's round-up, the account of the interminable workings of this commission and its ultimate and complete failure is to have a sense of the meaninglessness of much of Berlusconi's 'just-let-me-get-on-with-the-job' rhetoric, but also an awareness of the man's growing capacities as a peculiarly Italian politician.

Again the author is Gianfranco Pasquino. Rapidly, he sketches in the positions of the main players. The president of the commission, DS secretary Massimo D'Alema, was eager to show his statesmanship by achieving a definitive solution to the Italian problem, but behind him he had a party and above all a coalition historically opposed to a strong executive. Berlusconi was looking for a presidential system which would allow him to be directly elected as head of state. However, before he would agree to anything, he wanted the judiciary reformed in a way that would allow him to escape the now endless investigations into his past. D'Alema might have been willing to grant such a reform in return for sensible constitutional change, but knew that his party would object. On the right, Gianfranco Fini, the leader of the National Alliance, was willing to sign almost any deal merely for the legitimacy that would be conferred on him by having been seen to be involved in it. Ironically, he was D'Alema's staunchest ally. At the same time he couldn't irritate Berlusconi, since it was Berlusconi who had given him legitimacy in the first place by accepting him into his coalition. Fini was frightened that D'Alema and Berlusconi might resort to the classic Italian arrangement of forming an amorphous central coalition that would forever exclude him.

Meantime, the half a dozen central parties, mainly fragments of the ex-Christian Democrats, together with two 'green' parties and the far left Rifondazione Communista, were working hard to avoid any solution that would endanger their continued existence. They did this by constantly threatening to pull out of the government coalition and thus end the legislature if the commission produced an unfavourable constitution. Naturally, as leader of the opposition, Berlusconi had a certain interest in encouraging them to do this. The League, on the other hand, still in a radically separatist phase, was only interested in demonstrating that the nation state was unworkable. Having walked out of the commission at the beginning, they staged a dramatic comeback to swing a crucial vote in favour of a directly elected president, something D'Alema hadn't wanted and that the League itself had previously opposed. Seeing the work of the commission unexpectedly close to being concluded in the direction he wished, but without his having resolved his judicial problems, Berlusconi now claimed that the presidency envisaged did not have significant powers and so scuppered the whole process. Upon which D'Alema, after 480 hours of meetings, gave up in disgust. Pasquino comments: 'the real contents [of the reforms] always remained of marginal concern for the majority of the commission's members.'

I mention this episode (of which I have omitted the half), chosen from amongst many others of equally Byzantine complexity all excellently covered in the Istituto Cattaneo's reviews, to hint at what can and cannot be expected from any Italian government, whether its prime minister be Berlusconi or Prodi. Italy is a country where identity is largely structured around a person's membership of various groupings (geographical, cultural, economic) that are fiercely if often only theatrically embattled with other groupings. 'You exist only through your hate for us' writes a Verona football supporter, in local dialect, to traditional enemies Vicenza supporters on his club's website message board. It might just as well be the unions talking to the employers, the north to the south, state workers to the self-employed, ex-communists to ex-Fascists. Except in moments of extreme crisis, no central authority or even common good is recognised.

The inevitable result is that even more than elsewhere the defining experience of any political career is frustration. Of whatever colour, however led, each government seems able to offer no more than another version of Italian immobility, which, after all, is but the downside of a social structure that still makes this country an extremely attractive place in which to live, and not quite like anywhere else.

Mad at the Medici

[Lorenzo de' Medici]

When does it become justifiable to kill a political leader? Lorenzo de' Medici, otherwise known as il Magnifico, was the acknowledged if unofficial ruler of the city state of Florence from 1469 until his death in 1492. He was no Hitler or Pol Pot. He could not be compared with his close ally, the debauched despot Galeazzo Maria Sforza, Duke of Milan, who was assassinated in 1476. If his expansionist policies threatened the small, independent towns around Florence, this was absolutely the norm for the time and no more than was expected of him. Lorenzo wrote fine poetry, maintained and built up the Medici family's extraordinary art collection and was a brilliant conversationalist and diplomat. In April 1478 a rival Florentine family, the Pazzi, tried to assassinate Lorenzo and his younger brother Giuliano at Mass in the Florence Duomo. They got Giuliano but failed to kill Lorenzo and were themselves overwhelmed in the bloodbath of revenge that followed. History has given them a bad press. In his new book, *April Blood: Florence and the Plot Against the Medici*, the highly respected historian of the Italian Renaissance, Lauro Martines, sets out to find justifications for the Pazzi. Though he draws no analogies with modern or other times, the issue of political assassination is inevitably of enduring relevance.

Only twenty when he came to power, Lorenzo was the third Medici to dominate Florence. The regime began with his grandfather, Cosimo, in 1434 and thus had been going thirty-five years when his father, Piero, died of gout in 1469. On the December evening after Piero's death about 700 citizens met in the convent of Sant'Antonio and agreed that the 'reputation and greatness' of the Medici family must be preserved. 'By which they mean', explained the ambassador of Ferrara to his lord, 'that the secret things of this government will pass through Lorenzo's hands as before through his father's.' It was about two years earlier that Marco Parenti, a quiet opponent of the Medici, had given up trying to write a history of the period because of 'the difficulty of knowing the truth when those who govern keep things secret'. The Florentines, it seems, often used the expression 'the secret things of our town'. Yet officially Florence was a republic with a written constitution dating back two centuries. What was it that had to be kept secret and why? To grasp the motivation behind the Pazzi attempt to eliminate the Medici, we have to look at a process that had been developing over many years.

The Florentine constitution worked, or was supposed to work, like this. The city was governed by a *signoria* comprising nine men, that is, eight priors led by a *gonfaloniere della giustizia*, a kind of first minister. However, each *signoria* served only for two months and its members were not elected by popular vote, but chosen by lot, their names being drawn from a series of bags prepared in such a way that there would be two priors from each quarter of the town, and that six of the eight would be from the more important guilds, in short the wealthier classes, and two from the minor guilds, the artisan class. A certain limited representativeness was thus guaranteed.

Aided by two consultative committees, the sixteen *gonfalonieri* and the twelve *buonomini*, the *signoria* initiated all legislation, but this then had to be ratified by two larger councils, the *consiglio del popolo* and the *consiglio del comune*, each comprising about 200 members and serving for four months. All these bodies and many others too were, like the government, elected by drawing lots from various bags, each with its hundreds of name tags of men from different quarters and guilds.

The inspiration behind such a constitution should already be clear. Everybody – or everybody considered eligible – would serve in government for a brief period, but nobody would dominate. The system did not allow for the existence of the professional politician or the political party. Indeed, political association of any kind was forbidden and political gatherings, whether in private or public, were banned. Strictly speaking, in so far as it was not religious but political, the meeting of Medici supporters the night after Piero's death was illegal.

What happened then when conflicting opinions led to impasse, when the government, for the most part elected from the patrician class, insisted on passing legislation that the two *consigli* with their wider representation insisted on rejecting? In a crisis, the *signoria* could summon a 'parliament'. That is, a bell was rung, inviting the city's entire adult male population to gather in the Piazza della Signoria in the heart of the town; a proposal was then read out, usually recommending the formation of a *balìa*, a legislative body wielding unlimited powers for a limited period; the *balìa* would then resolve the impasse, and since its members were selected by the *signoria*, it would obviously do so in their favour.

But what if the parliament voted against the *signoria*'s recommendations? Throughout the fifteenth century no parliament did so. For it was at the parliament that 'the secret things of the town' came briefly and brutally to the fore. The citizens arrived in the piazza to find it surrounded by armed men, often foreigners, always called there by the government of the day. A yes vote was guaranteed. Like many other republics and democracies before and since, fifteenth-century Florence was characterised by a fatal gap between rhetoric and reality: for 'parliament' read '*coup d'état*'.

At once utopian and repressive, the constitution sought to eliminate the natural tendency to form groups for political purposes in the pessimistic belief that no group would ever act on behalf of the whole town, but would always be self-interested and family-based. Indeed, there is an obvious correlation between the republic's institution of a special police force – the 'agents of the night' – to pursue homosexuals, or young women who broke regulations on public modesty by wearing platform shoes perhaps, or too many buttons, and its determination to stamp out political parties. This was a radically Christian society where everything was seen in terms of good and evil and the only respectable answer to evil was to repress, never accommodate. All the same, it proved hard to recruit the 'agents of the night' from Florence itself, and this for the simple reason that in a fairly small town of 45,000 people no one wanted to become unpopular for harassing acquaintances. Evil or not, homosexuals abounded, girls were fatally attracted to anything that might enhance their charms and political factions thrived, indeed they ran the show. In its very idealism, the constitution was ill-equipped to deal with reality.

Thus in the early decades of the century, the two-monthly governments were largely guided in their decisions by the Albizzi family and their clients and friends. In the early 1430s the faction's dominance was threatened by the rapidly accumulating wealth of the Medici bank and in particular Cosimo de' Medici's use of that wealth to acquire friends in every area of society. Big money has a way of seeking to buy what cannot or should not be bought, be it a place in heaven or power in government. Cosimo wanted both and was charming and generous to boot. At the same time the lively interest of humanist scholars in the history of the classical world was turning up a wealth of political figures who had been great leaders without the benefit of royal blood. A heady procession of new role models was becoming available to men like Cosimo, models for which the Florentine constitution was quite unsuited.

Military defeat and drastic tax hikes put the Albizzi faction on the defensive and precipitated a crisis. But since the city was not officially ruled by faction there was no legal way for power to be transferred from one group to another. 'Every case that came before the magistrates, even the least, was reduced to a contest between the parties' Machiavelli tells us in his *Florentine Histories*, though supposedly no parties existed. Finally, Rinaldo Albizzi persuaded a favourable *signoria* to call a parliament, create a *balia*, accuse Cosimo of treason and have him and his allies exiled. A year later, though, with Albizzi fortunes at a new low, the luck of the draw turned up a *signoria* favourable to Cosimo. He was recalled and promptly had all *his* enemies exiled.

This see-sawing of political fortunes dependent on the selection of government by lot had an element of farce about it, grim farce for those on the losing side. Understandably, Cosimo set about making sure that he would not have to leave Florence again. Over the next thirty years, through a series of cautious experiments and ad hoc electoral measures he sought to subvert the republic in such a way that the electoral bags would never again throw up a *signoria* opposed to his interests. On the other hand, he never actually abolished the business of choosing the names of government members from electoral bags, nor ever sought to become the city's official prince or dictator. In a fragmented Italy where, centuries before other Western nations, the idea of a divine right of kings had ceased to carry conviction, Cosimo's modernity lay in his understanding that to hold power for any length of time one must appear not to hold it; or rather, all power must now seem to have the new legitimacy of popular consensus. It had become important for the Florentines, as it is important for us today, to imagine that they were equals in a process of collective self-government. Cosimo would do everything he could to preserve that illusion. His reforms concentrated on the electoral lists that decided which names would be put in which bags for which appointments, and then in exploiting moments of military or economic crisis to claim special powers that allowed a small group of bureaucrats to select just a very few names (rather than hundreds) to be put in the bags. Meantime the city's registers went on recording what was now a charade of a lottery as if nothing had changed.

Inevitably, there was popular resistance to this and new, often bewilderingly complicated tricks had to be invented with a certain frequency. In one debate among members of the regime over whether they must give way to popular pressure and return to the real lottery system, Cosimo agreed that the concession seemed inevitable but was at a loss to understand how it might best be done while preserving the regime. In any event, he warned, 'the greatest attention must be paid to *the technical aspects.*' Whenever, in a democracy, we see our nervous rulers obsessed with 'the technical aspects' of the electoral process, then we know we are getting close to the 'secret things of our town'.

Because of the extent of Medici power in the mid-fifteenth century, as the family bank reached its moment of maximum extension and Cosimo the height of his considerable manipulative powers, it has been suggested that the citizen of Florence was in much the same position as the subject of the surrounding principalities. This was not the case. Equally powerless, the Florentine was nevertheless mocked, or flattered, by the rhetoric of freedom and legality. He could not bow before his monarch in dignified fashion, saying: this is God's will; nor, alternatively, tell himself: this man is a usurper and I only bow down because brute force obliges me to. The regular electoral process, the continuing existence of the *consiglio del popolo* and the *consiglio del comune*, fired the Florentine imagination with ideals of political freedom which remained forever frustrated. Hence a very special state of mind developed: a fizz of excited and idealistic political thought frothed over the intransigent reality of protracted if veiled dictatorship. This state of mind, the exhilaration and humiliation of the fake democracy, at once so relevant to the modern world and so difficult to pin down, is the real subject of *April Blood* and the key to understanding the Pazzi conspiracy.

Between Cosimo's return to Florence in 1434 and his great-grandson, Piero di Lorenzo's, flight from the city in 1494 there were three serious challenges to the Medici regime, each ending in a parliament, the appointment of a *balia* with unlimited powers, and a new turn of the screw. In 1458 a challenge was launched through legal institutions in line with the constitution. The regime survived, but at the high price of showing itself for what it was. Troops from Milan were marched into town for a parliament. The gloves were off.

In 1466, two years after Cosimo's death, the opposition came from key members of his regime now determined to take the state from his ailing son, the gout-paralysed Piero. In so far as they used the institutions against Piero, they did so by manipulating them in much the same way they had manipulated them on behalf of his father. It is hard to gauge how much seriousness to ascribe to each man's claim that he was acting for freedom and republicanism. Perhaps all they wanted was to set up the electoral bags to guarantee a patrician oligarchy, since the older Florentine families had always loathed the Medici habit of bringing in 'vile new men' who would be loyal to the ruling family in return. In any event, this crisis ended with both sides appealing to foreign powers for military aid, but whereas the opposition was divided and uncertain over the use of force, the bedridden Piero was surprisingly determined and efficient. The Medici won the day, the 'conspirators' were exiled.

These two failures serve to explain why, in launching the third challenge to Medici power in 1478, the Pazzi family made no attempt at all to work through public institutions. There was no point. With the Medici bank now in drastic decline, perhaps due to a general downturn in trade, perhaps to Lorenzo's incompetence in this sphere, the Medici were no longer in a position to buy support with a constant flow of gifts and so had actually tightened their stranglehold on the electoral machinery as the only way of staying in power. The point had now been reached where, in a simulacrum of legality bolstered by constant propaganda, a group of Medici initiates voted each other onto all the legislative bodies turn and turn about without any threat of interference. You could join the group, but only if you offered unconditional support to the still young and arrogant Lorenzo, who was behaving more and more like a hereditary prince.

In his excellent and erudite book *Power and Imagination: City-States in Renaissance Italy*, Martines made it clear that he would not allow the traditional enthusiasm for Renaissance art to cloud his moral and political judgement. His considerable scholarship is always galvanised by an edge of personal engagement. So in *April Blood* he uses the melodrama of the attempt to assassinate Lorenzo in the Duomo first to lure a wider public to the subject of Florentine republicanism and then, more problematically, to defend those who were willing to resort to murder rather than go on working with an authoritarian regime.

The events leading up to that bloody day make for excellent narrative. The Pazzi family at the time comprised an ageing uncle, Iacopo, with no fewer than ten adult nephews associated in a complex web of international trading and banking activities remarkably similar to, and frequently intertwined with, those of the Medici. For the last thirty years the Medici had been indirectly responsible for promoting the Pazzi to positions of government, and Lorenzo's sister Bianca had been married to one of the nephews, Guglielmo.

But in the late 1460s something went wrong and by the time the names of those eligible for the highest offices were reviewed in 1472, the Pazzi were clearly being discriminated against. In 1473 when Pope Sixtus IV tried to borrow from the Medici bank to buy the lordship of Imola for his nephew, Girolamo Riario, Lorenzo refused, Imola being a possible object of Florentine expansionism. He warned the Pazzi bank to do likewise. The Pazzi, however, not only gave Sixtus the money but told him of Lorenzo's warning. In 1474 the Pope retaliated by making Francesco Salviati, a close ally of the Pazzi, Archbishop of Pisa, a town subject to Florence and eager to regain its independence. Offended, Lorenzo blocked Salviati's entry into Pisa for more than a year.

Largely thanks to the Pazzi, il Magnifico was now in open conflict with the Pope. Between 1474 and 1476 the Medici bank lost both its right to run the papal monopoly on the important trade in alum (crucial for the textile industry) and its function as the Pope's main banker. The Pazzi were given what the Medici lost. In 1477 Lorenzo hit back by interfering in a complex piece of inheritance legislation which effectively deprived one of the Pazzi nephews of a huge legacy. What is remarkable about the escalating quarrel, as Martines points out, is that the Pazzi should have been so bold as to take on the Medici regime, or so stupid as to commit political suicide, in this way.

Martines finds an explanation in the character of Francesco de' Pazzi. A small, choleric man, whose father reputedly died of drink and debauchery, Francesco was running the Pazzi bank in Rome and thus had most to gain from the Pope's favours while being poorly placed to observe Lorenzo's real power back in Florence. Perhaps prompted by the murder of the Duke of Milan in 1476, Francesco had the idea of seeing off the Medici and rapidly drew in Salviati, now in place as the Archbishop of Pisa. He secured the services of Count Montesecco, a military commander for both the Pope and his nephew Girolamo Riario, now Lord of Imola. The King of Naples came on board and the Pope in person, knowing full well that the plan was to kill, gave his blessing to the overthrow of the Medici 'but without anyone's death'. Back in Florence, the head of the Pazzi family, old Uncle Iacopo, was not so easily persuaded, but as a notorious gambling man he eventually decided to join the conspiracy on the grounds that Francesco had always been lucky.

After various failed attempts to lure Lorenzo down to Rome, the conspirators, nervous that their plot would soon be discovered, took advantage of the fact that the seventeen-year-old cardinal Raffaele Riario (nephew to the Lord of Imola and great nephew to the Pope, in short, nepotism incarnate) was visiting Florence. Armed men could be sent as his escort. The Medici brothers had offered the cardinal lunch at their villa in Fiesole; the plan was to murder them there. But Lorenzo's brother Giuliano didn't turn up. The conspirators were agreed that there was no point in killing one brother without the other.

So the appointment with death would have to be at lunch a

week later, after Sunday Mass, at Lorenzo's palazzo in the heart of Florence where the juvenile cardinal was now invited to inspect il Magnifico's famous collection of cameos. On the day, however, it again appeared that Giuliano wouldn't be eating with them. Desperate, the conspirators now agreed to do the deed at holy Mass, only minutes away. The change of plan was fatal. Count Montesecco, the most professional of the band and Lorenzo's designated assassin, declared that he would not kill in church. His place was taken, ironically enough, by two priests. Meantime, an army of papal soldiers were within striking distance of the town and the Bishop of Pisa with about thirty armed men from Perugia set off to take over the government building.

Thus the bare bones of a complex and ultimately incompetent conspiracy. The two priests failed to dispatch Lorenzo. The archbishop failed to take the government building. The papal troops failed to show and old Iacopo's cries of 'Liberty!' yelled from horseback as he galloped through the streets failed to impress the Florentine crowd. All too soon the conspirators, archbishop included, were being strung from the high windows of the government building, if not simply tossed into the piazza below. War broke out with Rome and Naples, Lorenzo was excommunicated, the Pazzi and their properties were pursued for years and the Medici regime eventually emerged much reinforced.

It does make for fascinating reading. But it is hard to imagine a scenario more resistant to Martines's desire to present the conspirators as noble republicans. The Pope and the King of Naples wanted to draw Florence away from Milan and into their sphere of influence. The Pazzi, in their determination to supplant the Medici bank in Rome, had reached a point where the only way back into Florentine politics was over Lorenzo's dead body. All the same, one contemporary commentator does come to Martines's aid. The patrician Alamanno Rinuccini, avid reader of classical history, hailing from a rich family of bankers and with a long record in highest office under the Medici, to whom he had dedicated various translations from the Greek, retired to his country villa in 1479 to write a *Dialogue on Liberty* in the classical style in which he argued that the state of Medici tyranny was such that the only thing an honest man could do was to withdraw from public life. Rinuccini spoke of the Pazzi as having undertaken 'the just and honest task of liberating their country'. It has to be said, however, that Rinuccini had recently fallen out with Lorenzo and that his life savings were held in the Pazzi bank. Shortly after writing the dialogue, which he did not publish, he went back to Florence and served the Medici regime in a variety of public offices for many years.

Martines imagines the core of Rinuccini's identity as being in the republican dialogue and his public life as an unhappy charade, 'helping to clean the face of a government which he condemned as criminal'. Similarly he identifies, rightly, a strong current of republican feeling running beneath the surface in Florence, but one in thrall to Medici manipulations. The insistently repeated assumption is that if only the Medici could have been eliminated, Florence would have enjoyed a freer, more productive, republican existence. It is on this point alone that one would wish to take issue with this intriguing book.

Every situation and character Martines presents to us in *April Blood* is of marvellous complexity: the learned Pope turned feverish nepotist, the hardened mercenary who will not kill in church, the lucid Lorenzo, who hates church nepotism and does everything he can to get his son made a cardinal; then the general picture of a religious age in love with transgression, of a republican citizenry avid for the trappings of hierarchy. It is as if every player in this story contained not one but, in differing degrees and according to the role destiny assigned them, *all* the contradictory impulses of the time, as if the Florentine constitution with its obvious inadequacies had been thought up precisely to be open to subversion. In the end it is not hard to imagine Lorenzo the poet, deprived of power, becoming a most eloquent republican, and even easier to see Francesco Pazzi in power as a dangerous tyrant. More generally, one has the constant suspicion that the people of fifteenth-century Florence, and perhaps people in general, did not, do not, find it so difficult to be liberal and virtuous in private while toeing an authoritarian line in public. It gave life an exciting tension, a sense of direction towards those brief and heady periods, as after the departure of the Medici, when some real republican freedom was enjoyed. Fortunately neither the historian nor the reader is obliged to reach a verdict on either Francesco Pazzi or Lorenzo il Magnifico. But it is a pleasure, and perhaps salutary, to reflect on possible analogies with the present time.

Anachronistically, I imagine the Florentine patricians solving their problems by learning the trick of rotating apparently opposed but in the end complicitous factions according to the whims of a complacently enfranchised *popolo* anaesthetised by mass media and consumer goods.

Love Letter

[Fleur Jaeggy]

When teaching the limits and possibilities of literary translation, one tends to consider those writers whose highly individual styles pose special problems. For some years I have been putting the following passage from Fleur Jaeggy's novel *Sweet Days of Discipline* before my students in Milan. The Swiss-born Jaeggy lives in Italy and writes in Italian, but her narrator here is speaking of her girlhood in a Swiss boarding school, presumably in the early 1950s:

I hardly got any letters. They were handed out at mealtimes. It wasn't nice not to get much post. So I began to write to my father, mindless letters saying nothing. I hoped he was well, I was well. He answered at once, sticking *Pro Juventute* stamps on the envelopes. He asked me why on earth I wrote to him so often. Both his letters and mine were short. Every month a banknote would be enclosed, my *argent de poche*. I wrote to him because I knew he was the only person who did as I asked, even though it was my mother who was legally in charge of me and it was to her decisions I had to submit. She sent her orders from Brazil. I had to have a German room-mate because I had to speak German. And I spoke to the German, she gave me presents, chocolates she was always eating, American chewing gum, and art books. In German. With German reproductions. Blauer Reiter. Even her underwear was German. And yet I can't find her name in the pigeonholes of my mind; girls lost in my memory. Who was she? She was such a nonentity for me, and yet I do remember her face and body. Perhaps, thanks to some malign

189

trick, those we didn't pay any attention to rise up again. Their features are more deeply impressed on us than those we did give time to. Our minds are a series of graves in a wall. Our nonentities are all there when the register is called, gluttonous creatures; sometimes they fly up like vultures to hide the faces of those we loved. A multitude of faces dwell in the graves, a rich pasturage. While I write the German girl is sketching out, as in a police station, her own particulars. What is her name? Her name is lost. But it's not enough to forget a name to have forgotten the person. She's all there, in her grave in the wall.

Like everything Jaeggy writes, the passage (in my translation here) accomplishes surprising shifts of register, tense and narrative focus with disconcerting ease, as if they were the most normal things in the world. It opens with an apparently straightforward realism, but reporting – and again this is common with Jaeggy – an absence rather than an abundance, a disappointment rather than a fulfilment. The girl received very few letters. To rectify the situation, she writes to her father. And we arrive at once at a second 'absence'. He is a dutiful correspondent, but has nothing to say. That he can't understand why she writes so often suggests she has nothing to say either. 'Both his letters and mine were short.' At this point we have only a comedy of anxiety for contact on the one hand and incomprehension on the other. That the stamps bear the slogan *Pro Juventute* (For Youth) is one of Jaeggy's constant and quiet ironies.

In place of all she is missing the girl finds money, 'my *argent de poche*'. The use of the foreign language here is significant, and not just to carry the authenticity of a polyglot Swiss education. Again and again, in Jaeggy's writing, the occasional surrogates offered for intimacy and understanding present themselves in fragments of French or, above all, German, and almost always in the form of some little cliché or commonplace. In the last line of the first paragraph of *Sweet Days of Discipline* we are given the word *Zwang*, a duty or imposition. How ominously it clangs in the liquid, multisyllabic

Italian. The last pages of Jaeggy's new novel, *SS Proleterka*, echo with the German composites *Wahrheitsleibe*, love of the truth, and *Leidtragende*, she who bears the grief. It is as if, whenever we hoped to arrive at something essential, an unhappy distraction is imposed from without, some disturbing splinter of a foreign tongue, not part of the narrator's native pattern of thought. It's not long before we suspect that in each of these two novels the narrator is the only person who is actually thinking in the language of narration. Her mind will never be integrated with the surrounding reality.

As if fearing she has given too much away, Jaeggy's narrator now supplies an alternative reason for her letter writing: she wrote to her father, not out of a need for contact, but because he was the only one who would do as she said. She presents herself as spoilt, manipulative, not fragile at all. But this characteristic defensive posturing, so convincing psychologically, never generates much plot. We never hear what the girl asks for or gets. On the contrary, the reflection brings her at once to her mother, who holds the real power. And here my English version parts company with the original, which, translated literally, reads: 'although my life had to be under the legal will of my mother'. It is hard in elegant English to convey the abrupt violence of this. Neither 'be under' nor 'submit' carry the punch of the Italian *sottostare*. The mother figure is at once remote ('from Brazil she gave her orders' is the way the original Italian puts it) and all powerful. She imposes German on a daughter she never sees, imposes a companion who is not the girl the narrator was eager to spend time with.

The bitter little comedy of the German room-mate with her German art books and underwear but American gum in her mouth (unwanted gifts with foreign names) then leads to one of those shifts of perspective so typical of Jaeggy's work. The girl's name is not available in the 'pigeonholes of my mind' (in Italian, *casellario*, a series of boxes, for filing). Yet her face flies up like a vulture to hide the faces of those she loved. For now the mind is no longer a filing system but a series of 'loculi' (originally, burial niches, but used in modern Italian to refer to the system of slotting coffins into cemetery walls). The rapid shift of thought, somewhat muddled in the English, from filing systems to school registers to graves, is now more characteristic of poetry than prose. The word I have translated as 'pasturage' could also mean dung, or the bait thrown to attract fish to the hook.

Then comes the most dramatic change of tense, the most unsettling switch of narrative focus. 'While I write the German girl is sketching out, as in a police station, her own particulars.' Just as we appreciate the point that systems of registration rather than recovering life seem to destroy it, and that the unwanted (with the complicity of such authorities as private schools and police forces) always substitutes itself for the intimate, so we reach the maximum narrative disorientation. The past will not stay in the past. The memory is not easily governable. At the same time, and largely because of these sudden, disturbing transitions, we become extremely anxious for the mental health of our storyteller. Has she survived her 'sweet days of discipline'? What has life brought her to?

All this by way of extended introduction to Jaeggy's most recent work, *SS Proleterka*†, which in many ways must be read as complementary to the earlier novel. The *Proleterka* is a Yugoslav passenger ship on which a fifteen-year-old girl will take a two-week spring cruise around the Mediterranean. The ship's name means, literally, proletarian girl, exactly what Jaeggy's at once moneyed and deprived alter ego in these two novels is not. If the Swiss boarding schools of *Sweet Days of Discipline* were places where experience was systematically denied ('there was always a shortage of men', we hear with characteristic wryness, 'in the areas around these schools'), the *Proleterka*, on the other hand, is the very 'locus of experience'.

---

†The original title is simply *Proleterka*. It thus presents itself to the Italian reader as one of those foreign and incomprehensible impositions. To add the reassuring *SS* to explain the word for the American reader indicates a sad loss of nerve on the part of the publishers.

Which is to say, its decks are stalked by swarthy Slav crewmen. The adolescent girl immediately sees her chance and seizes it. Having barely spoken to him, she has sex with the second mate. Nor does she stop there. 'By the time the voyage is over, she must know everything. At the end of the voyage [she] will be able to say: never again, not ever. No experience ever again.' Initiation, in Jaeggy's world, does not take a character through trial into fulfilment, a shared, purposeful life with other initiates, but into nothingness, withdrawal, even death. The spring cruise will not blossom into summer. Rather the reader senses an awful limbo stretching across the decades between the moment of experience and that of narration. Her life has been 'very easy' the narrator remarks, in the closing pages. In the sense, we fear, that there has been no life at all.

As in *Sweet Days of Discipline*, the main character of *SS Proleterka* is unnamed. She begins to speak in the first person, but constantly lapses into the third, apparently wary of identifying entirely with her narrated self. Similarly and with chilling, often satirical detachment, many of the characters will not be referred to by name, but by their role, or relationship to someone else: 'Johannes's former wife', 'Professor Z's son'. It is as if a process of bureaucratic classification were constantly obscuring whatever inner being there might be.

The girl's family is recognisably that of the earlier novel. There is an absent mother who exercises legal guardianship from South America. Vindictively, she restricts her daughter's contact with the divorced father to a minimum. But at least he has a name now: Johannes. Sick, close to death, Johannes is granted the right to take his daughter on a two-week cruise. The process of getting to know him will also be a farewell. In so far as *SS Proleterka* is a beautiful as well as a most disturbing novel, it is so because, precisely through the medium of its determined restraint, it reads as a passionate love letter, not to the Slav sailors, but to Johannes.

Johannes is not an easy person to know. Deprived early of the family business and fortune, all spent to nurse his twin brother through an incurable illness, he is a man who has lost the core of his life and, with it, all social potency. His 'expression is always the same, sad and distant'. Johannes is a member of a Swiss corporation, or guild, a kind of ancient Rotary Club, dating back to 1336. For years the only meeting permitted with his daughter was at a traditional guild procession. As always in Jaeggy, intimacy is suffocated in a straitjacket of tradition, as if in a vendetta protracted against us by our ancestors.

We paraded together through the streets of a city on a lake. He with his tricorne on his head. I in the *Tracht*, the traditional costume with the black bonnet trimmed in white lace. The black patent leather shoes with the grosgrain buckles. The silk apron over the red of the costume, a red beneath which a dark bluish-purple lurked. And the bodice in damasked silk. In a square, atop a pyre of wood, they were burning an effigy. The *Böögg*. Men on horseback gallop in a circle around the fire. Drums roll. Standards are raised. They were bidding the winter farewell. To me it seemed like bidding farewell to something I had never had. I was drawn to the flames. It was a long time ago.

It is the guild that has arranged the cruise on the *Proleterka* for its members, a collection of ageing, well-to-do Swiss. 'Stubborn and self righteous', geriatric and vain, entirely comfortable with their customs and language, the guild members epitomise the forces that are constantly denying the young girl contact with real life, supposedly 'for her [own] good. A venomous expression . . . You ought to watch your back when listening to diktats of this kind. When you are a hostage to good. A prisoner of good.'

Johannes, however, is endearing because he is not quite like the other members of the guild. Since he married an Italian, lost his wealth and then his wife, he has been tolerated rather than fully accepted. Above all, although this cruise was to be his one opportunity for getting to know his daughter, and despite specific instructions from his ex-wife to keep her in check, he doesn't prevent the girl from spending much of the time, and particularly the nights, with the sailors.

'Well, doesn't her father see? Doesn't Johannes see his daughter's behaviour? It is *unverschämt*, shameless. We are in the dining room. Johannes's best friend looks with commiseration at the corner table. The neglected table. Johannes is absent and indifferent. He tries to tell me something, I should not leave the table. Immediately his voice dies away. Without conviction. Do what you like, say his clear and wounded eyes. The room sways. The waiters bring the hors d'oeuvres. They too no longer want anything to do with the passengers of the guild. Politely, I get up, excuse myself. The dining room is a prison.'

Yet the kind of experience the girl has outside the prison of guild protection is hardly more positive: 'Nikola shoves me violently into the cabin. They must not see us. The captain can know, but he must not see us. He locks the door. He is violent on the bunk too . . .' Submitting to her first sexual experience, the girl's mind is seized by memories of a school friend who advocated such brutal encounters, so that the crucial moment is somehow stolen from her. 'I was behaving a little as if she were present. She was taking notes.'

Ostensibly on the cruise to get to know her beloved if vacant father, the girl is distracted by the crewmen, the call to life, distracted within that distraction by another's imagined reportage of events, then unceremoniously passed on to another man for sex when the first has had enough. This infallible mechanism of malign substitutions is beautifully captured when, on a visit to the Acropolis, another member of the guild insists that the girl must make every effort to be with her father and remember him. To aid that process he offers to take a photograph:

I walk among the ruins and try to remember. But it is the previous night [with the second mate] that appears. Johannes's friend laughs. His eyes are astute slits. The vegetation is in bloom, splendor blazing in the fields on its way to withering.

195

To brushwood. At Athens, in the Acropolis, Johannes's friend comes up with his camera. '*Du wirst diese Reise mit deinem Vater nicht Vergessen.*' I was remembering the Acropolis photographed by him.

Later, in the book's cruellest twist, long after the end of the cruise and her father's death, the narrator will receive a letter from a man who claims that he, and not Johannes, is her natural father. At the age of ninety, with unforgivable complacency, he reveals this secret, he claims, out of *Wahrheitsleibe*, love of the truth, when the only truth the book is establishing is the perverse process by which the life we desire is obscured and denied to us. Language itself is complicit: 'Two words accompany me like a refrain: "living" and "experience". People imagine words in order to narrate the world and to substitute it.' In one passage the book brings together the moment of learning to write with the birth of conscious memory. It is the beginning of a process of falsification, of stylish calligraphy. Hence the immense, even tortuous caution of Jaeggy's prose.

'The healthy', as Emil Cioran remarked, 'always disappoint'. Jaeggy, who does not disappoint, creates a mind, a vision, that is nothing if not unwell. Deprived of intimacy, or indeed of all that we would normally consider as making up a life – partner, work, friends – her narrator is disturbingly intimate with the inanimate world; she experiences rooms, objects, landscapes, as alive, malignant and predatory. She possesses the various certificates and documents of her father's dead parents as if this might keep a possible vendetta at bay. She imprisons her dead mother's piano in a small room, where no one can see or play it, as though visiting on the instrument a revenge for her own suffocated childhood. Nothing is ever properly past, nothing ever effectively exorcised. Some critics have imagined that behind all this lies a never-declared Freudian trauma. Such a reading is banal. The 'sickness' is absolutely structural to this mind's experience of the world and of language. And if Jaeggy is convincing, it is because, aside from the psychology of her narrator and the fine intrigue of her story, even the 'healthiest' reader will recognise, in some part of himself, that there are moments when experience, or its absence, assumes this form.

As for any writer with a highly individual, determinedly controlled style, Jaeggy's main enemy is mannerism, the complacent repeating of oneself. And in the struggle against mannerism her main ally is plot. Again and again, in *SS Proleterka*, she finds the twist that will confirm and communicate her vision without simply repeating her ideas. At Johannes's funeral, not long after the cruise, the proprietors of the hotel where he has been living, people who, beneath a veneer of politeness, despised and exploited him, send 'a sumptuous wreath of flowers'. Johannes's daughter, who has been passive throughout the funeral arrangements, suddenly reacts:

> No, I said. Send it back. I did not want the wreath. Miss Gerda flushed. I could not, I could not send a wreath back. Johannes's daughter can not send a wreath of flowers back, she says. According to Miss Gerda, Johannes ought to decide whether to accept the wreath or not. And Johannes has left no instructions about accepting flowers or not. Reluctantly, Miss Gerda takes a last look at the pompous wreath with the purple ribbon and the showy gilt lettering. She lets the staff take it away.

In stark contrast to this gaudy wreath, the daughter, prevented by Miss Gerda, executor of her father's will, from kissing Johannes's corpse, has placed a nail in his pocket, 'a little piece of iron' to accompany him in the fire of cremation. Though Jaeggy would never be so explicit, it is not hard to imagine the extravagant wreath with its gilt lettering as an image of the prose she has rejected, the nail burning in the corpse's pocket (she does not place it in his hands as there 'it would have been too visible') as emblematic of something she aspires too. If Jaeggy's novels are always short, it is because the combination of the spare, often paratactic sentence

197

with an extraordinary density of thought, plot and emotion would become unbearable if extended.

To ask a translator to reproduce the prose that has gone through the purging fire of Jaeggy's rejection of all public rhetoric and easy sentiment is to risk contamination. As any translator knows, language constantly invites us towards the commonplace, the standard, the conventional flourish. Overall Alastair McEwen is admirable in avoiding this. He has the courage to keep Jaeggy's unsettling tense switches, he appreciates that one of the book's pleasures lies in the reader's effort to imagine the mind that could make such strange leaps. A little bent, perhaps, a little less sharp, as is inevitable, Jaeggy's nail is nevertheless driven home.

Tales Told by a Computer

[Hypertext]

Among the many things the computer is supposed to change in our lives, one of the most profound, if the change were really to occur, is our experience of narrative. For the way we tell ourselves stories – our sense of the opening, development and closure of a plot – still largely determines the way we think of ourselves and of our progress, or otherwise, between cradle and grave.

We are not talking here about the e-book, the portable screen on which, page by page, traditional narrative can be read. That, in the end, offers only a more economic, if less attractive, way of giving us what we already have. Perhaps the only reasons to welcome the e-book are the possibility it offers to save on school texts, to travel light with a number of volumes in electronic form, and above all, for those like myself whose eyesight is not what it was, the possibility of choosing a larger type size than any printed book will offer.

No, the development that seeks to revolutionise the nature of storytelling is the so-called hypertext narrative, a product that, whether stored on CD or downloaded from the internet, can be experienced only through the computer, since access to the many choices and variations it offers can only be achieved through the use of keyboard and mouse. It cannot properly exist on the printed page. All over the world, websites and university courses promulgate and promote the phenomenon. Novelists of the stature of John Barth and Robert Coover have written enthusiastic essays and given lectures on how to become hypertext narrators. In an 'Endtroduction' to Katherine Hayles's new book *Writing Machines* the editor remarks: 'It's no wonder that one of the chief fetishes our society has produced is the book. But bibliomaniacal impulses are mutating in this world of multi-, trans- and re-mediation, and we need to establish new categories for describing the emotional and physical relationships readers have with what (and how) they read.'[†]

The hypertext narrative comes in so many forms that it is difficult to consider its potential with reference to just a few examples. All the same, two fundamental innovations immediately present themselves: the hypertext is free to mix the written word, whether narrative, poetry or essay, with sound, static images or even cinematic effects, and to deliver the text at whatever speed and in whatever form the author chooses. This is such a dramatic extension of the bookish tradition of illustration and illumination that in many cases the written part of the hypertext may lose much of its sense if separated from the dynamic within which it is presented.

However, by far the most revolutionary development of the hypertext has to do with the succession in which sections of written text are read. Hypertext dispenses with the linearity that invites us to proceed from page one of a book through to the end, front cover

[†] It is curious that Katherine Hayles's *Writing Machines*, which deals mainly with the 'materiality' (p.6), as she puts it, of the written text, seems unaware of the many writers across the centuries who have offered profound meditations on the physical aspects of text and language: Shakespeare, Swift (exhaustively), Browning, Joyce and Beckett, to name but an Anglo-Irish few. The omission of their reflections is emblematic of what we might call 'the provincialism of the contemporary' that dogs a great deal of criticism in the field. Though the range of sources may be geographically wide, it is chronologically restricted. 'My title, *Writing Machines*,' Hayles tells us, 'plays with the multiple ways in which writing and materiality come together' (p.26). She goes on to express her admiration for Milorad Pavic, Ursula Le Guin, Paul Zimmerman and Robert Coover, but seems unaware of Gulliver's encounter, almost 300 years ago, with the professor who invented the word machine on the fantastical island of Lagado. 'Roland Barthes', she tells us, 'uncannily anticipated electronic hypertext by associating text with dispersion, multiple authorship and RHIZOMATIC structure' (p.30). Published in 1704, Swift's *A Tale of a Tub* covered the same ground. If one wishes to disturb chronology, much of it could be read as a satire of recent literary enthusiasms. Hayles's demand at the opening of her second chapter, 'Why have we not heard more about materiality?' (p.19) thus rings hollow.

to back. Pages are not numbered and one cannot 'turn' them. Instead we are invited to use the computer mouse to click on any of a number of links ('hot' words or images in text on the computer screen or on the margin of it) to proceed to *a* (not *the*) following screen.

It is clear that with this innovation each reader's experience, at least in so far as the trajectory of plot or the accumulation of the work's reflections is concerned, will be different. He or she is obliged to construct a personal route through the text, and this largely at random and often without knowing how many pages there are, or whether there is still more to read or not. 'The traditional narrative time-line', wrote Coover, who makes it clear that he has a personal investment in 'fictions that challenge linearity', 'vanishes into a geographical landscape or exitless maze, with beginnings, middles and ends being no longer part of the immediate display.'

Shelley Jackson's *Patchwork Girl, or a Modern Monster* is an example of a fairly early hypertext (1995) which, in every respect but linearity, remains fairly close to the print-bound novel; it has only a very few illustrations and no sound or cinematic effects. An opening image, comparable to a book cover, shows an old-fashioned, Da Vinci-style drawing of the human body, a woman's, above the title '*Patchwork Girl*, by Mary Shelley and herself'. The reader is invited to click on various body parts or various areas of an anatomically represented brain. In each case he will see different sections of text varying from a brief sentence to a full, traditional page, many of which offer further links. What eventually emerges is a sequel, or addition, to Mary Shelley's *Frankenstein*. Taking her cue from the unhappy student's dilemma over whether or not he should make a mate for his monster, Jackson stitches together pieces of Shelley's work with convincing pages of pastiche to tell, for example, the stories of those whose corpses yield the body parts for the gruesome experiment and the story of the monstrous girl herself, her fugitive anonymous life as an outcast and freak and her erotic adventures. All of this in a decidedly nineteenth-century prose:

My left leg belonged to Jane, a nanny who harbored under her durable grey dresses and sensible undergarments a remembrance of a less sensible time: a tattoo of a ship and the legend, Come Back To Me. Nanny knew some stories that astonished her charges, and though the ship on her thigh blurred and grew faint and blue with distance, until it seemed that the currents must have long ago finished their work, undoing its planks one by one with unfailing patience, she always took the children to the wharf when word came that a ship was docking, and many a sailor greeted her by name.

My leg is always twitching, jumping, joggling. It wants to go places. It has had enough of waiting.

At every point the text insists on an analogy between the patchwork nature of the girl's body and the fragmented and non-linear hypertext, between her difficulty in establishing an identity from the many lives that have formed her and ours as we click back and forth looking for a thread to follow, often finding ourselves frustratingly confronted by a screen we have already read, unsure how to proceed or when to stop. In this regard, and like almost all hypertexts, *Patchwork Girl* seems obsessively conscious of its experimental medium, which it is eager to present in a positive light as a heightened form of realism, a metaphor for modern consciousness and, in this case, something peculiarly feminine, if not feminist. Digressions on the usually female task of quilting, for example, run alongside sections such as this:

Arranging these patched words in an electronic space I feel half blind, as if the entire text is within reach, but because of some myopic condition I am only familiar with from dreams, I can see only that part most immediately before me and have no sense of how that part relates to the rest. When I open a book, I know where I am, which is restful. My reading is spatial and even volumetric. I tell myself, I am a third of the way down a rectangular solid, I am a quarter of the way down the page, I am here on the page. But where am I now? I am in here and a present moment that has no history and no expectations for the future.

More romantically the narrator announces:

I hop from stone to stone and an electronic river washes out my scent in the intervals. I am a discontinuous trace, a dotted line.

Or again:

The past I collect like snapshots in accordion-pleated plastic sleeves. Perhaps I'd like it better riding a strong steady flow, guaranteeing that if I boarded a Mississippi steamboat at x I would certainly pass through y before disembarking at z.

At this point one has to say that, as Twain has amply shown, if you do embark on the Mississippi at, for example, St Louis, you will inevitably pass through Cairo before reaching Memphis. Only if you fall asleep, as Huck and Tom do, do you risk missing the place where you want to stop. Not for nothing did Jackson speak of 'some myopic condition I am only familiar with from dreams'. The hypertext, perhaps, has a vocation above all for the dreamlike. The linear progression of time, the unyielding contour of the familiar landscape, these, whatever enthusiasms one may have for the post-modern world, are still our standard experience in the hours of wakefulness.

Turning back for a moment to the traditional book, it's worth recalling that nothing obliges us to read it from front to back. When we pick up anthologies, or essay collections, we frequently ignore the order in which the pieces are presented. Many like to read the last pages of a novel first.

The linearity of the book, of the page, or even the sentence, is thus only a convention, not inherent in the form, but something we choose to submit to, or not, every time we decide to read. In the 1960s and 1970s there were various experiments with loose-leaf novels whose chapters could be read in any order. They were soon abandoned. In his novel *Watt*, at the point of his main character's maximum derangement, Samuel Beckett begins to invert the order of the words in the sentence ('Day of most, night of part'), then the letters in the words ('"Geb nodrap," he said, "geb nodrap"'). No sooner has he reminded us that such things are possible, that nothing obliges him to write from left to right, top to bottom, than he returns to standard prose. Why?

However much the mind, on occasion and generally unprompted, may sense the nearness of distant moments, the closeness of remote places, thus challenging our normal experience of space and time, nevertheless it is evident that much of the pathos of our lives has to do with the stark simplicity of chronology: birth, youth, maturity, death. A novelist may choose to start *in medias res* or at the last gasp, every kind of mental resistance to the harsh facts of passing time may be recorded, but over the work's trajectory the reader expects a chronology to be reconstructed. Indeed, such a reconstruction from the tangle of memory and imagination can be considered a conquest, synonymous with the achievement of a certain knowledge and central to the moment of 'recognition' which concedes to the author a valuable wisdom about the world we share. That achievement is there in *Don Quixote* as it is there in *Ulysses*, or even, though in a more problematic fashion, in Beckett's trilogy. Borges, one of the writers whom hypertext practitioners most admire, once wrote an essay, 'A New Refutation of Time', which, having embarked on a most energetic denial of the reality of the combined enemies substance and time, concludes with a brutal volte-face: 'The world unfortunately is real; I unfortunately am Borges.'

Our willing submission, then, to the convention that one reads a book from front to back, accepting whatever ordering of events the author chooses, partakes of an experience that we recognise from ordinary life: our inevitable submission to the unalterable succession of chronological events. The mind's frequent yearning for a freedom from linearity ('the tyranny of the line' Coover calls it), often expressed in the non-chronological ordering of events in the text, is thus held in fruitful tension with (indeed expressed through) the implacable forward movement of the numbered pages. A desire to be outside time, free from linearity, can only be expressed within time and the bounds of the line.

Criticism of the hypertext, still at a promotional stage, resists this acceptance of a fixed order of experience and a fixed narrative line; it champions instead the idea of choice, the notion of the reader's being involved, through interaction with the text links, in creating the story rather than submitting to it. A typical essay ('Telewriting' by Mark Taylor and Esa Saarinen) concludes: 'Though the network is shared, the course each individual follows is different. Thus, no hypertext is the product of a single author who is its creative origin or heroic architect. To the contrary, in the hyper-textual network, all authorship is joint authorship and all production is co-production. Every writer is a reader and all reading is writing.'

Two questions have to be asked here: is this really true of the hypertext? If it is true, is it desirable?

The answer to the first question is no. The traditional text was always 'interactive' up to a point, as the comments and glosses on ancient manuscripts suggest. I can (and do!) write in the margin, express my objections or admiration. I can come back years later and wonder in disbelief that I ever thought that way. Or I can read someone else's reactions and find that he has a totally different Leopold Bloom or Madame Bovary from mine, this despite the traditional form and the 'single author'. I never think of this personal view of the story as joint authorship.

In the hypertext, this simple form of engagement is denied me. I cannot scribble on the page. In compensation, when I have finished reading a page I can, or must, choose between a limited number of alternatives to proceed. Certainly it is unlikely that I will read the text in exactly the same order as anyone else. But to say that this makes me a co-writer, to the same extent as the author who prepared the texts and decided what links would be available to me, where and when, is nonsense. I have written nothing. As I choose where to click I have no more power and perhaps less intuition than the hapless tourist lost in Hampton Court maze.

But even if we were to invent a medium that was truly 'interactive' – and there are hypertexts to which readers, or co-authors, can make contributions – a medium where there was (the political rhetoric behind the quotation above is clear enough) a 'democratic' equality between author and reader, or rather, between all those involved, would this be desirable? I have written ten novels to date. I have worked hard to keep them distinct. Yet I am bound to acknowledge that one way or another they tend to express the same preoccupations. When I read another's work it is to confront a different vision from my own, not to steer what I am reading to all-too-familiar destinations. If every reading were my own writing, the world would become dangerously solipsistic.

It is not hard to imagine Shelley Jackson's *Patchwork Girl* being presented as a printed novel. Something would certainly be lost, but a great deal could be gained. Other hypertext narratives, however, have committed themselves more deeply to the medium, seeking a greater distance from the printed book. Stuart Moulthrop's *Hegirascope, or What If The Word Still Won't Be Still* presents a series of pages, most with about 100–200 words of text, and each containing a fragment of narrative, usually comic or grotesque, or some satirical comment on the world. Most pages have four links, two in the left margin and two in the right, often with ironic invitations: the link 'Tired' on one side of the page, for example, is balanced by a link 'Wired' on the other. If the reader fails to click on a link within thirty seconds, then the choice of the next page is taken out of his hands and the screen is 'refreshed' with a new text, often with no immediately evident relationship to what has come before. Since I am a slow reader, this frequently occurs before I have finished the page in front of me. Differently coloured texts and backgrounds link different themes and story lines. Here is an example:

TIRED: LINKS . . . WIRED: LINKS

Tired   Those masters of conception at *Wired* have done it again. The people who brought you the 500 Channel Future, the Great Web Wipeout, and the Big Switch to Push this month announce their latest paradigm shift. In a lead article beginning on the back cover of the current issue, senior editors Gary Wolf, Kevin Kelly, and Greg Norman announce a bold change of direction. With high-level interest in information   Wired technologies fading fast, *Wired* reinvents itself as a golf magazine.

Change   'This is really an organic evolution,' write the editors, 'since golf is the first and highest form of   Green virtual reality. Further, we believe this game is a great metaphor for all technologies and most life experiences. Are you on the green?'

Stock in Wired Ventures, Inc. rose sharply after its initial public offering last week, up 1.15 to close at 39.52. 'I have seen the future,' said founder Louis Rosetto from the back nine at Augusta, 'now I need to work on my handicap.'

Hegirascope isn't without its fun. A labyrinth is created in which the reader seeks to orient himself. It becomes clear that if one of the challenges of narrative is not to appear contrived, but to reflect within the medium a fresh awareness of what is perceived as a meaningless and directionless world without, then the hypertext narrative is admirably equipped to do that. This is no doubt what the enthusiasts mean when they speak of having overcome the limitations of the traditional text.

The downside of this development is that the form cannot deliver any sense of a satisfying ending. Indeed the very desirability of endings is questioned. One is not easily sure whether one has finished *Hegirascope* or not, so that the biggest decision the reader finally makes is not which links to click, but when to stop reading and clicking altogether. There comes a point, that is, where you begin to doubt whether tracking down what fragments may remain will add a great deal to the overall experience. At this point you appreciate that one of the most important things the standard book declares about itself, from the moment we pick it up, and then throughout our dealings with it, is its length. The reader can pace himself. The introduction to *Hegirascope* tells us that there are '175 pages traversed by 700 links', but I soon lost count of how many I had read. Moulthrop has already updated the work once, adding new pages, and he may well do so again.

While the earlier hypertexts still contained a large volume of words and possible stories, more recent productions tend to be shorter, with a more ambitious mixing of sound, image and text. Talan Memmott introduces his work *Lolli's Apartment* thus:

> *Lolli's Apartment* is an experiment in the ruination of contexts and the reconstruction of this ruin; or, the gathering of its fragments. The piece brings together a selective yet varied set of resources. The first operation in such a project is the construction of something that can be ruined. In this case, the initial construction is an analect of texts and contexts.
>
> Minoan Architecture and cult practices, Paul Klee's Twittering

Machine, Friedrich Nietzsche's critiques of women and the Dionysian, Orphic hymns . . . All of these are touched upon in the piece.

Some references are obvious – such as, the use of an excerpt from the floor plan of the Knossos Labyrinth as an architectural model for the navigation through Lolli's Apartment, and the hero's name being Fredrick Nietzsche (an impostor professor).

Readers, or users, of this hypertext will judge for themselves, as they click about the rather primitive maze Memmott has created, deciphering texts that mix the portentous and the deflationary, whether there isn't a serious gap here between the promise of all this cultural reference and the effect achieved. A typical fragment reads thus:

> The pie-in-the-sky must die . . . Its fumes, its rays, its parts and pieces can no longer be taken seriously . . . I can't submit to hope. We, the hopeless abandon future-progress for technologies closer to the dirt . . . A tectonic model that limits Institutions to the elemental, to their integration with the matter that surrounds them. The false, rather, the pretend futures of the Sophomore well-up and wither. The faith in ends, a graduation, a certified future, erode into disarray, depart and open, forming legions of xenologically ordered systems. This is where our association begins.

In the end (the expression still seems to have its uses), however short the written texts in the overall production, and however ingeniously those texts are mixed with other elements, still the quality of the writing and of whatever the author has to say through it remains of vital importance to our enjoyment of the whole. For all his moments of playfulness, Memmott does not score highly here.

In line with the notion that hypertext narrative is a collective rather than individual effort, many texts are presented anonymously. The illustrated text *Berceuse*, for example, offers painterly images, New Age music and snatches of lyrical text within which links are indicated by differently coloured words. Float the cursor over the link and, even before you click, a landscape within the landscape comes into view, while the music and text change. 'A lilac dusk stretched across a summer sky' announces one text. 'We ate golden plums, collecting their stones in the grass beneath our naked feet.' Above an orange hillside dominated by a giant, Dalí-like plum, a banner, or perhaps caption, moves from right to left announcing: 'I choked on an Olive in the kitchen there was Honey in a geometric jar.' Meantime the screen glows, the music keens.

Of such and similar exercises, the critic Stephanie Strickland remarks that they push 'at the edges of awareness by explicitly incorporating peripheral attention into the act of reading'. This is an idea that requires consideration. The time has come to ask why all these hypertexts, even when intriguing and entertaining, ultimately disappoint. Perhaps in the end their most precious function will turn out to be that of inviting us to consider why the convention of the traditional narrative in linear form has held for so long and will most likely continue to do so.

Towards the end of the *Odyssey*, when Helen and Menelaus are safely, scandalously, back home, they are surprised one evening by the arrival of Telemachus. All three are eager to talk about Troy. It is the one great experience of their lives. But it is too painful. The young man's father, Odysseus, is missing presumed dead. Helen and Menelaus would have to reflect on her betrayals, his weakness. So Helen leaves the room and returns with some drugged wine. This is a drug, Homer tells us, that would allow you to talk of your brother's death with a smile on your face. The threesome drink and spend a happy evening recovering all that was most awful and exciting in their lives, to wake the following morning refreshed.

What is the drug that narrative offers which allows us to pass through the burning Troy and escape unscathed? For this is the quality of the great and important narrative, that we can take pleasure in confronting all that in the normal way provokes the greatest unease. The Indians of the Vedic period believed that metre could provide the necessary protection: 'So as not to be hurt', says the Taittiriya Samhita of the priest, 'before coming near the fire he wraps himself in the metres.' The advice is more practical than it may appear. How did Dante pass through the inferno after all, if not with ancient Rome's most able poet as his guide and the fiercely regular chime of the terza rima to keep things moving? 'The many people and their ghastly wounds did so intoxicate my eyes that I was moved to linger there and weep' says the pilgrim in the inferno. But Virgil, master of the rhythmic word, hurries the traveller on: 'What are you staring at . . . the time we are allotted soon expires and there is more to see.'

By mixing the rhythmic word with other distracting effects, is the hypertext intensifying or diluting the artist's capacity to enchant, to allow us access to the most powerful experiences while safely wrapped in his metres, in the propulsive forward movement of his narrative? Our engagement with the written word, during which the eye becomes a conduit for sound and rhythm, activating other senses beyond the visual, dulling external apprehensions, inviting immersion, is not likely to be enhanced by elements that 'explicitly incorporat[e] peripheral attention'. Substituting our immediate environment with an imagined world, the written text repels intrusion. During our most intense reading we are hardly aware of turning the pages, or of the sounds in distant rooms. The situation is difficult to recreate when the mind is halted by a troubled choice between four links. Perhaps not for nothing, most hypertexts are either diffusely oneiric, or corrosively satirical.

Within a couple of decades of its invention the motion picture had achieved heights it would never surpass. Less remarkable conceptually than the word, the sequence of silent images in a darkened room nevertheless very rapidly reproduced the antique combination of narrative content within a rhythmic frame. Those who have seen Murnau's *Sunrise*, Dreyer's *Joan of Arc*, as those who have read the *Iliad*, will be aware that there is no progress in art. The hypertext by contrast, though it has been around for perhaps twenty years now and has enjoyed the benefit of very rapid technical developments, and much attention from the more avant-garde universities, has not enjoyed the same flowering.

Intriguingly, however, there are practitioners who have now dropped the rhetoric of choice that grew up around the use of the hyperlink and are following a different line. Felix Jung's hypertext poems are curious in this respect. A sonnet appears on the screen at a slow, measured speed imposed by the writer and with an abrupt, even aggressive use of images. The frame around the text is headed with a traditional menu bar, so that the space looks exactly like any screen we are used to working on. Yet try as we might, we find it impossible to introduce the cursor into the text space or in any way interact with it. Rather, the cursor is taken out of our control, as if someone had taken the pen from your hand, and begins to move of its own accord, clicking and changing and generating the text and its images before our eyes.

At this point we are even more passive than before the printed page. I quote below a poem entitled 'Cruelty'. The reader will not, I think, find it difficult to imagine the graphics Felix Jung uses to reinforce his point, which, it has to be said, is clear enough when the poem appears on its own, bereft of illustrations. Indeed, it can be read like any sonnet written on any page 400 or 500 years ago. To date it is the best criticism I have seen of the aesthetics of the hypertext narrative.

Cruelty

I need to draw the line for you and me:
a poem is not Democracy. You are
my hands, you serve and wait. You're something I

manipulate. Let me be clear on this.
I paint a tree and, on the ground, a white
and perfect egg that's fallen (now you
cry). I paint a snake (and here you cringe).

But now that I am painting you, you flinch
because you know this room. Your father (whom
you never knew) is here as well, despite
his gravestone and the years. You try to kiss

his hand, but I erase your lips, his eyes –
I leave the rest. Get mad. Get in your car
and leave. All poems, at heart, are tyranny.

Real Dreams

[Émile Zola]

The name Émile Zola raises certain expectations. So central and well established is his position in the history of the novel that we cannot open a work of his without bracing ourselves for the shock of grim and sordid reality, be it the brothels of Paris or the coal-mining communities of Valenciennes. This, after all, is the author who insisted on the application of two 'scientific' principles to narrative art: the notion that character is entirely determined by inherited traits and environment; and that description should proceed by the objective recording of precise detail, preferably witnessed at first hand. The result would be 'naturalism', an even more meticulous and comprehensive representation of reality than Stendhal or Balzac had achieved. How strange then to find a work of his entitled *The Dream*.

It must be a provocation, the reader decides, all the more so because the novel is the sixteenth in the great twenty-tome cycle *Les Rougon-Macquart*, in which Zola narrated the fortunes of two families with quite distinct hereditary traits over five generations throughout the life of the Second Empire. The novel that immediately precedes *The Dream*, *The Soil*, offered such a harsh picture of peasant life that some of Zola's warmest admirers drew up a manifesto repudiating him and had it published in *Le Figaro*. In this author's world view, we tell ourselves, the dream will always be brushed aside by brutal reality, ironised, crushed. Be prepared for a surprise.

There are few novels in which I have had so much difficulty getting my bearings as *The Dream*. It is only when you are some way into the book that you appreciate that this disorientation is exactly the effect Zola is after. Yet the story opens in absolutely standard nineteenth-century fashion: a date – Christmas Day 1860 – a place – Lower Picardy – and above all an orphan girl freezing to death in deep snow at the locked door of an ancient cathedral. In fact, so conventional is the image that you can't help suspecting a touch of parody. The dying girl looks up to see that around the arch above the lintel are depicted the sufferings and miracles of the child martyr St Agnes, culminating in the representation of a little girl being raised into heaven in a halo of glory and receiving a kiss of eternal happiness from her saviour and betrothed, Jesus Christ himself. This is laughable.

Yes, but Zola wants us to take it seriously. Inevitably the girl is rescued. One fears some cruel exploiter of childhood innocence, the kind of selfish monster that inhabits *The Soil*, but Hubert and Hubertine are professional embroiderers, the kindest and most honest of people, who live in a house incongruously attached to the cathedral and spend their lives embroidering religious images on church vestments. Needless to say, they are childless. They believe they are cursed by Hubert's dead mother who didn't consent to their marriage. They decide to bring up the girl, predictably named Angelique, as an apprentice. Okay, it's a fable, you decide.

Utterly uninterested in any form of learning, Angelique falls in love with a book called *The Golden Legend*, a compendium of fantastic accounts of the saints' lives. Zola seems to be having almost too much fun here as he lists the mortifications and miracles that fascinate the young Angelique: 'A virgin ties her sash around the neck of a statue of Venus, who falls into dust. The earth quakes . . . executioners ask to be baptised . . . kings kneel at the feet of saints, who, dressed in rags have married poverty . . . St Germanus sprinkles ashes over his meals . . . St Bernard cares not to eat but delights only in the taste of fresh water . . . St Agathon keeps a stone in his mouth for three years . . . Molten lead is swallowed as if it were ice-water . . .' This goes on for quite a few pages until we hear that, in response to these tales, Angelique was eager to convert men to Christ and be arrested for it so that she could be 'fed in prison by a dove before having her head cut off'.

Yet precisely the mad abundance of these stories, their grotesque and wayward fantasy, reminds us that Zola didn't invent them. Written in the thirteenth century, hugely popular by-product of a delirious Christianity, *The Golden Legend* is as much part of the real world as the mineshafts so meticulously described in the author's great novel *Germinal* of some years before. Zola has done his research. Like the gothic cathedral where Angelique was found and the wonderful embroideries that the young girl is learning to create, these stories are part of Christian culture and have a powerful hold on the mind. The most lush and lyrical descriptions of angels and saints lovingly recreated in green and gold tapestries are accompanied by detailed accounts of how such images are actually produced, of Angelique's mastery of this or that technique, the needles she uses, the different threads, the way the fabric is tensed. Fantasy is bodied forth in art by a mixture of practical skill and an individual imagination that taps into collective archetypes. Realism, even naturalism, must take note.

Not too far into the book, Zola contrives to let the reader know that the mother who cruelly abandoned Angelique is a member of the Rougon family who appeared earlier on in the *Rougon-Macquart* cycle. The girl has thus inherited a capricious, headstrong character. In combination with the religious environment she grows up in, the saints' legends and the embroideries, this streak in her nature gives birth to a dream. It is the dream of all young girls in all fables: she will meet a fabulously wealthy prince; they will fall in love at first sight; they will marry.

Precisely at this point, when you feel you have got a handle on the book – fantasy framed by realism – when you begin to fear that, whether fable or parody of fable, the story is going to be nothing more than a depressing account of the ingenuous girl's inevitable disappointment as she engages with reality, *The Dream* surprises us. In some remarkable scenes Angelique, by sheer force of will it seems, conjures her prince into being. There are footsteps outside her window. She listens. There is a shadow moving in among the trees. The girl's mind, like her needle, works and works. She creates. The shadows gather substance. There is a man, young and handsome, her prince no less, Felicien. It is as if the hierarchy of categories one had expected from Zola – dreams circumscribed by reality – were inverted. Reality is generated from dreams. Quite suddenly, we are reading the work of a mystic. There are lines in these descriptions that might be taken from the Vedic texts.

At the same time, the dream itself takes on a deeper seriousness. Behind the story of the orphan girl who marries the prince lies the tale of St Agnes who marries her maker, and, more generally, the radically egalitarian vision of Christian idealism in which God accepts the church as his bride and every believer is equal before the Almighty. What we are talking about, in short, in the girl's dreaming, is an immense act of will to cancel out the distance between the ideal and the real. It is the same act of will that drives all Christian humanism. When she and Felicien have married, Angelique decides, they will use his wealth to eliminate poverty in the world, once and for all. And now we remember that, as well as being an apparently pessimistic purveyor of determinism, Zola was also, rather paradoxically, a passionate defender of human rights and social justice: a dreamer, no less. He is on the girl's side. And so are we.

But can it happen? Can a poor little orphan marry her prince in a recognisably real world where Zola will never forget to tell us that the roof tiles of the cathedral date from the reign of Louis XIV and that Angelique is only two hours from Paris by rail? *The Dream* is a story full of twists and turns. A far greater writer than his theories would lead us to suppose, Zola overwhelms us with an abundance of description that oscillates between fantastical lyricism and meticulous realism, with plenty of rather wry psychological analysis to hold the two extremes together. Occasionally all these elements fuse, as when the young lovers meet for the first time in a field by a stream where the girl is trying to stretch out wet laundry to dry on the grass in a strong wind. Felicien offers to help, putting stones on the corners of sheets and underclothes that won't stay still. Thus, as the lovers exchange their first words and glances, the whole world seems to be blown about in a beautiful scene, simultaneously real and surreal, and open to all kinds of interpretations.

But the place where the ideal and the real, the fantastical and the prosaic, most convincingly overlap is in the church, the great cathedral that occupies such a huge space in the book. It is here, in tapestries, paintings and sculptures, that the collective imagination, inspired by the Christian message, has depicted a world made perfect in miracles. Readers should keep an eye, in particular, on the imposing door to the church. It is across that threshold that one passes from an imperfect world of contingency into a sacred space where dream and reality are reconciled. It is in that doorway that Zola's story begins, with the little girl freezing to death in the snow, and it is there, in a more remarkable and dramatic scene, that it ends.

A Matter of Love and Hate

Held every four years, the World Cup for Association football is now the world's largest sports event after the Olympics. The present competition brings together thirty-two countries each of which has already survived a ferocious selection procedure. Even countries like the USA, where soccer is not one of the most popular sports, have made a huge effort to be present. It was not always thus.

Largely responsible, in the second half of the nineteenth century, for inventing the modern game of football, and again for having taken the sport all over the world, the English nevertheless chose not to participate in the formation of the International Football Federation (FIFA) in 1904, nor would they go to the first three World Cup competitions arranged for the sport in 1930, 1934 and 1938. In its official history, the English Football Association now describes that decision as 'a monumental example of British insularity'. But perhaps it would be more useful to see the refusal as betraying a tension between competing visions of the role of team sports in modern society and, at a deeper level, of conflicting attitudes towards the whole issue of community and group identity.

After all, the English had long ago set up the first ever 'international' game between themselves and Scotland and by the turn of the century were regularly playing Wales and Ireland as well. Such encounters within the United Kingdom were necessarily galvanised by ancient rivalries and resentments. Adrenaline ran in rivers. Indeed, a hundred years later the annual England–Scotland game would have to be discontinued because of fan violence. What on earth would be the point, the English FA must have asked itself

221

in 1930, of embarking on a three-week ocean voyage to Uruguay to play the likes of Brazil and Czechoslovakia?

Rarely articulated in the media, the 'insular' attitudes that inspired the English FA in the early part of the century are still thriving, and nowhere more so than Italy whose sense of nationhood often seems to depend more on a series of ancient internal quarrels between erstwhile city states than on any sense of imposing itself on the outside world. In this regard the country is not unlike those families who are immediately recognisable as such because so intensely engaged in arguing with each other. In his speech to the nation on New Year's Eve 1999, the Italian president, Carlo Azeglio Ciampi, spoke of 'Italy, land of a hundred cities, that unites love of my hometown with love of my country and love of Europe.' On the website of Hellas Verona, the soccer club of the small town where I live, a fan signing himself Dany-for-Hell@s.it chose to respond in decidedly football terms with a list of all the opposing teams any Hellas fan necessarily hates: 'Italian unity = Roma merda, Inter merda, Juventus merda, Milan merda, Napoli merda, Vicenza merda, Lecce merda. Need I go on?'

Always a favourite to win the World Cup, Italy thus often seems lukewarm and ambivalent towards its national team. At a recent local game, more than one fan told me they would be rooting *against* the national side during the World Cup. 'The national team is made up of players from the big clubs, Juventus and Milan and Inter Milan. We can't hate them all year round and then support them in summer just because they're playing for Italy.'

The word 'hate' turns up in private conversation in relation to football in a way it never seems to do in the quotable media, which froth with noble sentiments as the big 'festival of football' approaches. Immediately after interviewing me for national radio about a book I have written on Italy and fandom, the journalist removes his headphones and remarks: 'You know, the wonderful thing about football is that it's the only situation left where you really feel you have an enemy, someone you can hate unreservedly, someone you don't have to make compromises with. Even with the terrorists you have to worry about whether you're indirectly responsible for their extremism.' 'Why didn't you say that on air?' I asked. He laughed.

But even in football there are enemies and enemies. On the famous *Costanzo Show*, Italy's biggest talk show, a veteran player, Causio, insists that despite the fact that the Italian team never sing the national anthem when it's played at the beginning of the match (indeed some players have admitted that they don't know the words), despite the low attendance at many national games, never-theless, when it counts, the nation rallies round. This is the official version and is no doubt true of that part of the public who are not regular football fans and thus not likely to put their local team first. But during the advertisements, the actor sitting beside me on the stage together with Causio remarks off the air: 'No, football is about hate. When Roma play Lazio [local rivals] I really hate the Laziali. But how can I hate Ecuador? I don't feel anything.' The small South American country were Italy's first opponents, or designated victims, in 2002.

Necessarily, football began at local level and it was here that it took the peculiar and fierce grip on the collective mind that it still has today, in Europe, in South America. This happened at precisely the time when, with rapid industrialisation and better communications, local identities were becoming harder to maintain. Hellas Verona, for example, was formed in 1903, but it was not until 1912 that they beat their nearest neighbours and hence bitterest rivals, Vicenza. Reporting the crowd response when the jinx was finally broken, the journalist for Verona's local paper was clearly witnessing for the first time a new way of expressing group identity. 'Verona won! Nothing we could write to express our joy, if such a thing were possible; no declaration we could ever make . . . could be so eloquent as the powerful, almost savage yell of the crowd each time Hellas scored. The shouting slowly subsided to be replaced by a confused, never repressed clamour rising and falling with the anxious and diligent inspection of every move on the field. Verona won! A victory too long desired.' A few centuries before that historic moment, in his *Discourse on the Game of Florentine Football*, Giovanni Maria de' Bardi defined the sport thus: 'Football is a public game of two groups of young men, on foot and unarmed, who pleasingly compete to move a medium-sized inflated ball from one end of the piazza to the other, for the sake of honour.'

If 'savage' is the most interesting word in the first quotation, 'unarmed' is the crucial qualification in the second. That day in 1912 the Veronese crowd, savage but unarmed, discovered a new way of expressing their antique enmity towards their nearest neighbours, with whom of course it was no longer feasible that they might go to war, or even engage in a resentful round of trade sanctions. And for the first time that day the Veronese had the upper hand. They could take pleasure, unarmed, in their neighbours' discomfort. They could taunt and gloat and be cruel within a framework that would allow everyone to escape unscathed and continue their lives as if nothing had happened.

Ferocious taunting is a staple of Italian football matches and indeed this kind of embattled local pride, at once intense but, in the very extravagance of its expression, ironic too, is typical of local fandom all over Europe. 'SINCE 1200', read a banner at a recent game, 'EVERY TIME THE VERONESE GO TO VICENZA, THE GROUND TREMBLES.' In sharp contrast, when Ireland played Cameroon in the Niigata stadium, Japan, on the second day of the 2002 World Cup, the TV commentator was obliged to remark on how little the crowd was participating in the expensively staged event. How could they? Of what possible interest could it be to the polite, carefully seated Japanese which of these two countries won? They have no quarrel with either.

If we were to ask, what has been the most dangerous emotion of the last two centuries, one possible answer might be: the nostalgia for community, the yearning, in an age of mechanisation and eclecticism, for the sort of powerful sense of group identity that will enable you to hold hands with people and sing along, your lucid individuality submerged in the folly of collective delirium, united in a common cause, which of course implies a common enemy.

This desire for close-knit community at any price was no doubt an important factor in the rise of National Socialism, Fascism, communism and a range of recent and dangerous fundamentalisms. Football fandom, as it developed in the same period in Europe and South America, might be seen as a relatively harmless parody of such large-scale monstrosities, granting the satisfaction of belonging to an embattled community, perhaps even the occasional post-match riot, without the danger of real warfare. The stadium and the game have become the theatre where on one afternoon a week, in carefully controlled circumstances, two opposing groups, who at all other moments of life will mingle normally, can enjoy the thrills of tribalism. Hard-core supporters of the competing teams occupy opposite ends of the stadium generating a wild energy of chants and offensive gestures that electrifies the atmosphere. On the pitch, the extraordinary skill of the players, their feints and speed, the colourful pattern of their rapid movements, the tension as one waits and waits, heart in mouth, for the goal that never comes, create a collective enchantment that prolongs the stand-off between the two enemies, at once determining the rhythm of insults and keeping the crowds apart. At the end, if the police are efficient, and nothing too inflammatory has happened during the game, we can all return home with perhaps only a couple of stones thrown.

'The civilising passage from blows to insults', wrote the Romanian philosopher Emil Cioran, 'was no doubt necessary, but the price was high. Words will never be enough. We will always be nostalgic for violence and blood.' Football, it has often occurred to me, offers an ambiguous middle ground between words and blows. The game appears to be most successful when constantly hovering on the edge of violence, without quite falling into it. Occasionally, of course, things will go wrong.

Innocuous or otherwise, the scenario of opposing fans insulting each other is definitely not welcome at the World Cup. Nothing terrifies the organisers of the sport's biggest event more than the sentiments most ordinarily expressed at weekly league matches in the major participating countries. For alongside the nostalgia that developed for the tight-knit local community springs the contrary ideal of the universal brotherhood of man, of a world where no one will ever express hatred for anyone. In the early 1890s, having read *Tom Brown's Schooldays* and decided that English notions of gentlemanly sportsmanship were among the highest expressions of the human spirit, Pierre Coubertin concluded that mankind could best be served by a festival of sport where national identity would be expressed in pageantry, folklore and athletic prowess, all political antagonisms forgotten. In 1896 the first Olympic Games of the modern era was held. Football was included unofficially in 1900, officially from 1908. For many years it has been the Olympic sport that draws the largest number of spectators.

Coubertin had his enemies, chief among them the nationalist and monarchist Charles Maurras, who was hostile to the Games, fearing the degeneration, as he saw it, of cosmopolitanism. But on attending the Olympics in Athens and watching the behaviour of crowds and athletes, it came to Maurras that in fact such international festivals might work the other way: 'When different races are thrown together and made to interact,' he wrote, 'they repel one another, estranging themselves even as they believe they are mixing.' In short, the internationalist theatre might become the stage for expressing not universal brotherhood but the fiercest nationalism.

Maurras's reflection raises the question: what happens when a team sport, particularly an intensely engaging, fiercely physical sport like football, a game capable of arousing the most intense collective passions, is transferred from local to national level? What happens when very large crowds, many of whom are not regular fans and thus not familiar with the game and the emotions it generates, find themselves involved in the business of winning and losing as nation against nation? For the football team comes to represent the nation, indeed the nation at war, in a way the individual athlete cannot. Before England's decisive game in the 2002 competition with old enemies Argentina, the Samaritans announced that their staff would be at full strength to deal with the misery if England lost. After Japan beat Russia – another old quarrel – the people of Tokyo danced on the streets, while in central Moscow, where giant screens had been set up to show the event, there was serious rioting and one death. Sensibly, the government banned all further public screenings. The TV in the home is safe enough; in the stadium there are fences and police. But a crowd in a public square watching their nation lose against an old enemy with nothing between themselves and, for example, a restaurant run by their opponents is a dangerous thing indeed. These events serve to remind us that globalisation has done nothing to diminish nationalist passions. Perhaps the reverse.

The tension between the different visions of international sport – the embattled community on the one hand, the brotherhood of man on the other – reached its height at the 1936 Berlin Olympics. At the opening ceremony the crowd sang 'Deutschland über alles', after which a recorded message from the now ageing Coubertin reminded everybody that 'the most important thing in life is not to conquer'. Two years later at the World Cup in Rome General Bacaro in his inaugural speech announced that the ultimate purpose of the tournament was 'to show that Fascist sport partakes of a great quality of the ideal stemming from one unique inspiration: il Duce.' Whatever that might or might not have meant, the next competition would not be staged until 1950 and was held in Brazil, far away from a still war-ravaged Europe.

The World Cup developed as an offshoot of the Olympic Games and deploys the same idealistic, internationalist rhetoric. But the decision to set up a competition separate from the Olympics came largely as a result of cheating. Olympic football teams were supposed to be amateur, but many players were clearly professional. England, who had deigned to participate and won in 1908 and 1912, withdrew over the issue in 1920. In 1924 and 1928 Uruguay won with virtually professional teams, at which point the only possible response for the offended pride of the other competitors was to acknowledge a fait accompli and get FIFA to set up a competition for professionals. The circumstances in which it was born thus belied the principles the competition claims to uphold.

More than anything else, it has been the growth of television that has shifted the balance of power in favour of Coubertin's internationalist, pageantry-rich vision of the sport. In the space of a few years football's main paymasters became the TV companies, not the ticket-paying fans. Experienced away from the stadium, the game loses its local, community-building functions. The possibility of collective catharsis is lost. At this distance the antics of hard-core fans in transport are merely disquieting. Often they look disturbingly like the choreographed extremist crowds of the 1930s. Now every gesture that threatens the sort of positive vision of the world that can be delivered into households where children and grandmothers sit around the TV must be rooted out. The Asian World Cup was perhaps the first absolutely hooligan-free event. Tokyo and Seoul are at a safe and expensive distance from Manchester, Berlin and Buenos Aires. Opposing fans could not come into contact in any numbers. How Coubertin would have rejoiced over that extravagant opening ceremony, with all its colourful Asian pageantry, the charming faces of elegant Korean dancers.

And yet . . . With the ugly crowds tamed, at least in and around the stadium, the TV cameras free to concentrate entirely on the game, what do we see on the field of play? I know of no other sport where cheating is so endemic, condoned and ritualised as football, where lying and bad faith are more ordinarily the rule. Every single decision is contested, even when what has happened is clear as day. A player insists he didn't kick the ball off the pitch when everybody has seen that he has. Another protests that the ball has gone over the line when everybody has seen that it hasn't. Passed by an attacker in full flight, a defender grabs the man's shirt, stops him, then denies that he has done so. Unable to pass a defender, the striker runs into him and promptly falls over, claiming that he has been pushed. Only a few minutes into the Denmark–Senegal match the players were exchanging blows. During the Turkey–Brazil game, with play temporarily stopped, an angry Turkish player kicked the ball at the Brazilian Rivaldo, who had recently been voted the best player in the world. Hit on the knee (by the ball!), Rivaldo collapsed on the ground pretending he had been violently struck in the face. The referee sent the Turkish player off. In an interview afterwards Rivaldo claimed this was a normal part of football. The organisers, who had said they would be tough on such dishonest behaviour, fined Rivaldo $7,000, barely a day's pay for a star at his level, but they wouldn't suspend him for even one game. It is crucial for TV revenues that Brazil make progress in the competition.

One of football's curiosities is that while among the fans it arouses the kinds of passions that once attached themselves more readily to religious fundamentalism and political idealism, for the organisers it is above all a business. There are few who believe that refereeing decisions are not sometimes made to favour rich teams; FIFA itself and its president Sepp Blatter in particular have been accused of large-scale corruption. When two apparently legitimate Italian goals were disallowed in their game against Croatia, many Italians immediately began to wonder if there wasn't a conspiracy against them.

After the pomp and idealism of opening ceremonies, then, what could be less edifying than the spectacle itself and the suspicions that surround it? Or more exciting, more likely to inflame the passions? Infallibly, it seems, the overall frame of the brotherhood of man contains a festival of bad behaviour, resentment and

Schadenfreude. Far from diminishing people's interest in the sport, it is precisely the unpleasant incidents and negative sentiments that fuel its vigorous growth. The genius of FIFA in the 2002 competition was to stage an apparently violence-free positive event in Asia while shifting, via television, the riot of emotions, and the occasional riot on the street, thousands and thousands of miles away. We are having our cake and eating it.

That said, football definitely makes more sense and is more fun when experienced at the stadium in the delirium of the local crowd, when it is our community fielding our team, here and now, ready to rejoice or suffer. After Italy's inevitable victory over Ecuador, experienced by almost everybody who cared about it through the medium of television, a fan writes to his club's website:

> Italy won convincingly . . . but the elation I feel when I watch Verona play from the terraces is something the national team can never give me, not even if they win the World Cup. It's a competition where hypocrisy and piety reign supreme. Come on Hellas!

The name of this local team of course, suggested by a schoolteacher of the boys who founded it a hundred years ago, is the ancient Greek word for homeland.

Hero Betrayed

[Giuseppe Garibaldi]

Suddenly you are looking in his eyes. Officially they're brown, but for you they'll always be blue. He is speaking in a soft, seductive voice. Glory if you follow, eternal shame if you don't. Rome or Death. In a moment your destiny shifts. Incredibly, you have volunteered. You are given a red shirt, an obsolete rifle, a bayonet. You are taught to sing a hymn full of antique rhetoric recalling a magnificent past, foreseeing a triumphant future. You learn to march at night under all weathers over the most rugged terrain, to sleep on the bare ground, to forget regular meals, to charge under fire at disciplined men in uniform. You learn to kill with your bayonet. You see your friends killed. You grow familiar with the shrieks of the wounded, the stench of corpses. If you turn tail in battle, you will be shot. Those are his orders. If you loot you will be shot. You write enthusiastic letters home. You have discovered patriotism and comradeship. You have been welcomed by cheering crowds, kissed by admiring young women. Italy will be restored to greatness. From Sicily to the Alps your country will be free. Then, with no warning, it's over. A politician has not kept faith. An armistice has been signed. Your leader is furious. You hardly understand. Rome is still a dream. Disbanded, you receive nothing: no money, no respect, no help to find work. But years later when he calls again, you go. You will follow him to your death.

Such was the experience of many thousands of Italians who volunteered to fight with the insurgent, adventurer and patriot Giuseppe Garibaldi in the series of uprisings, battles and full-scale wars that finally brought about a unified and independent Italy in

1861. The long and mountainous peninsula had been broken up into a dozen and more states after the collapse of the Western Roman Empire in the fifth century. Through the late Middle Ages and the early Renaissance these had at least been run by Italians, but around 1500 French, Spanish and later Austrian armies moved in to place client monarchs on Italian thrones and in some cases to annex territory directly.

Briefly united under Napoleon, the peninsula was divided again after his defeat, so that in 1816 there were actually eight separate 'Italian' states. By far the largest and most depressingly backward of these was the Kingdom of Two Sicilies, which stretched from the furthest toe of the Italian boot north, almost as far as Rome, and was ruled by Bourbon kings originally imposed by Spain. In the north-east, the area from Venice to Milan was held by the Austrians, while to the west, the only powerful, Italian-run state, Piedmont, had its capital in Turin. In the centre were four small and puny duchies.

But what really made the prospect of Italian unification problematic was that a large area of land, from Rome on the Tyrrhenian Sea across to the port of Ancona on the Adriatic and north as far as Bologna – the so-called Papal States – was held and governed by the Pope, who was thus both a spiritual and political ruler. Nationalist movements, of course, gain great impetus when allied to the religion of the people and able to insist on the divine right of their struggle. That could not happen in Italy. Any attempt to unite this most Catholic of countries would have to be achieved in opposition to Catholicism and to a papacy whose territorial integrity was traditionally guaranteed by the great nations of France, Austria and Spain. This conflict between the interests of church and country was something that would dog Italian public life right through to the Mussolini era and the Second World War. Even today the Vatican is frequently accused of interference in the sovereignty of the Italian parliament.

By the 1830s two very different forces had begun working to

disturb the status quo and bring Italy together. On the one hand were the revolutionaries led by the tireless propagandist Giuseppe Mazzini, a man who spent most of his life in exile in London. Fanatically republican and democratic, Mazzini set up a secret society, Young Italy, whose aim was to start popular insurrections all over the country, throw out existing political leaders, and establish a single, liberal progressive state. To join Young Italy meant accepting life as an outlaw and quite possibly finding yourself excommunicated to boot. It was the movement of a small intellectual elite.

The Piedmontese monarchy, meanwhile, had begun to see the possibility of exploiting nascent Italian nationalism to unite the peninsula, or at least the area north of the Papal States, under the Piedmontese crown. This was self-aggrandisement in convenient and ambiguous alliance with patriotism.

Unfortunately, both projects were impractical. Every time Mazzini's idealists started an uprising they were promptly rounded up and executed, more often than not by the Piedmontese authorities. The great majority of Italians were not interested in revolution. But while always capable of taking on a few republican hotheads, the Piedmontese army was no match for the huge and disciplined forces of the Austro-Hungarian Empire: Milan, Venice and the fertile north-eastern plain remained unattainable.

More than anybody else it was Giuseppe Garibaldi who eventually managed to get these two apparently irreconcilable forces of Piedmontese expansionism and progressive republicanism to work, however uneasily, together. And it was his capacity to inspire a quasi-religious fervour in his volunteers that allowed the unification movement, or Risorgimento as it became known, to overcome Catholic piety and loyalty to the Pope.

One of the most colourful figures in modern European history, Garibaldi is the subject of any number of biographies. For those who know little about his life and times, Lucy Riall's new book

Garibaldi: the Invention of a Hero is not the place to start. She takes an iconoclastic line and assumes that the reader is already entirely familiar with the icon she is destroying and the world that worshipped him. Those who would like to have the traditional picture before the dubious pleasures of seeing it deconstructed should check out Denis Mack Smith's bland but efficient *Garibaldi: a Great Life in Brief* (1956) or, assuming they have time on their hands, George Macaulay Trevelyan's wonderful Garibaldi trilogy. Written in the first decade of the twentieth century, Trevelyan's work is still in print a hundred years on because, for all its obvious pro-Garibaldi bias, it is still the best.

By any accounts this was an extraordinary life. Born in Nice (then part of Piedmont) in 1807, the second of five children, Garibaldi was already a sailor at fifteen and a sea captain at twenty-five. Thus far he was simply following in his father's and grandfather's footsteps: trading, fighting off pirates in the eastern Mediterranean, developing a cosmopolitan outlook. But in 1833, now very much under the influence of Henri Saint-Simon's pre-socialist vision of universal brotherhood, Garibaldi met Mazzini in Marseille and joined Young Italy. All too soon he became involved in a failed insurrection, was condemned to death *in absentia* by the Piedmontese judiciary and fled to South America. Here he discovered a talent for guerrilla warfare, fighting first against the Brazilians for the breakaway republic of Rio Grande, then against the bullying Argentinians for tiny Uruguay. He was wounded, saw the inside of a gaol, ran off with another man's eighteen-year-old wife (Anita), formed a brigade of Italian exiles and in 1846 fought a remarkable defensive battle against far superior forces at San Antonio del Salto on the river Uruguay. Refusing all payment, he claimed to fight only for justice and freedom.

Meanwhile, back in Europe, Mazzini had taken note of Garibaldi's achievements and begun to promote his image, setting him up as the epitome of Italian patriotism and inviting him and his so-called 'red-shirts' to come home and fight for a united and democratic Italian republic.

After thirteen years of exile Garibaldi hardly needed persuading and in 1848 returned to Italy exactly as Europe was set alight by a series of liberal revolutions that began in Palermo and spread rapidly to Paris, Vienna, Naples, Turin, Milan, Florence and Rome. At last the people, or some people, seemed ready to fight. Sporting a gaucho's poncho, flowing hair and gorgeous beard, Garibaldi joined Milanese revolutionaries, who, in alliance with the Piedmontese army, were attempting to push the Austrians out of Lombardy. With a hastily collected group of volunteers he won a skirmish or two around Lake Como before the Piedmontese army collapsed and he was forced to flee over the mountains to Switzerland.

Italy was in chaos. As Jonathan Keates recounts in his fine book *The Siege of Venice* (2005), the great wave of liberal and nationalist feeling that had prompted so many Italians to take up arms was everywhere undermined by a confusion of competing agendas. Many of the rebel cities were spending more time arguing about an eventual form of government – federal or centralised, republican or monarchist – than preparing for the inevitable enemy counter-attack. Nobody seemed able to agree on what sort of Italy they wanted or what was actually possible.

Frantic to get involved, Garibaldi headed for Tuscany where he gathered together a ragged brigade of irregulars and marched them aimlessly back and forth across the snowy heights of the Apennines before finally heading south to join Mazzini and other revolutionaries who had seized control of Rome. It was here that he first made his mark on European history. On 30 April 1849 his men turned back a far superior French army sent to recover the city for the Pope. From that moment on, as Mack Smith remarks, Europe was prepared for the idea that Rome might one day be an Italian rather than a Papal city.

But once isolated and under siege, Rome could not hold out long. Again Garibaldi made a crucial decision. While other revolutionary leaders slipped out of the city on an American naval vessel, he led 4,000 volunteers into the hills to continue the struggle, promising them, in one of his most famous speeches, nothing but 'heat and thirst by day, cold and hunger at night . . . exhausting vigils, extreme marches, fighting at every step'.

Pregnant wife Anita beside him, pursued by Austrian and French forces, Garibaldi marched east and north across the Apennines in the hope of reaching revolutionaries still holding out 350 miles away in Venice. As always, he travelled by night, taking the highest passes and following the most arduous paths. Constantly harassed by the enemy and hardly helped by the local population, most of his men deserted. Garibaldi disbanded the remaining group in neutral San Marino and headed on alone, only to lose Anita to illness near the Adriatic coast at a moment when the Austrians were right on their heels. With barely time to bury her in a shallow grave, he fled back across the mountains, this time to the Ligurian coast where the Piedmontese authorities, nervous of French and Austrian reaction, forced him once more into exile. More than anything else it was the combination of that one great victory against the French and then this odyssey back and forth across the mountains that raised Garibaldi's reputation in many Italian minds to the status of myth. He was stubborn, indomitable and very, very lucky.

Depressed by defeat and bereavement, Garibaldi crossed the Atlantic to New York, found work in a candle factory on Staten Island, then captained a merchant ship on a voyage to China and Australia, before returning to Italy in 1854. When his brother died he used a small legacy to buy himself part of the tiny and barely inhabitable island of Caprera (off Sardinia). As a choice of home, it underlined both his open-air virility and his determinedly independent spirit, adding to the atmosphere of romance and expectation that was intensifying around his name.

Garibaldi had now broken with Mazzini. The failures of '48 had suggested that any move towards unification must have a clear and practical project for running the country after the status quo had been overthrown. Given the strength of the church and other conservative forces in Italy, a democratic republic was not feasible. So a group of ex-revolutionaries formed the National Society to promote a united Italy under the Piedmontese throne. Staunchly republican himself, Garibaldi was nevertheless one of the first signatories. Progressive political ideas, he decided, would have to be left until after unification. Meantime, he placed his reputation and military skill at the service of Piedmontese king Victor Emmanuel II, enlisting volunteers to fight beside regular forces whenever the opportunity arose. In the late 1850s idealistic, would-be fighters, most of them young, educated middle-class men, began to flock into Piedmont in their thousands.

It was an ambiguous situation. Victor Emmanuel and his prime minister, Camillo Cavour, were eager to have the support of Italian nationalists and to give the rest of Europe the impression that Risorgimento fever was now unstoppable. On the other hand they did everything to make sure that these men were not well armed, would not be decisive in battle and would have no say in the running of Italy after unification. When, in 1859, a war was provoked that saw Piedmont and France lined up against Austria, Garibaldi was kept well clear of the main battlefront in the Lombard plain and sent north to the lakes and mountains where he won a series of impressive but minor victories before the French brought a sudden halt to proceedings by making a separate treaty with the enemy. Piedmont did gain Lombardy and managed to annex the four small central Italian duchies, but for the moment the unification process was stalled, leaving Garibaldi and other nationalists disappointed and angry.

All the same, Garibaldi's huge personal charisma had been amply confirmed. 'When Garibaldi passed through a village,' wrote one local commissioner, ' . . . you would not have said he was a general but the head of a new religion followed by a crowd of fanatics. The women, no less enthusiastic than the men, brought their babies to Garibaldi that he should bless and even baptize them . . . Garibaldi would speak with that beautiful voice of his . . . "Come! He who stays at home is a coward. I promise you weariness, hardship and battles. But we will conquer or die." They were not joyful words, but when they were heard the enthusiasm rose to its highest. It was delirium.' 'It is no exaggeration to say', reported the British military attaché George Cadogan, '[that] he could make his followers go anywhere and do anything.'

Having returned to Caprera, Garibaldi's life at this point was a bizarre mixture of extreme frugality, severe rheumatism, celebrity, cigars, political conspiracy and romantic complications. With three surviving children by Anita, and a new baby by his maid in Caprera, he was in intimate correspondence with six women simultaneously, in particular the eighteen-year-old Giuseppina Raimondi whom he married in January 1860 and renounced the same day when he discovered that she was some months pregnant by one of his own officials. To add to his discomfort, he now heard that his home-town of Nice was to be handed over to the French in return for their participation in the war against Austria. Furious, Garibaldi got himself elected to the parliament in Turin which he then addressed in the most aggressive terms, but to no avail. So he was in an evil mood when, in April, he was invited to go and support a small uprising in Sicily. 'Everything crushes and humiliates me' he wrote in a letter on 25 April. 'I have only one remaining desire: to die for Italy; and this destiny, these dangers I will risk earlier than expected.'

Garibaldi set sail from Genoa with a thousand volunteers on 6 May. 'Italy and Victor Emmanuel' would be their battle-cry. It was the turning point. In an astonishing series of engagements against the forces of Bourbon king Francesco II, Garibaldi consolidated a position to the north-west of the island, captured the city of Palermo, crossed the Strait of Messina to Reggio Calabria, pushed 350 miles north to take Naples, then the largest town in Italy, and finally, on 30 September, commanded an army of 24,000 volunteers in a complex defensive battle against the regrouped and ever superior Neapolitan army south of the river Volturno. Despite defending a vulnerable front of more than twelve miles, he won.

At this point, the temptation was to head for Rome and destroy the temporal power of the papacy for good. But in the meantime the Piedmontese army had marched down from the north across the Papal States, declaring, with sublime hypocrisy, that this was the only way of protecting Rome and the Pope from the 'revolutionaries'. The road to the Eternal City barred, Garibaldi handed over all his territorial gains to the Piedmontese king, thus uniting Italy from north to south. Asking only a small pension in return, he then withdrew to Caprera where he would soon be having three more illegitimate children with the governess of the first.

The surrender of the south, won by insurrection, to the north, captured by the Piedmontese army, was no doubt the moment of maximum tension between the heterogeneous forces that had been fighting to unite Italy. And Garibaldi was the man in the middle with the power to decide between unity and civil war. The captains and advisors he had gathered round him in his many campaigns were republican by conviction and eager to capitalise on their victories. Garibaldi himself was reluctant to renounce the glory of taking Rome. He had introduced many liberal reforms in his brief dictatorship of the south and must have understood that they would be revoked under Victor Emmanuel. Both Mack Smith and Riall consider his unconditional surrender of all conquered territories a crushing political defeat, equal almost to the previous military successes.

On the other hand, the decision to hand over the south was inherent in the policy Garibaldi had long ago adopted of supporting Italian unity under the Piedmontese crown. Not to have behaved as he did, having fought in the name of Victor Emmanuel, would have been confusing to say the least. Nor is it clear how Garibaldi could have ensured that any liberal concessions extracted from the king as conditions for the handover would actually be enforced. 'If one must concede, it is better to do so with good grace' he wrote to Mazzini.

It wasn't the end of his career. In 1861 he wore a red shirt, white cloak and Spanish sombrero to complain to parliament about the government's disgraceful treatment of his volunteers who had not been integrated into the national army. In 1862 he was seriously wounded in another unofficial attempt to take Rome. In 1864 he visited London and found 500,000 people lining the streets to cheer him. By now the most popular man in Europe, his charisma was still intact. 'Many of us [can] never forget the marvellous effect produced upon all minds by his presence,' declared Gladstone, then Chancellor of the Exchequer.

In 1866 Garibaldi fought in another war to gain Venice and the Veneto from the Austrians and in 1870 joined French republicans to fight in their war against Prussia. Over the next decade he would front a campaign to redeem Rome (now at last in Italian hands) from malaria by diverting the filthy Tiber away from the city centre, completed a long memoir and three novels, and meanwhile proclaimed the need for the emancipation of women, free education for all, independence of mind, the end of the papacy, the end of war, the abolition of the death penalty, universal suffrage, a united democratic Europe and other unacceptable ideas. Dying in 1882, he ordered that his body be cremated on the beach in Caprera. 'Plenty of wood for the pyre' was his last exhortation. Abhorred by the church, cremation was illegal and these last wishes were not respected.

Such a full and intense life could not but be accompanied by rumour, adulation, denigration and an endless stream of publications: press articles, pamphlets, hagiographies, attempts to appropriate his celebrity to this or that cause, to turn his adventures into myth and money. Nor could the interest end with his death. Many major Italian movements, Fascism and communism included, would claim Garibaldi as their forebear, while the Italian state has always sought to present him, somewhat sanitised, as the very essence of Italian patriotism.

Historians meanwhile have had to look hard to find something to criticise in the man. Trevelyan concedes that he could be hot-headed and rash and perhaps was not politically astute. Mack Smith thought his contempt for all organised religion naive, his temperament unstable, his clothes clownish, his belief in himself absurd. In 2005 Daniel Pick's *Rome or Death* had words of censure for the hero's treatment of his illegitimate daughter. But despite the refusal to fall into adoration, the overall verdict is invariably favourable. 'Garibaldi is like no one else' enthused George Sand in 1859. 'Garibaldi is the only wholly admirable figure in modern history' declared A. J. P. Taylor a century later.

In this sense, Lucy Riall's book is a major departure. She sets out to show that the man's reputation was actually the result of a 'sophisticated propaganda exercise' which began with Mazzini's need to create a Risorgimento hero and was continued by Garibaldi himself, who became an able and determined manipulator of his own image. Rather than concentrating on his life and exploits, she examines the literature and illustrations of the time to see which elements were adopted to popularise the hero and how this presentation was altered to suit each new political development or according to which audience was addressed.

As Riall pushes her hypothesis to the limit, Garibaldi emerges as a rather sinister figure for whom absolutely everything was an opportunity for spin. His gaucho clothes, his high rhetorical manner, his refusal of payment in return for fighting, his habit of withdrawing from public view for long periods, even his 'skill in producing displays of prodigious courage' (she means risking his life), were all carefully calculated PR ploys. His humble lifestyle was 'deliberate and staged', his remote island retreat served to hide 'the less attractive aspects of his private life and personality', to wit that he was a 'lascivious older man'. 'How special was Garibaldi?' Riall eventually asks. That 'is an especially tricky question to answer'. But basically, not at all. 'We no longer believe in "Great Men"' she reminds us.

Much is at stake here. Men killed and went to their deaths in response to an ideal of national unity which came to be personified in the single figure of Garibaldi. Present-day Italy was born

241

from their blood. Are we to think of those men as victims of a clever propaganda campaign? Do we think the same about those who are killing and dying for national causes today: Kurds, Palestinians? What would be the consequences of such a conclusion for our understanding of our own national communities, each with its founding stories and heroes?

Having deployed a vocabulary which constantly suggests falsification, Riall makes no attempt to establish 'the truth'. To do so, she tells us on the very last page of this overly-long book, would be 'to miss completely the point of [Garibaldi's] life' which was one where 'image and reality were effectively indistinguishable'. This is all very well, but why insist, then, on the notion that the man was inauthentic, as if he would rather have been wearing a dinner jacket in downtown Turin than a poncho on lonely Caprera? Surely his soldiers would have seen through such posing at once. And why not distinguish between evidently mendacious propaganda campaigns, such as the papal pamphlets telling stories of Garibaldi atrocities, and the letters home from Garibaldi's volunteers in Sicily, all bubbling with idealism and excitement, of which Riall ungenerously remarks: 'the epistolary evidence suggests a general consensus to construct . . . an exemplary Risorgimento narrative.' Why not compare the cult that grew up around Garibaldi with, say, that which would later support Mussolini, where the gap between spin and performance was all too evident?

Riall is at her best when she looks at Garibaldi's career after unification. Unlike most historians, she takes him seriously and is convincing about his long-term influence on Italian politics. But on the whole her book is bound to be dull because she is scared of examining what actually happened. She offers not one close account of the many battles when Garibaldi's decisions *did* affect the course of history. She has nothing to say about the passions that moved him. She is deeply suspicious of any expression of collective excitement, seemingly embarrassed by accounts of his seductive voice and magnetic eyes, which so many supporters were convinced were blue. Everything must be deprived of its intensity and 'deconstructed' as self-serving or shown to be appropriated from second-rate fiction or popular illustrations, as if there wasn't always a constant back and forth between invented narrative and the lives people create for themselves.

Looking at the present international situation, the fanaticism, brutality and sheer ugliness of some forms of insurgency, it's not hard to guess why Riall feels as she does. We must be sceptical, she seems to be saying, of any concept of heroism, for such notions are tools in the hands of those seeking to manipulate our collective destiny with callous disregard for bloodshed. One can feel sympathy for this position. All the same, it might have been timely to dwell on the merits of an insurgent who did not use torture, suicide attacks or indiscriminate killing, who did not want to enslave people to a creed or regime, whose image, however carefully cultivated, encouraged people to believe in the possibility of independent thought and action, and, above all, who having achieved power by conquest handed over all his gains, as promised, without any desire to wield power long term or even to get rich.

Riall dismisses Garibaldi's memoirs as 'undeniably badly written'. Well, I deny it. They are exciting and give a powerful sense of the confusion surrounding political and military events during the Risorgimento. At one point Garibaldi remarks: 'A tree is judged by the quality of the fruit it bears, and individuals are judged by the benefits they can bestow on their fellow-human beings. Being born, existing, eating and drinking, and dying – insects do all this as well. In times like those in 1860 in southern Italy men are truly alive and their lives in the service of others. This is the real life of the soul!'

One imagines the young men and women who sit in Professor Riall's classes at the University of London. One wonders if she finishes her lectures as she does the chapters of this book with a section headed 'Conclusion' in which she wearily repeats what was said in the previous pages in case you weren't paying attention. Outside the window, perhaps, in the busy city, there is a call to arms, there are people urging us to take up a struggle. Perhaps a young man's head lifts. He wants to be involved in the world. Should he answer the call? Should he submit to the enchantment of the embattled community? Is the struggle ugly? Is it beautiful? Is it worth a life? These questions are not resolved by deciding that all communication is propaganda.

Siege of the Serenissima

[1848]

In the thirteenth century, Florence banned its noble families from holding public office and instituted a republic. The names of a few hundred select citizens were placed in leather bags and every two months a new government was drawn by lot. In more conservative Venice a group of nobles simply elected one of their number as monarch or doge for life. There was no question of hereditary succession. Even where there were dukes and kings, in Milan and Naples, dynastic rivalries and reversals eroded any belief in divine right. 'No trace is here visible', wrote Jakob Burckhardt in his great study of the Italian Renaissance, 'of that half religious loyalty by which the legitimate princes of the West were supported.'

The removal of the apex of the medieval hierarchy did not lead to the system's total collapse. In the fourteenth century an attempt by Florentine woolworkers to get rid of the wealthy oligarchs who themselves had ditched the nobles was short-lived. The plebs were put back in their place. The city actually ran two currencies to separate the realms of the rich and the poor. In such circumstances, the question 'On what principles of legitimacy is power to be held?' was constantly to the fore. In this sense Italy was at the vanguard of political thought. Needless to say, wealth and fear threw up various alibis to make sure control remained in a limited number of hands.

But if the important Italian states all had different forms of government, they were nevertheless agreed on what constituted the basis for a sovereign territory. It was the city and the agricultural land surrounding and supplying it. When Venice or Florence or

Milan launched wars of expansion they extended taxes but not voting rights to the subject towns they acquired. Venice was superior to Padua and Verona, Florence to Pisa, Milan to Brescia. There was no question of shared sovereignty. Nor, despite recognising that they had 'Italianness' in common, was there any movement among the larger cities towards unification. Such a prospect would anyway have been problematic since a large swathe of central Italy was held by the papacy, which apparently needed to exercise temporal power in order to fulfil its divine mission. One has to wait till Mussolini to find an Italian leader who puts the land as a whole and the people of the countryside before the cities.

This fragmentation meant that Italy never developed a unified approach to the problem of how power was to be legitimised. Different traditions flourished. It also led to the peninsula's being overwhelmed by foreign invasions at the end of the fifteenth century, but again not unified under occupation. With the exception of Venice, the republics disappeared to be replaced by client monarchies and dukedoms that sought an aura of legitimacy in grandiose monuments and public works while keeping a lid on political debate. It was a state of affairs which could only welcome the Counter-Reformation.

During the next three centuries of foreign domination the desire for a free and united Italy very gradually took shape. Liberation, it was understood, was a common cause and would be achieved and sustained only through collective action. By the end of the eighteenth century, secret societies promoting the idea of an Italian state were common, though there was no agreement on the political form such a state would have. The brief unification of the country under Napoleon from 1805 to 1814, with the introduction of many republican ideas and the Napoleonic code of law, gave impetus to the patriots, but the Congress of Vienna re-established the old status quo and in particular granted the whole of the Veneto and Lombardy to the Austrian Empire, the then superpower of central Europe. Once again the lid was clamped down on nationalist aspirations.

But by now the pot was coming to the boil. In 1848 patriotic rebellions broke out all over Italy. Jonathan Keates's *The Siege of Venice* examines the most long-lived of the rebel states that came into being. With its broad view of the 1848 experience across Italy and its detailed account of political developments and divisions in Venice during the city's eighteen months of independence, the book offers a fascinating picture of Risorgimento Italy and plenty of opportunity to reflect on continuities with the present day. It also makes an excellent story.

Writing in 1826 of the dispiriting nature of Italian public life, the poet Giacomo Leopardi remarked: 'It is as marvellous and apparently paradoxical as it is true that no individual or people can be so cold, indifferent and insensitive . . . as those who by their nature are lively, sensitive and warm.' That is, Leopardi explains, the lively, sensitive Italian nature, when exposed to the ugly 'reality of things and men', particularly as manifested under Italy's abysmal rulers, is prone to fall into a 'full and continuous cynicism of mind'. What the poet suggests is a psychology oscillating dramatically between positive and negative states, a condition that 'the northern peoples', less warm, and hence 'less swift to disillusion', could not understand.

Generalising as it is, Leopardi's observation will serve as a frame for reading the relationship between the Austrians and Italians as it unfolds in Keates's book. Among the Italians there are extremes of idealism and cynicism that fizz together in the constant and universal obsession that others are betraying the cause. To this rather hysterical dynamic the Austrians reply with the uniform and dogged determination of a society that, six centuries after the birth of the Italian republics, still believes in the absolute right of the Habsburg dynasty to rule over all its subject territories, regardless of language and ethnicity and whatever the quality of the dynasty's representative at any given moment. Emperor Francis I would never have been chosen as a leader by any electoral body.

* * *

Keates opens his book with the story of the Bandiera brothers and at once poses the question: what does it mean to sacrifice one's life for a cause even when no practical benefits immediately accrue? Italian officers in the Austrian navy, Attilio and Emilio Bandiera became fervent patriots, tried to lead an insurrection in the navy, were betrayed, deserted, subsequently attempted, in 1844, with only twenty followers, to stir up an insurrection in Calabria, were again betrayed and arrested, shortly after which they met the firing squad with shouts of '*Viva l'Italia*'.

Keates speaks with some irony of the brothers' ineptitude and bungled plans, but then admits that precisely 'their rashness afforded them an imperishable glamour'. And indeed many a piazza in Italy is still named after i Fratelli Bandiera. Their story points up the eagerness of the mind, particularly the youthful mind, to attach itself to ideals that give life meaning. Above all, it warns us that whenever people are willing to sacrifice their lives for a cause, the rest of us, however indifferent or hostile, must sit up and take notice. Inept, bungled and irrational self-sacrifice can be seductive and inspirational, especially in the cynical public world which Leopardi describes. These extremes call to each other.

One man who certainly took notice was the hero of Keates's book, Daniele Manin, who four years later would find himself at the head of the Venetian rebellion. Keates is troubled throughout his long tale by the reflection that Venice in general and Manin in particular have not been afforded the celebrity they deserve in the history of Italy's Risorgimento. They were overshadowed by events in Rome and by figures like Mazzini and Garibaldi. His determination to set the record straight gives the book a touchingly personal note, if only because the reasons for Manin's and indeed Venice's relative obscurity in the liberation process are soon all too evident to the reader.

Born in 1804, his grandparents Jews converted to Christianity, Manin was an able lawyer of liberal leanings deeply committed to the commercial life of Venice and to improving its plight under an

Austrian regime that tended to favour the port of Trieste and responded even to constructive criticism with censorship, if not worse. Bespectacled, short of stature and of ever uncertain health, Manin fought his city's corner with courage, confronting the Austrian authorities with demands for administrative devolution and favourable trading conditions. He was concerned above all that unrest arising from worsening poverty and harsh Austrian government would lead to serious public disorder if concessions were not made. The Venetian mob, it should be said, is perhaps the second most important character in Keates's book, a loud background noise always threatening to break in on any orderly political debate or military endeavour. Rather than seeing Manin as a moderate with whom they could do business, the Austrians arrested him on 18 January 1848 and held him in prison even after a trial had absolved him of any wrongdoing.

The rapid succession of liberal protests and uprisings in 1848 from English Chartism, through revolutionary Parisian republicanism to the many rebellions in Austria, Hungary and Italy suggests how much modern communications were transforming Europe into a place where what happened at one end of the continent could immediately, if unpredictably, affect the other. A sense of the chronology of the uprisings is thus essential for an understanding of Manin's and Venice's story. Here is a brief summary of the first phase of events.

In January 1848 Palermo rebelled against its Bourbon, Naples-based king, who was obliged to withdraw his forces from Sicily. In February, Paris rose against its government. In March the Viennese did likewise and the arch-conservative Metternich was dismissed. Monarchs in Naples, Turin, Florence and Vienna all promised their people constitutions. On 17 March a demonstration in Venice forced Manin's release and on 22 March a rebellion by shipbuilders in the Arsenale led the Austrians to withdraw from the city. That this happened with very little bloodshed was largely thanks to Manin. During the same few days the Milanese pushed out the occupying

Austrian army led by their senior general, Radetzky. Vicenza, Padua, Treviso and Udine all gained their freedom. On 23 March Charles Albert of Piedmont announced an invasion of Lombardy and the Veneto. In April Hungary gained a measure of autonomy within the Austrian Empire, which was now close to total collapse. In May the emperor fled Vienna.

If there is a tide in the affairs of men, this was the moment to take it at the flood. Austria was on her knees. The major powers of northern Europe were preoccupied with their internal affairs. In a reversal of previous papal policy, the recently elected Pope Pius IX had declared himself in favour of Italian national aspirations and in so doing had become a hero for thousands of patriots. It seemed there was nothing to prevent Italian unification.

But to form a single state would mean to agree on a political system and, perhaps more crucially, to accept the subordination of one's home city to a national government, whether republican or monarchical. These matters had never been thrashed out. There were rival views. Charles Albert was marching into Lombardy as much to bury republicanism as to further unification. Pope Pius had been enthusiastic about the idea of Italy and the popularity his patriotism brought him, until he began to appreciate what the reality would mean in terms of the papacy's relationship with Catholic Austria and the inevitable involvement in a struggle with republicans in Italy. As the battle against Austria began in earnest in Lombardy and the Veneto, he sent an army north but told his commanders not to cross the Po, then called them back. They disobeyed and advanced anyway. As international events in our new millennium have shown, to dismantle the status quo without a clear sense of what will replace it can lead to a long period of turmoil.

Concentrating on the Venetian experience, Keates's book now offers a fascinating dramatis personae encompassing more or less every shade of opinion and emotional response to the new situation that had so suddenly developed, a group of men and women whose inter-action illustrates how, despite great physical courage, honesty, idealism, adequate resources and considerable powers of organisation, defeat can nevertheless be snatched from the jaws of victory.

Manin had become the idol of the crowd, but his quiet charisma lay above all in his ability to face a mob down and restrain people from acts of public disorder. What appears to have mattered to him more than anything else was that Venice demonstrate its right to liberty through a show of civilised restraint. He rapidly put together an administration that was extremely successful in managing the city's resources but unimaginative in its response to the inevitable Austrian counter-attack. Manned by Italians who could have been encouraged to mutiny, the Austrian fleet was allowed to escape and would return months later with different crews to blockade the Venetian lagoon. Appeals for military help from the surrounding towns of the Veneto were not generously met. Very soon the ancient *campinilismo* re-emerged, with Padua, Vicenza and Treviso all suspecting that Venice intended to lord it over them.

Manin was assisted and hindered in his work by the wonderfully tetchy writer Niccolò Tommaseo, an outspoken and provocative misanthrope with a genius for taking offence. While Manin supported a moderate republicanism, the Catholic Tommaseo believed fervently in an Italy led by the papacy. Further to the left were patriots supporting more extreme forms of republicanism and even communism. Among the business community many pressed for fusion with Piedmont under the conservative rule of Charles Albert, while the city's Cardinal Monico was not alone in hoping for the return of the Austrians, a sympathy that would lead to his house being stormed and looted.

All these positions were intensely and eloquently argued in a plethora of newspapers and assemblies while the Austrians, who, though demoralised, knew exactly what they were about, regrouped to the east. In April the Irish general Nugent led Austrian forces into Friuli and the Veneto in an attempt to link up with Field Marshal Radetzky, who had retreated to a defensive position in the town of Verona, midway between Milan and Venice.

The campaign was long and complex. One is struck, reading Keates's entertaining account, by the international nature of the forces on both sides. The Austrian army was largely Croat, but there were also Hungarians, Slavs of every kind, Romanians and indeed many Italians who kept their oath to the imperial flag and the very simple, even 'natural' view of the world it allowed. On the Venetian side were soldiers who had deserted from the Papal army, from Naples and Calabria, from Tuscany and Romagna, but also a contingent of Swiss volunteers and stray adventurers from as far abroad as England.

It is also striking to learn, through Keates's many mini-biographies, how many of the men involved, whether professional soldiers or volunteers, switched sides and ideologies both before and after this campaign. Personalities seemed to metamorphose under the pressure of rival political visions and sudden changes of context. Men who had fought for Bourbon kings now fought valiantly for republicans, but would perhaps return years later to shooting down unarmed political demonstrators. Clearly there was a passion and enthusiasm in these heady days of liberation that carried along many in a *raptus* of collective sacrifice that would later seem inexplicable. Yet conscription was not introduced and even after the military situation in Venice became desperate there were many young men who did not volunteer to fight and presumably remained indifferent to the outcome of the war. On the other hand there were many women whose contribution went beyond nursing and knitting blankets to offering themselves as soldiers.

For months the outcome hung in the balance. The Piedmontese achieved early successes in Lombardy and on the borders of the Veneto. Supported by a variety of Papal, Tuscan, Neapolitan and Venetian troops, the people of Treviso and Vicenza fought courageously. But again and again one force let down another, professional soldiers showed their contempt for volunteers, local groups and new arrivals failed to co-ordinate. Town by town, the dogged Austrians regained control. Every failure on the Italian side led to recrimination and suspicion of treachery. There were so many agendas. Above all, the Italians lacked a man who possessed both political and military vision and the mandate to use it. The much-envied Garibaldi might have been that man, but he was given a small force of poorly equipped volunteers and dispatched by the Piedmontese on a pointless diversionary excursion north of Milan.

The Venetians waited. Keates repeatedly and admiringly remarks on how meticulously the city's accounts were kept throughout this difficult period when a population of 100,000 and more had to be fed and armed despite a tightening blockade. But careful accounting was a minor quality beside what was now required and hardly likely to inspire future generations of patriots. In July 1848, fearful of Austrian successes, a democratically elected assembly of Venetians voted for fusion with Piedmont in the hope that Charles Albert could offer protection. Manin resigned from the city's government, unable, he said, to serve in a monarchy, thus revealing that he put his political ideals before a united Italy. Ironically, only three weeks later the Piedmontese army was beaten at Custoza (just south of Lake Garda). Milan capitulated shortly afterwards and very soon Charles Albert was making a peace which did not even recognise the Venetians as ever having been part of his kingdom. This betrayal brought Manin back into government again, though with little idea as to how his city's independence might now be saved aside from futile appeals to liberal opinion in France and Britain. At this confused moment, however, events in Venice were decidedly upstaged by those in Rome.

When one considers the rise and fall of the various European powers in the modern age, it is hard to overestimate how much Britain's potential was enhanced by that superimposition of faith and patriotism achieved through the invention of the Church of England. On most matters, British political and religious leaders could speak with one voice and in the event of European war only a small percentage of Catholic citizens might feel their loyalties were divided. This was emphatically not the case in Italy and the events of 1848 were to confirm a rift between faith and patriotism that would plague the country into the 1930s.

There were those who had hoped that Pius IX could bring religion and national sentiment together. 'If Pius IX wishes it,' wrote Massimo d'Azeglio, later to be prime minister of Piedmont, 'if he consents to what public opinion is making of him, the papacy will become the century's guiding force.' To encourage the Pope to show his hand, he penned a proclamation for the commanders of the Papal army on their arrival at the Po in April 1848. It declared that the struggle against Austria was a holy war on a par with the crusades. The plan backfired. Far from coming on board, Pius recalled the army and shortly afterwards bade all Catholics obey their foreign rulers. When in November his chief minister was murdered by demonstrators the Pope fled to take refuge with the reactionary King of Naples. From that moment on the split between the official church and Italian patriotism was irremediable.

Into the vacuum left by the Pope came Mazzini and Garibaldi. They headed a revolutionary government. Neither was from Rome. Having lived much of their lives as exiles, they were attached above all to the idea of Italy and had no particular allegiance to any one town. Although important social reforms were passed, their main aim was to use this moment to advance the cause of a united Italy. Over a period of four months Garibaldi won two major engagements against French and Neapolitan armies and then led a spirited defence against a massive French siege. Always aware that the city couldn't be held, he then fought his way out of it and took what was left of his army into the hills so that the fall of the town should not be seen as a final defeat. Keates repeatedly points out that the siege of Venice lasted so much longer than that of Rome, yet this is hardly the point. There was a clarity of patriotic intention, a simplicity of gesture in the defence of Rome that was far more likely to capture the imagination than the drawn-out vicissitudes of the siege of Venice. One was a watershed in Italian consciousness, the other was not.

*   *   *

With the fall of Rome in July 1849, Venice was now the only rebel town in Italy. The Austrian army were dug in on the terra firma all around the town and they controlled the sea, if not the lagoon; capitulation was only a matter of time. As Keates's story draws to a close his language grows more coloured and emotional, attractively so. He seems to have forgotten now his irony at the expense of the Bandiera brothers and their futile sacrifice. Close by inclination to the peace-loving and pragmatic Manin, he has nevertheless been seduced, as his readers will be too, by the heroism and excitement of the final, futile Venetian defence, particularly the disciplined resistance of Fort Marghera at the landward end of the railway causeway, where for many days a mixture of Neapolitan artillerymen and Venetian and Swiss volunteers sacrificed their lives under the fiercest bombardment, killing large numbers of enemy troops as they did so.

A section of the railway causeway is blown up to prevent the Austrian advance across the lagoon. Cannonballs rain down on the city's ancient churches and monuments. Little boys collect the iron balls to restock Venetian munitions. Artists are present to paint the smoke and fires reflected in the lagoon. Other more priceless paintings are destroyed. Patriotic operas are performed. Food is scarce. The hospitals groan with amputees. Cholera victims are dying in their hundreds. The people demand that ancient religious icons be brought out and paraded. The soldiers engage in orgies with prostitutes, male and female. Syphilis is rife. Meanwhile, trapped in a rhetoric of last-ditch heroism, everybody is afraid to advocate surrender. Defeatists have been beaten and lynched. Manin himself wavers. At the last, it's hard to avoid the impression that the diminutive bespectacled lawyer with his frock coat and fussy beard is finally and officially installed as dictator only so that the responsibility for capitulation can rest on the most popular man's shoulders. The final image of the gondola bearing the white flag reminds us how Venice transforms almost any event, however desperate, into an aesthetic experience.

Had Venice become part of a free and unified Italy as a result of the heroics of 1848, then Manin would doubtless be a major presence in Italy's collective memory. He was a man without glaring defects. He had none of Garibaldi's ferocious anti-clericalism, Mazzini's inflexible fanaticism. He was not a subtle and ambiguous politician like Cavour, nor a pompous incompetent like the kings of Piedmont. But it didn't happen. Venice was added to a united Italy in the most humiliating way possible. After yet another Piedmontese defeat at the hands of the Austrians in 1866, Vienna nevertheless handed Venice to Paris who passed it on to Italy. So today, if I ask my children, educated from start to finish in Italian schools, who Manin was, they have only the vaguest notion. But then they have very little notion of the Risorgimento at all. Indeed it is hard to think of a single hero who is wholly revered in Italy in the way, say, Nelson has recently been admired in England. One problem perhaps is that almost every episode of the Risorgimento recalls divisions that are not entirely resolved today, in particular the tension between state and church, ideologies and nationalism. Exiled from Italy after the siege, Manin died in Paris in 1857. He was fifty-three. After unification his body was returned to Venice where the church authorities denied him burial in the Basilica of San Marco. 'Every Italian', Leopardi reflected in 1826, 'is more or less equally honoured and dishonoured.'

The Superman's Virgins

[Gabriele D'Annunzio]

Nothing drives a narrative better than repression. When we hear in Shakespeare's *Measure for Measure* of Angelo's ruthless purity we are already determined that it be corrupted. This man must be humiliated by lust. Nothing else will satisfy us. When we see a story entitled 'The Virgins', we are tensed for the deflowering. All the stories in this book are essentially tales of awakening, but not the kind that brings enlightenment. Rather, the lucid mind is over-whelmed by a compulsion before which every rule and taboo is suddenly obsolete. A river, usually no more than a distant murmur, has broken its banks. The everyday world is submerged in sensu-ality, utterly sexualised. Sensory perceptions fantastically enhanced, the will drowns in a flood of feeling.

Transgression is usually taken as a sign of authenticity in a writer. The poet's sins assure us that he is the real thing. Not so with D'Annunzio. On the rare occasions he does nudge his way into the Anglo-Saxon consciousness, it is always for the wrong reasons. He is the rabid nationalist who urged Italy to join the First War. He is the egocentric adventurer whose mad volunteers, in defiance of international law, occupied Fiume on the north Adriatic coast in 1919. He preached the superman (along with Carlyle and Nietzsche and Shaw), was friends with Mussolini. Even his sexual trespasses win him little credit. There is something farcical about the ageing man who orders the bells of his villa to be rung when-ever he achieves orgasm with the nth mistress. An old alliance between piety and caution, between church and socialism – some-thing we have recently learned to call political correctness – has

257

written off D'Annunzio as a monomaniac. His style, they tell us, is excessive, verbose. They don't want us to open his books. I was kept away for years.

A dozen pages of 'The Virgins' will dispel these prejudices. D'Annunzio surprises. One of two unmarried sisters is dying of typhus. These young women have given up their lives to God and to the community, teaching catechism and basic grammar to children in their home. The priest arrives to give extreme unction. The host is placed on a tongue dark with blood and mucus. The evocation of a suffocatingly religious, peasant household, of a mortal sickness in all its ugliness, stench and mental stupor, is dense and marvellously paced. Sentence by sentence, we are waiting for the woman to die, begging for it to be over.

Giuliana doesn't die, and D'Annunzio is not just another practitioner of nineteenth-century social realism. Far from cancelling out the old Adam and ushering another soul through the pearly gates, the last rites appear to have returned Giuliana to a state before the Fall. She is back from the dead and intensely sensitive to the mystery of her healing body, as if experiencing the throes of a second puberty. A subtle symbolism informs the plot but, as with Hardy's or Lawrence's finest work, it springs naturally from the world we know, offering but never imposing a possible order. In the shameless hunger of first convalescence, Giuliana searches the house for food while her sister is away at Mass. She finds an old apple and bites deep to the seeds. A heady, rosy perfume is released. Giuliana laughs, as anyone returning to health would laugh, and laughter is of the devil. She finds a mirror, studies her face, then, more boldly, her naked body. All at once we have a fiercely sexed young woman, adult and virgin, dangerously innocent, living and sleeping beside a sister who, in her repressive religious devotion, seems 'the corpse of a martyr'. It is Camilla who is dead. Not Giuliana.

At last the convalescent goes to the window and draws back the curtain. The smell of fresh bread drifts up seductively from the bakery below, the blast of the trumpet sounds the hours from the nearby barracks where the soldiers whistle to the passing girls. The reader is gripped by a powerful sense that something tremendous is about to happen.

Place is important. Pescara is at the same latitude as Rome on the Italian peninsula, but on the opposite coast, the Adriatic. Busy, provincial, backward, the town forms a ribbon of chaotic life between coastal pine woods and rugged hills that rise steeply to the high plateaux of the Abruzzo mountains. Winter rains and snow fill the streets with rushing water. Spring is an explosion of rich smells. The violent summer sun glares off white limestone, tortures the dark vegetation, glitters on the sea. Himself in love with extremity, D'Annunzio has an uncanny ability to capture every manifestation of climate and landscape, bucolic or grotesque, threatening or lush. Far from being superfluous, his descriptions set in motion the brooding drama of a huge and inexorable natural process, against which the moral pretensions of religion and society are increasingly felt to be meaningless. In one of these stories a bleeding woman stumbles into a house to collapse and die, while a solitary, blind old man taps uncomprehendingly about the corpse with his stick. Nothing could better express D'Annunzio's sense of the fatal elusiveness of life and death to rational enquiry.

Altered states of mind, sickness, passion, delirium are the norm. A woman and her husband's brother are pampering her young daughter in the presence of his elderly mother. Adult fingers meet by chance in the child's thick blond hair; unplanned and unwanted a passion begins that sweeps away the claims of parenthood, the duties of son to dying mother. 'Aren't you afraid of having a spell cast on you?' one character asks in another story. You should be, is D'Annunzio's answer. It is this apprehension of the mind's subjection to the magic of the world, or to organic processes if you like, coupled with a conviction that established prescriptions for good behaviour are quite obsolete, that will ultimately lead D'Annunzio to his cult of the superman, the figure whose will is so strong that

259

he can stamp new patterns of value on life. That dangerous figure is absent from these stories, which present us rather with life's victims, yet latent all the same, and understandable.

Teaching proper Italian to their infant pupils, the two virgin sisters broke up the language into its constituent parts – *la*, *le*, *li*, *lo*, *lu*, they made the children repeat, *nar*, *ner*, *nir*, *nor*, *nur* . . . Returning to new life after her terrible illness, Giuliana listens to her sister repeating these formulae – *ram*, *rem*, *rim*, *rom*, *rum* – and finds them intolerable. She sobs and beats her fists on the pillow. These rigid patterns and divisions are death to those truly alive. The moment can be considered emblematic of the birth of modernism. From now on everything is to be mixed and fizzing with life: male and female, ugly and beautiful, sacred and profane, poetry and prose, above all good and evil. The most unexpected words appear together, sacred images disclose all their eroticism, erotic gestures are made in complete innocence. Decades before their day, this is the world of Lawrence and Joyce.

A Pagan in Italy

[Lawrence and Italy]

Wake up! This is the experience. At any moment Lawrence may say something startling. It could be brutal: 'If I were a dictator I'd hang that man.' It could be hilarious: the Sicilians 'pour over each other like melted butter over parsnips.' Or it might be at once surreal and rivetingly exact: 'Cypresses are candles to keep darkness aflame in full sunshine.' But whatever the nature of the surprise, Lawrence infallibly reproduces the sensation he himself seeks when he travels: sudden confrontation with strangeness, that special alertness aroused by phenomena that demand explanation. 'I was startled into consciousness' he tells us of one encounter. Or again. 'I went into the church. It was very dark, and impregnated with centuries of incense. It affected me like the lair of some enormous creature. My senses were roused, they sprang awake in the hot, spiced darkness. My skin was expectant, as if it expected some contact, some embrace . . .'

We mustn't ask Lawrence for information. It's not a kind of knowledge he's interested in. He won't give us hard facts about Italy. They can be found in a guidebook. Surprised and touched by what he sees, he wants to touch and surprise us. 'Rather gentle and lovely', he tells us of a painting in an Etruscan tomb, 'is the way the man touches the woman under the chin, with a delicate caress. That again is one of the charms of the Etruscan paintings: they really have the sense of touch; the people and the creatures are all really in touch. It is one of the rarest qualities, in life as well as in art.'

But one wouldn't want this kind of abrupt and intimate contact

261

with just anybody. 'I should loathe to have to touch him' Lawrence tells us of a particularly ugly character at the train station in Messina. So if we're going to get involved with a writer whose embrace more often feels like that of the wrestler than the friend, we need to know where he's coming from. With Lawrence, biography is vital.

Invalided out of teaching, or indeed any form of strenuous employment, by an attack of pneumonia in 1911, the twenty-six-year-old Lawrence at once plunged into the most strenuous love affair. In 1912, after only a few weeks' acquaintance, he ran off with the German wife of his ex-professor at university. Six years his elder, a mother of three, Frieda Weekley, née Richthofen, was not sure how serious the affair was until, without her permission, Lawrence wrote to her husband and told him what was going on. She immediately and openly betrayed her presumptuous lover with a German friend.

Lawrence and Frieda were staying with her family in Germany. Having prised her away from husband and children, Lawrence now dragged her from her new man and her mother to take a strenuous walk across the Alps from Bavaria to Italy. They set off with two male friends and Frieda promptly betrayed Lawrence with one of them. But on arrival at the northern tip of Lake Garda on the Italian side of the Alps, their friends went off and at last Lawrence had Frieda to himself. With the excuse that their finances were tight, he managed to rent cheaply in a small village on the western shore of the lake, the less frequented side. This is steep and rugged country between the alpine lake and the icy peaks. They had arrived in autumn with the empty, tourist-free winter ahead. It was hard to see where Frieda would find another lover now.

Given all this drama – fidelity or betrayal, marriage or freedom, public morality versus private conviction – it's not surprising that Lawrence tended to think of the world in terms of polarities. Ensconced in a house called Villa Igea, facing east across the lake, he now embarked on the most strenuous work programme. In the space of seven months he wrote the final version of *Sons and Lovers*, the story of the conflict between his father and mother, of his personal battle to become his mother's favourite, then his battle against his mother to be allowed to have girlfriends. He also wrote two plays and much of the poetry collection *Look! We Have Come Through!* about his love and conflict with Frieda. And he also began the great novel *The Rainbow*, and another, *The Lost Girl*. Where, then, did he find time to learn Italian and write a travel book as well? And why, living in an area renowned for the electric sharpness of its bright air, did he call that book *Twilight in Italy*?

Walking over the Alps, Lawrence notices the wayside crucifixes. Carved by untutored peasants, they depict a Christ absolutely trapped in his earthly, sensual existence yet eternally exposed to the empty brightness of the alpine snows and sky. Aside from the opposites set up here, the sensual life against the mental, dark and light, intensity and nullity, what at once has the reader alert is how Lawrence looks at these artefacts without any reference to Christian orthodoxy. The real world is always ready to take on symbolic sense for him, but it is a sense that arises from his concentration on the object itself. So even when he is in danger of becoming didactic, his eye is simply too open to be trapped in any scheme. Intensely observed, the landscape trembles with a readiness to be seized and transformed by the creative mind: 'There was a blood-red sail,' he tells us, looking from a parapet over Lake Garda, 'like a butterfly breathing down on the blue water, whilst the earth on the near side gave off a green-silver smoke of olive trees, coming up and around the earth-coloured roofs.' On the other hand, we are always reminded that the hills are steep to climb and the air is cold.

Opposites attract and repel each other, creating a force field of excitement and fear. So for many readers the essential Lawrence experience is that described in the poem 'The Snake' written a few years later in 1919. Going to get water from a drinking trough, the writer is startled by a snake. There is a powerful awareness of the otherness of the reptile; man and serpent share the same world and the same need for water, yet each inhabits a realm of consciousness unknowable to the other. It was the kind of encounter Lawrence had already described on a number of occasions, but perhaps most notably in *Twilight in Italy* in his meeting with the old woman spinning wool above Gargnano. It is from his reflections on this episode that we have the twilight of the book's provocative title.

On a terrace high above the lake, Lawrence finds an old woman, her back against a wall, head 'tied in a dark-red kerchief, but pieces of hair, like dirty snow, quite short, stuck out over her ears. And she was spinning.' The more Lawrence concentrates on the woman, the more she becomes emblematic of a different order of consciousness, or rather unconsciousness. 'She was spinning spontaneously, like a little wind . . . All the time, like motion without thought, her fingers teased out the fleece . . .'

Lawrence tries out his still rudimentary Italian on the spinner but she is not interested. 'She remained as she was, clear and sustained like an old stone upon the hillside.' And the difference between the two of them essentially is this: while Lawrence appreciates that her way of being lies outside his mental grasp, and hence is bound to accept that he lives in a multifarious world teeming with potentially disturbing encounters, for the old woman there is only her own knowledge, her own language, her own reality and environment, in which she is totally integrated. She doesn't take on board his otherness. True, she hasn't seen him before, but only in the same way that there are parts of her body she has never seen. 'There was nothing which was not herself, ultimately.'

So in rural Italy Lawrence finds a form of pre-modern consciousness, something that always fascinated and attracted him. What happens when eternal opposites meet? At best, fireworks. Escaping from the woman because fearful that she will 'deny [him] existence', evening falls, the sun turns red and, very briefly, day and night become one: 'on the length of mountain-ridge, the snow grew rosy-incandescent, like heaven breaking into blossom.' This, for Lawrence, is the fleeting consummation of alien worlds, a brief and magical manifestation of the oneness behind opposites.

But just as that beautiful sunset flames across the peaks, in the valley below him Lawrence sees two monks pacing back and forth together between 'bony vines' in their 'wintry garden'. It's a place bereft of either sunlight or shadow, not a consummation of opposites, but an annulling of all differences in a twilit world of sterile mental reflection. 'They did not touch each other . . . as they walked' he notices. 'Their hands were hidden . . . in the long sleeves . . . of their . . . robes . . . Yet there was an eagerness in their conversation.' Then Lawrence produces one of those extraordinary, almost mad paragraphs in which, from a close observation of real phenomena, he leaps to the most fanciful conclusions.

'Neither the flare of day nor the completeness of night reached [the monks], they paced the narrow path of the twilight, treading in the neutrality of the law. Neither the blood nor the spirit spoke in them, only the law, the abstraction of the average. The infinite is positive and negative. But the average is only neutral. And the monks trod backwards and forward down the line of neutrality.'

Any big idea in Lawrence is set up to be shot down. Never take anything as Bible. He hated the book. All the same, the concept here is central: there is a fruitful and natural way for polarities to encounter each other in conflict, consummation, intensity: a flaming sunset, a red-hot argument with Frieda; and there was a negative, merely destructive way, the mind coldly and mechanically neutralising opposites in arid codes of thought and manipulation. This was the territory of Frieda's respectable husband, of contemporary intellectual individualism, of industrial mechanisation. Only Lawrence, it has to be said, could have seen the world's modern ills symbolised in the crepuscular back and forth of two monks in an Italian garden.

Twilight in Italy proceeds with a gallery of local characters, the fascinating, sometimes hilarious account of the performances of a local theatre company, the sensual excitement of an evening's dancing between local peasants and two visiting Englishwomen. On every page Lawrence's ability to capture physical presence is remarkable: 'The Bersaglieri sit close together in groups, so that there is a strange, corporal connection between them. They have close-cropped, dark, slightly bestial heads, and thick shoulders, and thick brown hands on each other's shoulders ... And they are quite womanless. There is a curious inter-absorption among themselves, a sort of physical trance that holds them all and puts their minds to sleep ... They are in love with one another ...'

At times his indiscretion takes the breath away. Is there any writer today who would follow a sympathetic description of his foreign landlord and landlady with a profound analysis of their imagined sex life and the way the meeting of their bodies is expressive of their different relationships with the land and the community? It is this that most astonishes about Lawrence: the naturalness, almost insouciance, with which he goes deeper than you would have thought possible.

Yet beyond, or rather through, these character studies, what he is writing about is the twilight, as he sees it, of a certain Italian mentality: the shedding of the old oneness of man and land in a hierarchical community – the world of the spinner – and the movement towards an obsession with all that is countable and mental and egalitarian, the modern money-driven neurotic life. Hence his concentration on the local Gargnano men who have been or dream of going to America: the peasant who went and came back and remained completely untouched by the modern world – in a sense was never really away from his vines and olive trees – and the younger man whose encounter with New York has made life in rural Gargnano impossible and who is about to abandon a newly wedded wife to cross the ocean once more. Profound changes of the spirit are in the air, even in this tiny Italian community. Lawrence understands that. And the reader understands that below the surface Lawrence is seeking to see these things in relation to his own escape from England with Frieda.

So it's appropriate that *Twilight in Italy* should end with another walk across the Alps in which Lawrence encounters a number of Italian emigrants working in a textile factory in Switzerland. They are escaping conscription. They are looking for money. They are nostalgic for home, for the soil and the food and the sun, but that nostalgia isn't strong enough to take them back. It's moving, among all the chatter and comedy of these episodes, how profoundly and personally troubled Lawrence is by these people and above all by their strange readiness to embrace everything mechanical. 'Give a man control of some machine', as he says elsewhere, 'and at once his air of importance and more than human dignity develops.' This would be one of the great themes of *The Rainbow*. As he walks back from Switzerland into Italy, watching the spread of roads and railways and factories eating into the mountain landscape, he gives us reflections that might have been written, less eloquently, by some proponent of the anti-globalisation movement of today:

> It is the hideous rawness of the world of men, the horrible deso-lating harshness of the advance of the industrial world upon the world of nature that is so painful. It looks as though the indus-trial spread of mankind were a sort of dry disintegration advancing and advancing, a process of dry disintegration. If only we could learn to take thought for the whole world instead of merely tiny bits of it.

Frieda is barely mentioned in *Twilight in Italy*. It's as if Lawrence were still too insecure to let us make her acquaintance. He keeps her to himself, writing poems about her, about how they have over-come their problems. In a way they are coercive poems, informing Frieda and the world that Lawrence's determination for the couple to make a success of it has indeed won the day. In 1913 they returned to England to be married.

But by the time we get to *Sea and Sardinia*, everything has changed. True, Lawrence had seen lean times in the First War. In 1915 *The Rainbow* had been banned for obscenity almost as soon as it was published. Too frail to be a soldier, he was nevertheless repeatedly called up and subjected to humiliating medical examinations. In 1917 he and Frieda were evicted from Cornwall on suspicion of spying for Germany, this as much a punishment for Lawrence's pacifism as Frieda's nationality. In the same year – an even more ridiculous error – his publishers rejected *Women in Love*.

But with the end of the war came the chance to shake the dust of England from their feet and almost immediately the Lawrences were in Italy, first on the island of Capri and then in Taormina on the eastern slopes of Etna looking back across the sea to mainland Calabria. And despite all the setbacks, Lawrence now had a reputation. *Sons and Lovers* had won critical acclaim. Above all, he himself had understood the importance of *The Rainbow* and *Women in Love*. He was thirty-six. Much had been achieved. Ideas that had still needed to be thrashed out and validated a decade ago were now thoroughly thought through and could be allowed to fall into the background. So there is a different kind of confidence about *Sea and Sardinia*; we can be allowed to meet Frieda.

Lawrence didn't travel to write travel books. 'Comes over one an absolute necessity to move' he tells us in the first startling sentence of this book. Perhaps writing all day, living frugally in remote locations, he needed travel for the stimulus of confrontation. 'I love trying things,' he once famously remarked, 'and discovering how I hate them.' Certainly he hated much of what he found in Sardinia.

Where *Twilight in Italy* is a collection of largely disconnected moments, character studies and descriptions held together by theme and style, *Sea and Sardinia* is a rapid, blow-by-blow account of a dozen nightmare days on the move – Sicily to Sardinia and back – a classic collision between exuberant high spirits and repeated disappointments. In this sense it is a comedy of the *Three Men in a Boat* variety. Except that where Jerome K. Jerome's charming threesome entertained ordinary middle-class yearnings for a quiet break in idyllic surroundings, Lawrence was once again looking to Sardinia to give him examples of a pre-modern community of dignified manhood. Indeed, he and Frieda had half a mind to set up home there. Naturally, the greater the expectations, the greater the comedy of disappointment . . .

With masochistic energy the Lawrences depart from their remote villa before dawn. They have packed their 'kitchenino', a little food hamper, with bacon sandwiches and a Thermos flask (an object of mystery to the Italians). Lawrence carries their clothes in a knapsack, another imported novelty that brings such stares from the Sicilians that he might as well be 'riding on a pig'. The description of the dawn commuters on the platform at Catania is sublime, likewise the experience of the packed train from Messina to Palermo, the interminable delays, the inexplicably numerous officials: 'You know them by their caps. Elegant tubby little officials in kid-and-patent boots and gold-laced caps, tall long nosed ones in more gold-laced caps, like angels in and out of the gates of heaven they thread in and out of the various doors.'

On the boat from Palermo, too, the multitudinous crew are only occasionally and casually involved in the business of navigation. Their real task is to make life miserable for the passengers. Again and again Lawrence launches into rhapsodies: how he loves the freedom of the sea, how he appreciates Sicilian baking, only to be quickly and comically deflated by seasickness, rudeness and squalor. When he and Frieda get off the boat at Trapani in search of some nice little cakes they find that the city that 'looked so beautiful from the sea . . . is a cross between an outside place where you throw rubbish and a humpy unmade road in a raw suburb with a few iron seats, and litter of old straw and rag.'

Never actually named, Frieda is referred to at first as 'the queen bee', which is as much as to say: she who is ministered unto by all while rather grandly doing nothing herself. But what the queen bee does do is to offer a foil to Lawrence's ups and downs. When Lawrence is disgusted by the begging of a filthy little girl pushing a fat baby against him, Frieda kindly talks to the girl, asks the baby's name. In fact, Frieda talks to everybody who irritates Lawrence and seems to dislike everyone he likes. Perhaps it's because of this that 'queen bee' very quickly becomes just 'q-b' in the ironic shorthand of the now established marriage.

The climax of the trip comes when, after many vicissitudes, they reach the tiny village of Sorgono, deep in the Sardinian interior. Lawrence has been enthusing wildly about the 'lovely unapproachableness' of the Sardinian peasants in their traditional dress and strange black stocking caps: 'they wear them as a sort of crest, as a lizard wears his crest at mating time . . . A handsome fellow with a jaw of massive teeth pushes his cap back and lets it hang a long way down his back. Then he shifts it forward over his nose, and makes it have two sticking-out points, like fox ears, above his temples. It is marvellous how much expression these caps can take on. They say only those born to them can wear them. They seem to be just long bags, nearly a yard long, of black stockinette stuff.'

Lawrence loves this. He loves the fact that these men still refuse to accept 'the world's common clothes. Coarse, vigorous, determined, they will stick to their own coarse dark stupidity and let the big world find its own way to its own enlightened hell.'

This is fantastic. And the way they treat their women, brusque, hostile almost, as befits people who accept 'the defiant, splendid split between the sexes' makes our champion of polarities even more appreciative. No twilight here. Sex is about opposites, about kissing and strife, as he once wrote. 'Give me the old, salty way of love. How I am nauseated by sentiment and nobility, the macaroni slithery slobbery mess of modern adorations.'

Then they arrive in Sorgono where the only hotel is filthy and cold, the proprietor is filthy and rude, and the streets are filthy and smelly, for the simple reason that they are used as toilets. Lawrence now falls into a sort of John Cleese rage, a wonderful send-up of himself: 'I cursed the degenerate aborigines, the dirty breasted host who dared to keep such an inn, the sordid villagers who had the baseness to squat their beastly human nastiness in this upland valley. All my praise of the long stocking-cap vanished from my mouth. I cursed them all, and the q-b for an interfering female.'

Yet the more things go wrong the more, deep down, Lawrence seems pleased, as if the most frightening scenario would have been to find what he was looking for, the ideal place for himself and Frieda to live. Indeed, *Sea and Sardinia* has a great deal to say about fear, and it is this that establishes its centrality in the writer's oeuvre. Everywhere he goes Lawrence is concerned he will be cheated, robbed, badly served, badly fed, bored by hangers-on, harangued by ignorant people blaming him for the British government's foreign policy ('I am not the British Isles on two legs!'). He immediately picks up on such details as shoes left outside a hotel room, or doors left open on the streets, as indications of the level of local honesty. Towards the end of the book, afraid of not finding a cabin on the night steamer from Naples back to Palermo, he and Frieda try to save time by making their own way to the docks while the train is still stopped in the station. Afraid now of being fleeced, they reject the idea of a taxi – 'I am weary of that boa-constrictor, a Naples cabman after dark' – and walk alone through 'the vast black quicksands of that harbour road', where 'one feels peril all around'. Did Lawrence go to Italy, one sometimes wonders, precisely because it had a reputation for being dangerous?

When they reach the ticket office, he plunges 'into the fray. It is literally a fight. Some thirty men all at once want to get at a tiny wicket in a blank wall.' Lawrence constantly has to look to his wallet. Yet he is not upset: 'Somehow or other, waking and sleeping, one's spirit must be on its guard nowadays. Which is really what I prefer, now I have learnt it. Confidence in the goodness of mankind is a very thin protection indeed . . . Therefore, tight on my guard, like a screw biting into a bit of wood, I bite my way through that knot of fellows, to the wicket, and shout for two first class. The clerk inside ignores me for some time, serving soldiers. But if you stand like Doomsday you get your way. Two firsts, says the clerk. Husband and wife say I . . .'

To 'stand like Doomsday'! Isn't this how Lawrence had won

Frieda? Isn't this how he had convinced the publishers to accept his work? And how he survives in Italy? An act of sheer will, of fear turned into desperate forcefulness. 'Husband and wife' indeed. What a proud proclamation! With all its comic encounters, little disasters, raptures, and above all its exhausting search for decent food and shelter, *Sea and Sardinia* is the book that most candidly reveals Lawrence as he must have been on his many travelling adventures, friendly one moment, aloof the next, then belligerent, and always up or down according to whether Frieda was down or up. One thing in particular that emerges is the tension between his enormous appetite (for food and life) and an incredible parsimoniousness: he was determined to save every possible penny. Hence it's an added twist to discover that the original manuscript of *Sea and Sardinia*, written over a matter of weeks immediately after the trip, was thereafter consumed as toilet paper.

Turning to *Sketches of Etruscan Places*, the last of Lawrence's travel books, we find that Frieda has disappeared again. We are six years on, Lawrence is forty-two, and everything has changed. The two of them have travelled in Asia, Australia, the USA and Mexico. Vast amounts of writing have been done. Lawrence is recognised as one of the great novelists of his time, of any time. But his health is collapsing. In 1924 he suffered a serious bronchial haemorrhage. In 1925 tuberculosis was diagnosed. In 1926, back in Italy again, Frieda had taken a lover, Angelo Ravagli, a man twelve years younger than herself. Now, in early April 1927, she left Lawrence in their rented accommodation near Florence to visit her family in Germany, but quite probably, as her husband no doubt understood, stopping in Trieste on the way to see Ravagli.

Partly to console himself, Lawrence set off with an old friend, Earl Brewster, on a tour of the Etruscan tombs in various small towns fifty or so kilometres north-west of Rome on the Tyrrhenian coast. If *Twilight in Italy* was written from the excitement of his first home with Frieda and *Sea and Sardinia* in the heyday of their relationship as they searched for a new home and lifestyle, *Etruscan Places* more sombrely but very beautifully describes a different kind of house hunt: the exploration of a number of underground chambers and tunnels 'cut out of the living rock', yet 'just like houses'. The houses of the dead. Returning to the antique past, Lawrence was looking to his own future. He was dying. Tuberculosis was not an enemy against whom one could stand like Doomsday. It was Doomsday. Before very long there would be no impediment to Frieda Lawrence becoming Frieda Ravagli.

Lawrence's interest in the Etruscans, whose many city states thrived in central Italy before the founding of Rome, was not new. For many years he had seen this forgotten people as emblematic of the sort of pagan consciousness he admired and emulated. Most emblematic of all was their total destruction at the hands of, as he saw it, a mechanistic, militaristic Rome. Having just finished a second draft of the polemical *Lady Chatterley's Lover*, Lawrence opens *Sketches of Etruscan Places* in the same argumentative spirit. In particular, he is eager to underline the deep alliance throughout history between the brutal will to power and puritanical morals, an alliance, as he sees it, still alive in 1927 both in imperial Britain and Fascist Italy. The Etruscans loved the symbols of the phallus and the ark (the womb) and displayed them everywhere. Small stone phalluses are placed in niches outside the tombs of all the men. This, Lawrence says, is why Etruria had to be wiped out. 'Even in their palmy days the Romans were not exactly saints. But they thought they ought to be. They hated the phallus and the ark, because they wanted empire and dominion and, above all, riches: social gain. You cannot dance gaily to the double flute and at the same time conquer nations or rake in large sums of money.'

But gradually the polemics fade and *Etruscan Places* finds a rhythm all its own, becoming, before too long, the most serene and unstrained of Lawrence's books. It is the spirit of the landscape and the spirit with which the Etruscans approached death that alter the tone.

273

'There is a stillness and a softness in these great grassy mounds with their ancient stone girdles, and down the central walk [of the burial ground] there lingers still a kind of loneliness and happiness ... The same when we went down the few steps, and into the chambers of rock, within the tumulus. There is nothing left. It is like a house that has been swept bare ... But whoever it is that has departed, they have left a pleasant feeling behind them ...'

All his adult life, Lawrence had sought to live as a pagan in the modern world. Not an atheist, atheism being, as he saw it, just a negative dogmatism brought into being by monotheistic religion. He had looked for a way out of repressive Christian morality, while never seeking to be either immoral or amoral. And he had likewise looked for a way out of the general scramble for money and social status. But the supreme test of any life comes with the imminence of death. Reconstructing the mindset of these people who left us almost nothing but their tombs, yet whose tombs impart a deep sense of peace, Lawrence is seeking to prepare himself for the final journey.

It's a beautiful story. Crawling into one burial chamber after another with his friend, a guide and a couple of candles, Lawrence examines the many paintings on the ancient walls, conjuring up from their strange detail and symbolism the Etruscan way of life, their aesthetic sense, their religious practices, social hierarchy, how they lived in intimate contact with their bodies and nature. 'The things they did,' he remarks, 'in their easy centuries, are as natural and as easy as breathing. They leave the breast breathing freely and pleasantly, with a certain fullness of life.'

For a man who suffered such severe lung problems, this was an achievement to yearn for. Finally, Lawrence had found a pre-modern culture that did not disappoint him as, over recent years, Sardinia, Ceylon, Mexico and New Mexico had all in their different ways disappointed. The reason is obvious. The Etruscans are no longer around to bother Lawrence with poor food, indifferent table manners and dodgy sanitation.

Or are they? The key to a reading of *Etruscan Places* is the idea of continuity. 'Death, to the Etruscan, was a pleasant continuance of life, with jewels and wine and flutes playing for the dance. It was neither an ecstasy of bliss, a heaven, nor a purgatory of torment. It was just a natural continuance of the fullness of life. Everything was in terms of life, of living.'

If a sense of continuity is the right approach to death, then Lawrence will reproduce the principle in his book. Where another writer would have focused entirely on the Etruscans, on the tombs and their paintings, he moves freely between the artefacts of past millennia and the modern Tuscan landscape outside, between reflections on migration in the fifth century BC and the boy who drives him and his friend across the low, windy hills in a pony cart, and then the hotel proprietors, the waiters, the part-time guide who works on the railways, the young German archaeologist at once so knowledgeable and so unimpressed. With a sureness of touch that isn't quite there in the earlier works, Lawrence leaves it to the reader to grasp the connection between the Fascist busybody determined to examine his passport in Civitavecchia and the Romans who destroyed the Etruscans. And he is entirely convincing when he finds in the faces and manners of the local village women the same traits he has seen in the underground paintings. One way or another, he decides, the Etruscans will always be with us. And slowly but surely this ease of movement between ancient and modern, burial chamber and hotel room, begins to establish a curious mood of alert tranquillity, something as far from the Doomsday defiance of the earlier Lawrence as one could possibly imagine.

An Etruscan prince, Lawrence tells us, would have 'a little bronze ship of death' on the stone bed beside his sarcophagus. The prince, unlike his people, was an initiate in the mysteries of the cosmos, and above all in the 'mystery of the journey out of life and into death'. He was at once a ruler and a priest. 'Try as you may,' Lawrence remarks, and certainly he had tried, 'you can never make the mass of men throb with full awakedness ... Only a few are initiated into the mystery of the bath of life, and the bath of death.'

Now, visiting the tombs of the Etruscan princes, Lawrence feels a growing identity with these ruler priests. He too is an initiate in life's mysteries. He too would build his ship of death, a vessel that might take him across the stormy waters beyond the final horizon of being. *Etruscan Places* marks the moment when Lawrence consciously began to build that boat. It would not be complete until, on his deathbed, he wrote the extraordinary poem 'Ship of Death'. As with *Etruscan Places*, the tone was one of quiet, unblinkered acceptance. 'Oh build your ship of death,' runs one short stanza,

> . . . your little ark
> and furnish it with food, with little cakes, and wine
> for the dark flight down oblivion.

Reading these lines, it's hard not to remember the kitchenino of *Sea and Sardinia*, so carefully packed for the voyage out, hard not to think of the little cakes that he and his queen bee sought so avidly in Trapani and Cagliari, and indeed of all the dark wine drunk, chapter after chapter, in these three remarkable books on Italy. As with the Etruscan paintings he so lovingly described, the sense of continuity between life and death is powerful. Perhaps, at the very end, Lawrence had managed to become truly pagan.

The Fighter

Places and dates of first publication

Lawrence – The Fighter: *New York Review*, September 25, 2003
Bassani – Gardens and Graveyards: *New York Review*, July 14, 2005
Dostoevsky – After the Struggle: *The Nation*, June 14, 2004
Mussolini – The Illusionist: *New York Review*, April 7, 2005
Hardy – Fear is the Key: *New York Review*, April 12, 2007
The Disenchantment of Translation: Paper delivered at Katha Utsav, Delhi, January 6, 2004
Beckett – Still Stirring: *New York Review*, July 13, 2006
Bernhard – Genius of Bad News: *New York Review*, January 11, 2007
Jelinek – Let Sleeping Beauties Lie: *New York Review*, July 19, 2007
Cioran – A Polished Pessimism: *Spectator*, 1996
Machiavelli – True Scandal: Introduction to *The Prince*, The Folio Society, London, 2006
A Model Anomaly: *New York Review*, October 18, 2001
Lorenzo – Mad at the Medici: *New York Review*, May 1, 2003
Fleur Jaeggy – Love Letter: *New York Review*, February 12, 2004
Hypertext – Tales Told by a Computer: *New York Review*, October 24, 2002
Zola – Real Dreams: Introduction to *The Dream*, Hesperus Press, London, 2005
World Cup Football – A Matter of Love and Hate: *New York Review*, July 18, 2002
Garibaldi – Hero Betrayed: *New Yorker*, June 2007
1848 – Siege of the Serenissima: *London Review of Books*, December 1, 2005
D'Annunzio – The Superman's Virgins: Introduction to D'Annunzio, *The Book of Virgins*, Hesperus, 2003

Lawrence and Italy – A Pagan in Italy: Introduction to *D. H. Lawrence and Italy: Etruscan Places, Sea and Sardinia, Twilight in Italy*, Penguin Classics, 2007

References

The first number in the left column refers to the page, the second to the line on which the quotation ends.

The Fighter

1   3   D. H. Lawrence, *Apocalypse* (London, Penguin, 1995), p.60
1 10   D. H. Lawrence, *The Letters of D. H. Lawrence*, Vol. IV (Cambridge, Cambridge University Press, 1979), p.108
1 22   Ibid., VIII, p.114
2   1   Jeffrey Meyers, *D. H. Lawrence: A Biography* (New York, Cooper Square Press, 2002), p.17
2   2   Ibid., p. 17
2   7   Michael Squires and Lynn K. Talbot, *Living at the Edge: A Biography of D. H. Lawrence & Frieda von Richthofen* (Madison, University of Wisconsin Press, 2002), p.199
2 31   Meyers, p.18
3   6   D. H. Lawrence, *Women in Love* (London, Penguin, 1982), p.541
3 15   Meyers, p.27
4 11   Ibid., p.52
4 20   Ibid., p.54
4 23   Ibid., p.50
5 13   Lawrence, *Letters*, VIII, p.3
5 22   Philip Callow, *Body of Truth: D. H. Lawrence – The Nomadic Years, 1919–1930* (Chicago, Ivan R. Dee, 2004), p.xii
6   4   Ibid., p.x
6   7   Anne Fernihough, *The Cambridge Companion to D. H. Lawrence* (Cambridge, Cambridge University Press, 2001), p.7
6 24   Callow, p.155
6 28   Geoff Dyer, *Out of Sheer Rage* (London, Abacus, 2003), p.113

7   4   Lawrence, *Letters*, V, p.519

7 13   *Cambridge Companion to D. H. Lawrence*, p.34

8   7   D. H. Lawrence, *Lady Chatterley's Lover* (London, Penguin, 2006), p.328

8 12   Ibid., p.332

9   4   D. H. Lawrence, *The Complete Short Novels* (London, Penguin, 1982), p.155

9 23   *Women in Love*, p.431

9 25   Ibid., p.397

9 29   Fiona Becket, *The Complete Critical Guide to D. H. Lawrence* (London, Routledge, 2002), p.51

9 33   *Cambridge Companion to D. H. Lawrence*, p.7

10   2   D. H. Lawrence, *Studies in Classic American Literature* (Cambridge, Cambridge University Press, 2002), p.14

10   9   Squires and Talbot, p.274

10 16   Meyers, p.241

10 25   *Lady Chatterley*, p.101

10 28   Lawrence, *Letters*, III, p.92

10 31   Lawrence, *Studies*, p.17

11 23   Callow, p.83

12 18   *Critical Guide to D. H. Lawrence*, p.61

13 27   D. H. Lawrence, Foreword to *Women in Love* (New York, Thomas Seltzer, 1920)

13 32   Lawrence, *Letters*, V, p.201

14 10   *Women in Love*, p.349

14 18   Meyers, p.109

Gardens and Graveyards

Quotations are from the Italian edition of *Il giardino dei Finzi-Contini*, and translated by myself.

17 25   Giorgio Bassani, *Il giardino dei Finzi-Contini* (Turin, Einaudi, 1999), p.39

24 14   Ibid., p.128

28 30   Ibid., p.263

After the Struggle

29 3 Leonid Grossman, *Dostoevsky, His Life and Work*, trans. Mary
         Mackler (Indianapolis, Bobbs-Merrill, 1975), p.552

29 11 Joseph Frank, *Dostoevsky, The Seeds of Revolt, 1821–1849*
          (Princeton, Princeton University Press, 1976), p.270

29 14 Grossman, p.495

29 23 Fyodor Dostoevsky, *Notes from Underground*, trans. Richard
          Pevear and Larissa Volokhonsky (London, Everyman, 2004), p.5

30 7 Fyodor Dostoevsky, *Notes from Underground*, trans. Jessie
          Coulson (London, Penguin, 1972), p.18

30 12 Loc. cit.

30 16 Loc. cit.

30 23 Joseph Frank, *Dostoevsky, The Stir of Liberation* (Princeton,
           Princeton University Press, 1986), p.252

31 22 *Notes* (Pevear and Volokhonsky), p.54

32 7 Frank, *The Star of Liberation*, p.57

32 31 *Notes* (Coulson), p.29

33 16 *Notes* (Pevear and Volokhonsky), p.6

33 18 Ibid., p.7

33 22 Ibid., p.6

33 29 Ibid., p.7

34 14 Ibid., p.11

36 15 *Notes* (Coulson), p.54

36 20 Ibid., p.59

36 31 Loc. cit.

37 16 Ibid., p.60

37 23 Ibid., p.61

38 18 Grossman, p.396

39 4 *Notes* (Coulson), p.100

39 32 *Notes* (Pevear and Volokhonsky), p.118

40 5 *Notes* (Coulson), p.123

40 32 *Notes* (Pevear and Volokhonsky), p.94

41 3 Frank, *The Star of Liberation*, p.295

41 11 *Notes* (Coulson), p.122

41 17 Frank, *The Star of Liberation*, p.224

43 4 *Notes* (Coulson), pp.50–1

The Illusionist

47   6   Nicholas Farrell, *Mussolini: A New Life* (London, Phoenix Press, 2005), p.32

47   19   Ibid., p.37

48   33   *Encyclopaedia Britannica*, entry on Mussolini

49   5   Richard Bosworth, *Mussolini* (London, Hodder Arnold, 2003), p.116

50   29   Farrell, p.113

50   33   Ibid., p.124

51   26   Ibid., p.120

52   8   Ibid., p.126

52   28   Ibid., p.7

53   10   Bosworth, p.114

53   12   Peter Neville, *Mussolini* (London, Routledge, 2003), p.36

53   20   Ibid., p.12

54   3   Giacomo Leopardi, *Discorso sopra lo stato presente dei costumi degl'italiani* (Milan, Feltrinelli, 1991), p.47

54   13   Ibid., p.51

54   19   Farrell, p.111

54   33   Renzo De Felice, *Mussolini il duce, Gli anni del consenso, 1929–1936* (Turin, Einaudi, 1996), p.50

55   11   Denis Mack Smith, *Garibaldi: A Great Life in Brief* (Greenwood Press, 1982)

55   22   De Felice, p.48

55   24   Farrell, p.111

55   27   Ibid., p.46

55   34   Ibid., p.101

56   2   Bosworth, p.262

56   3   De Felice, p.20

56   7   Ibid., p.51

56   13   Farrell, p.305

56   26   De Felice, p.50

56   32   Bosworth, p.296

57   17   Ibid., p.216

58   21   Farrell, p.93

59   21   Ibid., p.359

62   2   Ibid., p.304
62   6   Ibid., p.305
62 21   Bosworth, p.346
62 24   Ibid., p.340
62 26   Ibid., p.338
62 34   Ibid., p.342
63 10   Farrell, p.311
64 26   Ibid., p.112

Fear is the Key

65   3   Claire Tomalin, *Thomas Hardy* (New York, Penguin Press, 2006),
          p.222
65 13   Ibid., p.223
65 17   Ibid., p.222
66 26   Ibid., p.288
66 30   Ibid., p.24
66 31   Ibid., p.323
66 34   Thomas Hardy, *Jude the Obscure* (New York, Signet, 1999),
          p.17
67   8   Thomas Hardy, *Tess of the D'Urbervilles* (London, Penguin,
          2003), p.24
67 11   Ibid., p.49
67 18   Tomalin, p.27
68   3   Loc. cit.
68 11   Ibid., p.40
68 14   Ibid., p.46
69   7   Ibid., p.82
69 20   Ibid., p.70
70   2   Ibid., p.64
70 21   Loc. cit.
71 31   Thomas Hardy, *The Complete Poems*, ed. James Gibson (London,
          Palgrave, 2001), p.312
72 10   *Tess*, p.74
72 21   Ibid., p.200
74   9   Tomalin, p.273

75   5   *Tess*, p.169

75   6   Tomalin, p.228

75   28 *Tess*, p.123

75   29 Ibid., p.183

76   6   Ibid., p.151

76   6   Ibid., p.170

76   7   Ibid., p.152

76   25 Ibid., p.225

76   31 Ibid., p.229

76   32 Loc. cit.

77   1   Ibid., p.182

77   2   Ibid., p.234

77   8   *Poems*, p.237

77   12 Tomalin, p.247

77   20 *Poems*, p.313

77   26 Tomalin, p.231

77   28 *Tess*, p.xix

77   29 Ibid., p.xx

79   3   Thomas Hardy, *Far From the Madding Crowd* (London, Penguin, 2000), p.8

79   9   Thomas Hardy, *The Return of the Native* (New York, Bantam, 1981), p.5

79   14 Ibid., p.47

79   30 *Tess*, p.85

79   32 Loc. cit.

80   9   Ibid., p.226

80   19 Tomalin, p.224

81   2   Loc. cit.

81   11 Ibid., p.259

82   1   Ibid., p.239

82   5   Ibid., p.170

82   10 *Thomas Hardy's Personal Writings* (New York, University Press of Kansas, 1969), p.124

84   4   *Poems*, p.346

84   9   Tomalin, p.322

85   21 *Poems*, p.553

The Disenchantment of Translation

91 15 Quoted in Barbara Milberg Fisher, *Noble Numbers, Subtle Words: The Art of Mathematics in the Science of Storytelling* (Madison, NJ, Fairleigh Dickinson University Press, 1997), p.32

91 16 Loc. cit.

91 27 Paul Celan, *Gesammelte Werke* (Frankfurt, Suhrkamp, 1983), Vol. III, p.175

95   9 Ernest Hemingway, *The Snows of Kilimanjaro* (Milan, Mondadori Parallel Texts, 1992), p.132

96 20 D. H. Lawrence, *Women in Love* (London, Penguin, 1982), p.430

99 10 J. M. Coetzee, *Disgrace* (London, Vintage, 2000), p.117

Still Stirring

101   1 Samuel Beckett, *The Grove Centenary Edition*, Vol. IV, p.492

101 23 E. M. Cioran, *Anathemas and Admirations*, trans. Richard Howard (London, Quartet, 1992), p.129, footnote 1

102   3 *Beckett Remembering, Remembering Beckett*, ed. James and Elizabeth Knowlson (New York, Arcade, 2006), p.295

102   5 Ibid., p.293

102   7 Ibid., p.189

102 10 Ibid., p.299

102 24 Cioran, p.135

103 26 Beckett, *Centenary Ed.*, I, p.3, footnote 2

104 14 Ibid., IV, p.503

104 33 Samuel Beckett, *Disjecta* (London, Calder, 1983), p.171

105   8 Loc. cit.

105 19 Beckett, *Centenary Ed.*, I, p.27

105 32 Ibid., II, p.407

106   4 Ibid., IV, p.472

106   8 Ibid., I, p.164

106 19 S. E. Gontarski and Anthony Uhlmann, *Beckett After Beckett: Essays* (Gainesville, Florida University Press, 2006), p.67

106 29 Beckett, *Centenary Ed.*, I, p.205

107 30 Ibid., I, p.211

109   6   *Beckett Remembering*, p.113

109 22   Ibid., p.105

109 26   Ibid., p.109

109 29   Anne Atik, *How It Was: A Memoir of Samuel Beckett* (New York, Shoemaker & Hoard, 2001), p.95

110 30   Beckett, *Centenary Ed.*, I, p.370

111 18   Ibid, p.369

111 18   Ibid., p.379

112   8   Ibid., II, p.190

113 20   Ibid., IV, p.430

114 18   *Beckett Remembering*, p.174

115 18   Beckett, *Centenary Ed.*, III, p.40

116   1   Cioran, p.129

116 16   *Beckett Remembering*, p.166

Genius of Bad News

117 16   Gitta Honegger, *Thomas Bernhard: The Making of an Austrian* (New Haven, CT, and London, Yale University Press, 2001), this is the quotation that opens the book, page unnumbered

117 21   Ibid., p.xiii

119   5   Thomas Bernhard, *The Lime Works*, trans. Sophie Wilkins (Chicago, University of Chicago Press, 1986), p.47

121   5   Honegger, p.8

121 24   Ibid., p.31

122 33   Ibid., p.42

123   5   Loc. cit.

123 28   Ibid., p.57

124   2   Ibid., p.64

125 15   Thomas Bernhard, *Frost*, trans. Michael Hofmann (New York, Knopf, 2006), p.9

125 23   Ibid., p.15

125 30   Ibid., p.94

126 24   Thomas Bernhard, *Gargoyles*, trans. Richard and Clara Winston (Chicago, University of Chicago Press, 1986), pp.12, 13

128 11   Ibid., pp.181, 182

129 33 Honegger, p.118

130 18 Ibid., p.36

130 25 Ibid., p.13

131   9 Ibid., p.142

131 25 Ibid., p.141

132   3 *Gargoyles*, p.680

133   4 Honegger, p.267

133 22 Ibid., p.295

Let Sleeping Beauties Lie

135   9 Elfriede Jelinek, *The Piano Teacher*, trans. Joachim Neugroschel
         (London, Serpent's Tail, 1999), p.141

135 12 Ibid., p.90

135 18 Ibid., p.74

136   7 http://nobelprize.org/nobel_prizes/literature/laureates/2004/
         index.html

136 10 http://en.wikipedia.org/wiki/Elfriede_Jelinek

136 27 Hans-Jürgen Heinrichs, *Schreiben is das bessere Leben* (Munich,
         Kunstmann, 2006), p.21 (my translation)

137   6 Elfride Jelinek, *Women as Lovers*, trans. Martin Chalmers
         (London, Serpent's Tail, 1994), p.9

137 13 Ibid., p.22

137 16 Ibid., p.9

137 22 Ibid., p.153

138   6 Ibid., p.32

138 32 Elfriede Jelinek, *Wonderful Wonderful Times*, trans. Michael Hulse
         (London, Serpent's Tail, 1990), p.16

139 11 Elfreide Jelinek, *Greed*, trans. Martin Chalmers (New York, Seven
         Stories Press, 2007), p.192

139 12 Ibid., p.136

139 20 Elfriede Jelinek in interview with Gitta Honegger in the journal
         Theater 36(2) (Durham, North Carolina, Duke University Press,
         2006), p.29

139 23 Loc. cit.

139 28 Loc. cit.

139 32 *Wonderful*, p.20
140 18 *Greed*, p.11
140 21 Ibid., p.39
140 22 Heinrichs, p.17
140 33 *Piano*, p.24
140 33 Ibid., p.14
142   5 Ibid., p.243
142   5 Ibid., p.251
142   7 Ibid., p.193
143 11 Ibid., pp.176–7
143 24 Heinrichs, p.23
144   1 Elfriede Jelinek, *Lust*, trans. Michael Hulse (London, Serpent's Tail, 1992), p.3
144 12 Ibid., pp.14–15
144 17 Ibid., p.18
144 20 Ibid., p.22
145 12 *Theater* 36(2), p.26
146   4 *Greed*, p.117
146 11 Ibid., p.193
146 18 Ibid., p.323
146 29 Ibid., p.73
148   2 Ibid., p.135
148 25 http://en.wikipedia.org/wiki/Elfriede_Jelinek
149 14 *Greed*, p.13
149 15 Elfriede Jelinek, *Gier* (Hamburg, Rowohlt, 2005), p.15
149 30 Heinrichs, p.49

A Polished Pessimism

151   2 E. M. Cioran, *La Chute dans le temps* (Paris, Gallimard, 1964), p.1
151 12 Ibid., p.35
151 18 Ibid., p.36
151   6 Ibid., p.37
151   7 Ibid., p.167
152 19 E. M. Cioran, *History and Utopia*, trans. Richard Howard (London, Quartet, 1966), p.90

152 25 Ibid., p.88
152 30 Ibid., p.89
152 31 Ibid., p.96
152 34 Ibid., p.91
153 7 Ibid., p.61
153 19 Ibid., p.75
153 21 Loc. cit.
153 30 Ibid., p.136
153 31 Loc. cit.
154 4 Ibid., p.69
154 12 Ibid., p.67

True Scandal

156 17 Niccolò Machiavelli, *The Prince*, trans. George Bull (London, Folio Society, 2006), p.77
156 21 Ibid., p.81
156 28 Ibid., p.57
156 30 Loc. cit.
156 32 Ibid., p.59
157 11 Ibid., p.87
157 32 Ibid., p.96
158 21 Ibid., p.36
159 7 Ibid., p.43

A Model Anomaly

161 3 *Italian Politics, The Faltering Transition*, eds. Mark Gilbert and Gianfranco Pasquino for the Istituto Cattaneo (New York/ Oxford, Berghahn Books, 2000), these titles listed on pp.v, vi
161 16 Marco Travaglio, *L'odore dei soldi, Origini e misteri delle fortune di Silvio Berlusconi* (Rome, Editori Riuniti, 2001), p.9
161 27 Anna Cento Bull, *Social Identities and Political Cultures in Italy* (New York, Berghahn Books, 2000), p.2
162 10 Loc. cit.
162 20 Travaglio, p.15
162 23 *The Economist*, 26 April 2001

163 1 Bull, p.3

163 2 Ibid., p.225

163 18 *Satyricon*, RAI 2, 14 March 2001

164 22 Travaglio, p.50

165 23 Ibid., p.28

167 24 Ibid., pp.275–6

169 27 Bull, p.219

172 24 Silvio Berlusconi, *L'Italia che ho in mente* (Milan, Mondadori, 2000)

173 7 *Corriere della Sera*, 15 March 2000

176 3 *Italian Politics, The Return of Politics*, eds. David Hine and Salvatore Vassallo, for the Istituto Cattaneo (New York/Oxford, Berghahn Books, 1999), p.110

176 12 Guest book of Hellas Verona official website, now deleted (www.hellasverona.it)

Mad at the Medici

178 1 Nicolai Rubinstein, *Il governo di Firenze sotto i Medici (1434–1494)* (Milan, La Nuova Italia, 1999), p.232

178 5 Loc. cit.

178 8 Mark Phillips, *The Memoir of Marco Parenti: A Life in Medici Florence* (Toronto, Encore Editions, 2000), p.223

180 34 Niccolò Machiavelli, *Florentine Histories*, trans. Laura F. Banfield and Harvey C. Mansfield, Jr (Princeton, Princeton University Press, 1988), p.176

182 6 Rubinstein, p.33

185 20 Lauro Martines, *April Blood: Florence and the Plot Against the Medici* (London, Jonathan Cape, 2003), p.158

187 6 Ibid., p.216

187 14 Ibid., p.220

Love Letter

190 10 Fleur Jaeggy, *Sweet Days of Discipline*, trans. Tim Parks (New York, New Directions, 1993), pp.23–4

192 27 Ibid., p.13

192 29 Fleur Jaeggy, *SS Proleterka*, trans. Alastair McEwen (New York, New Directions, 2003), p.87

193 6 *Proleterka*, p.87

193 12 Ibid., p.114

194 3 Ibid., p.88

194 19 Ibid., pp.6–7

194 22 Ibid., p.93

194 27 Ibid., p.39

195 12 Ibid., p.83

195 16 Loc. cit.

195 20 Ibid., p.84

196 4 Ibid., p.92

196 14 Ibid., p.78

196 18 E. M. Cioran, *La Chute dans le temps* (Paris, Gallimard, 1964), p.1

197 13 *Proleterka*, p.106

197 22 Ibid., pp.106–7

197 25 Ibid., p.109

197 30 Ibid., p.3

Tales Told by a Computer

200 6 N. Katherine Hayles, *Writing Machines* (Boston, The MIT Press, 2002), p.138

201 15 Robert Coover, 'The End of Books', *New York Times Book Review*, 21 June 1992

202 12 Shelley Jackson, *Patchwork Girl* CD-ROM (Eastgate Systems Inc., 1995)

203 4 Loc. cit.

203 7 Loc. cit.

203 12 Loc. cit.

204 33 Jorge Luis Borges, *Selected Non-fictions* (New York, Viking Penguin, 1999), p.332

205 5 Coover

205 21 Mark C. Taylor and Esa Saarinen, *'Telewriting' Imagologies: Media*

Philosophy (New York, Routledge, 1994), p.6. Also available at http://hypertext.rmit.edu.au/essays/crossroads/saarinen/saarinen2.html

207 27 Stuart Moulthrop, *Hegirascope*, http://iat.ubalt.edu/moulthrop/hypertexts/HGS/HGS243.html

209 7 Talan Memmott, *Lolli's Apartment*, http://www.heelstone.com/meridian/talan/preface.html

209 22 Ibid., http://www.heelstone.com/meridian/talan/f.html

210 10 Zahra Safavian, *Berceuse*, http://www.drunkenboat.com/db3/safavian/berceuse.html

210 14 Stephanie Strickland, 'Dalí Clocks: Time Dimensions of Hyper-media', *Electronic Book Review*, 2001, http://www.electronicbookreview.com/thread/webarts/hypertext

211 6 *Mundaka Upanishad*, I, p.1

211 11 Dante, *Inferno*, trans. Robert & Jean Hollander (New York, Doubleday, 2001), Canto XXIX, ll.1–3

211 14 Ibid., ll.11–12

213 11 Felix Jung, 'Cruelty', http://webdelsol.com/Synesthesia/2/cruelty.html

Real Dreams

216 34 Émile Zola, *The Dream*, trans. Andrew Brown (London, Hesperus Press, 2005), pp.21–4

217 3 Ibid., p.29

A Matter of Love and Hate

221 15 B. Butler, *The Official History of the Football Association* (London, Queen Anne Press, 1991)

222 13 Carlo Azeglio Ciampi, televised address to the nation, broadcast RAI 1, 31 December 1999

222 19 Guest book of Hellas Verona official website, now deleted (www.hellasverona.it), 1 January 2000

224 3 Adriano Raganella et al., *Il calcio a Verona* (Verona, Unione Stampa Sportiva Italiana, 1999), p.25

224　8　Ibid., p.14

225　32　E. M. Cioran

226　27　Ian Buruma, *Voltaire's Coconuts* (London, Weidenfeld & Nicolson, 1999), p.176

227　26　Ibid., p.178

230　18　Guest book of Hellas Verona official website, now deleted (www.hellasverona.it), 5 June 2002

Hero Betrayed

236　3　Lucy Riall, *Garibaldi: Invention of a Hero* (New Haven, CT, and London, Yale University Press, 2007) p.83

238　3　G. M. Trevelyan, *Garibaldi and the Thousand*, (Phoenix Press, London, 2001), p.112

238　5　Riall, p.175

238　23　Ibid., p.183

238　25　Trevelyan, p.210

239　33　Riall, p.306

240　9　Ibid., p.339

240　21　Denis Mack Smith, *Garibaldi* (Italian edition), p.220

241　7　Mack Smith (Italian edition), p.241

241　8　From the back cover of *Garibaldi and the Thousand*, Trevelyan

241　12　Riall, p.14

241　25　Ibid., p.213

241　26　Ibid., p.346

241　28　Ibid., p.181

241　29　Ibid., p.206

241　30　Ibid., p.391

241　31　Ibid., p.291

242　11　Ibid., p.392

242　21　Ibid., p.244

243　19　Ibid., p.155

243　28　Giuseppe Garibaldi, *My Life* (London, Hesperus Press, 2004), p.126

Siege of the Serenissima

245 11 Jacob Burckhardt, *The Civilisation of the Renaissance in Italy* (London, Penguin, 1990), p.27

247 13 Giacomo Leopardi, *Discorso sopra lo stato presente dei costume degl'italiani* (Milan, Feltrinelli, 1991), p.70

247 15 Ibid., p.57

247 16 Loc. cit.

247 19 Loc. cit.

248 12 Jonathan Keates, *The Siege of Venice* (London, Chatto & Windus, 2005), p.17

254 7 Keates, p.174

256 23 Leopardi, p.50

The Superman's Virgins

258 31 Gabriele D'Annunzio, *The Book of the Virgins*, trans. J. G. Nichols (London, Hesperus Press, 2003), p.36

259 29 Ibid., p.57

260 8 Ibid., p.15

A Pagan in Italy

261 3 D. H. Lawrence, *D. H. Lawrence and Italy: Etruscan Places, Sea and Sardinia, Twilight in Italy* (London, Penguin, 1972), p.10

261 4 Ibid., p.7

261 6 Ibid., p.81

261 10 Ibid., p.4

261 15 Ibid., p.21

261 25 Ibid., p.45

262 1 Ibid., p.10

263 25 Ibid., p.21

264 8 Ibid., p.22

264 12 Ibid., p.23

264 15 Ibid., p.23

264 24 Ibid., p.25

264 29 Ibid., p.26

264 31 Ibid., p.30

265   2 Ibid., p.28

265   8 Ibid., p.29

265 16 Ibid., p.30

266   6 Ibid., p.76

267   8 Ibid., p.34

267 20 Ibid., p.154

268 22 Jeffrey Meyers, *D. H. Lawrence: A Biography* (New York, Cooper Square Press, 1990), p.280

269   8 *Lawrence and Italy: Sea and Sardinia*, p.7

269 15 Ibid., p.11

269 26 Ibid., p.31

269 28 Ibid., p.4

270 14 Ibid., p.90

270 18 Ibid., p.91

270 21 Ibid., p.67

270 25 Loc. cit.

270 34 Ibid., p.100

271   9 Ibid., p.48

271 19 Ibid., p.189

271 24 Loc. cit.

271 33 Ibid., p.190

273   4 *Lawrence and Italy: Etruscan Places*, p.9

273 29 Ibid., p.14

274   7 Ibid., p.12

274 27 Ibid., p.9

275   6 Ibid., p.12

275 29 Ibid., p.10

275 32 Ibid., p.52

276   1 Ibid., p.51

276 14 D. H. Lawrence, *Complete Poems* (London, Penguin, 1993), p.718